The Alaska Cruise Handbook

A MILE BY MILE
GUIDE

The Alaska Cruise Handbook

A MILE BY MILE GUIDE

BY JOE UPTON

Coastal Publishing
Bainbridge Island, WA

The maps in this book are not to be used for navigation.

2005 Edition

Coastal Publishing
15166 Skogen Lane, Bainbridge Island, WA. 98110

Editing by Glenn Hartmann and Joe Upton
Illustrations by Russ Burtner and Christine Cox
Maps by Joe Upton
Design by Martha Brouwer

Photographs by Joe Upton unless noted with the following abbreviations:
AMNH - American Museum of Natural History, New York
BCARS - British Columbia Archives and Records Service.
BCRM- British Columbia Royal Museum.
CRMM - Columbia River Maritime Museum, Astoria, Oregon
MOHAI - Museum of History and Industry, Seattle.
SFM - San Francisco Maritime Museum.
THS - Tongass Historical Society, Ketchikan, Alaska.
UAF - University of Alaska, Fairbanks
UW - University of Washington Special Collections.
WAT - Whatcom County (WA) Museum of History and Art

ISBN 0-9645682-8-4

Printed in China

For
Mary Lou, Matthew,
and Katherine Anne,
mariners all.

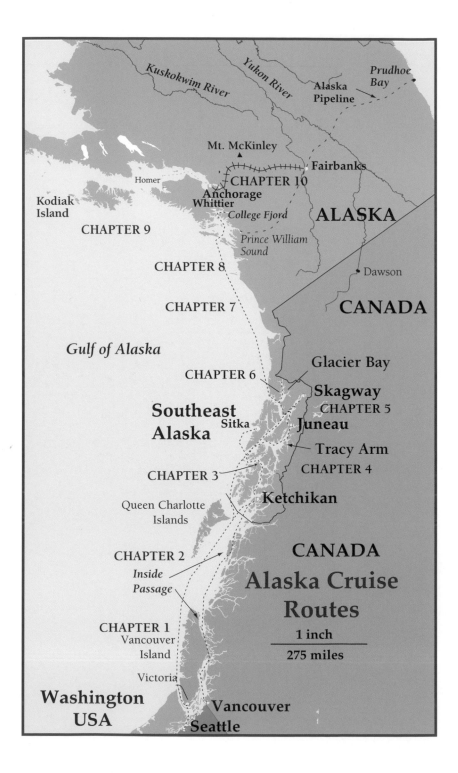

Kuskokwim River

Yukon River

Prudhoe Bay

Alaska Pipeline

Mt. McKinley

Homer

CHAPTER 10

Anchorage
Whittier
College Fjord

Fairbanks

ALASKA

Kodiak Island

CHAPTER 9

Prince William Sound

Dawson

CHAPTER 8

CHAPTER 7

CANADA

Gulf of Alaska

CHAPTER 6

Glacier Bay

Skagway

CHAPTER 5

Southeast Alaska

Sitka

Juneau

Tracy Arm

CHAPTER 3

CHAPTER 4

Queen Charlotte Islands

Ketchikan

CHAPTER 2

Inside Passage

CANADA

Alaska Cruise Routes

1 inch
―――――
275 miles

CHAPTER 1
Vancouver Island

Victoria

Washington USA

Vancouver

Seattle

Contents

Wrangell Narrows, Alaska, 1975

To the Alaska Traveler

On a June night in 1965, I felt a hand on my shoulder in the dark fo'c's'le of the *Sidney*, a 90' fish buying boat on which I'd just gotten my first Alaska job. I was 19.

"C'mon up, kid," Mickey, the 70-year-old mate rasped, nodding up at the pilot-house stairs, "You gotta' see this."

He was right. We were lying almost motionless in a little bight in a steep and forested shore. Ahead of us in the thin light I could make out a torrent of water, like rapids in a river, pouring out of a gap in the trees.

"W-w-we're going in there...?" I stammered, awed at the sight, inexperienced, and totally new to the Inside Passage.

"It used to be really bad" came the soft-voiced answer, "That's Seymour Narrows. There was a rock right in the middle. They blew it the hell out of there."

Two days later we arrived at our cannery in a remote fishing village, to join a large fleet of workboats. It was Alaska in capital letters—we saw icebergs, eagles and whales. And everywhere we traveled, old Mickey had a story—about the steamer that stranded there in 1920, and how the passengers just waited on shore for the next boat and kept going. And about the square rigged ships that used to sail up from San Francisco to the canneries, and about the northern fisheries and working in the pack ice. Mickey shared tales from his life as a trapper, a fisherman, and a mail boat skipper. The old gentleman took me under his wing, teaching me about the lore and legends of The North.

That long season in The North and that kindly old Alaskan instilled in me a lifelong interest in northern places and history, especially the inland waterways that form the Inside Passage and Southeast Alaska.

Eventually I bought a used 32-footer and began fishing salmon, along the sheltered waterways of Southeast Alaska. In the cove where British Explorer George

Vancouver and his men found desperately needed shelter in 1793, my wife and I built a cabin and a float. Nearby was a tiny, roadless, fishing settlement.

Our store and post office each floated on a log raft in the harbor, our vehicles were our outboard boats. It was a unique community, where a person could make a living fishing with an open skiff, get a piece of waterfront land with little money, and build a home with local lumber. Our store was also a floating bar, which eliminated the nasty problem of negotiating that steep walkway down to your boat at low tide. The drinks were whiskey and water, whiskey and coke, and whiskey and Tang.

Mickey and me, aboard the Sidney, 1965.

The people of the community welcomed new blood—showing us the best fishing places—and helping us build our home. Just 200 yards from our house the humpback whales hung out all summer, and at night, if it were still, we could hear them breathing as they surfaced.

In the spring we fished the windy outside coast. In the summer, we worked nearby Sumner Strait. In the fall we traveled north to the natural wind tunnel called Lynn Canal, for the 10-dollar-a-fish chum salmon. And in the long, kerosene lantern-lit winters, there was time for visiting.

And during these last three decades, in a hundred little coves up and down the coast, from the very edge of the Arctic down to Puget Sound and Seattle, when the storms came, we anchored up in our little boats, waiting for the wind to stop.

Sometimes it blew for days, and while we waited, the stories came out. The experiences of my friends, and those before them, an oral history of the coast. And in my travels I sought out the little-visited communities, the out-of-the-way places.

I was an amateur photographer, and a bit of a writer. "Write a book," my friends said, "Tell our story." One book became another, and another after that.

When I first started fishing, cruise ships were few and small. Then more ships began traveling the coast, and I designed a series of illustrated maps to better share with these new visitors the drama and beauty of The North.

When I traveled on board cruise ships, I found many passengers found it very hard to simply find out where they were as they traveled up the coast. To make it easier, I developed a route numbering system based on Seattle as Mile Zero. On many ships your position will be announced using these milemarker numbers. The book and map are keyed together with milemarker numbers on the top right hand pages to make it easier for you to follow your progress.

For me the books and maps are a way to share with you a sense of the mystery and the power of this place that has become such a big part of my life.

So, come, take this journey through this land that remains much as it was when the first explorers passed through.

Launch Foxy *in Puget Sound, Washington, about 1920. By picking their route and weather carefully, skippers of such small craft could travel to Alaska via the Inside Passage.*

The Inside Passage

To a mariner, "inside" means "protected," and when the Pleistocene glaciers scoured out the fjords and canyons of the northwest coast a million years ago, they created "protected" waters and a boater's paradise.

Behind the eight large islands between Cape Flattery, Washington, and Cape Spencer, Alaska, is a roughly northwest-southeast route that has become known as the Inside Passage. Stretching for a thousand miles from Seattle, Washington, to Skagway, Alaska, it allows small and large craft alike to travel in protection and comfort.

The Inside Passage was explored, charted, and named in the 1790s by a British Navy captain, George Vancouver, who sought a sea route from west to east.

In some places, vessels have a choice of routes. For the purposes of this book, the "Inside Passage" means the traditional route laid out for small- and medium-size craft in the *Hansen Handbook*—now out of print but an essential navigational guide for mariners before the days of modern electronics.

The Tides

In few waterways of the world does the tide so influence mariners as it does along the northwest coast. From the tipsy sailor who exits a tavern, only to face the 45-degree ramp down to his boat, to the skipper of a 6,000-horsepower tug who steams to the side of Johnstone Strait when the current is against him, the mariner here must always consider the tide.

In the Kvichak River of western Alaska, propellers of boats at anchor are turned by the tide. In Sergius Narrows, near Sitka, Coast Guard buoys disappear underwater, pulled down by the current when the tide is running.

In some constricted passages, the tide rushes with a force like rapids in a river. In Seymour Narrows and Yuculta Rapids, British Columbia, safe passage is possible only briefly each day: at slack water, the top or the bottom of the tide.

Tides are caused by the moon's gravity (and to a lesser extent the sun's) pulling the earth's oceans into bulges on either side that attempt to follow the moon. Because the moon takes one day plus 50 minutes to orbit the earth, each tide is 50 minutes later than the day before.

Tides on this coast have a great range of rise and fall, from 10 feet in Seattle to 18 feet in Ketchikan, Alaska. At certain times of the year, the alignment of moon, sun, and planets create tides higher and lower.

A channel marker in Wrangell Narrows at Petersburg. Here savvy mariners tie up their boats before they put their engines into neutral. At times the current past the docks can run at four knots (about four and a half miles an hour) which is almost faster than you can walk.

The Arrival of Vancouver

"April 29, 1792. At four o'clock [a.m.] a sail was discovered to the westward standing in shore. This was a very great novelty, not having seen any vessel but our consort, during the last eight months. She soon hoisted American colors and fired a gun to leeward." —Captain George Vancouver, *A Voyage of Discovery to the North Pacific Ocean and Round the World.*

This was a singular day for the British captain and his two ships and crews. They had sailed from England 15 months earlier to seek the Northwest Passage from the Pacific Ocean to the Atlantic. Vancouver had his doubts. Captain Cook hadn't found it and Vancouver was with him. For 6,000 miles, almost to the southern tip of Chile, the Pacific coast was a wall, with no interior straits and few good harbors.

Captain Robert Gray, a Boston fur trader, in the American vessel *Columbia*, assured Vancouver that the strait existed; it was a few miles to the north. Around noon on the 29th the rain and the mists parted and Vancouver saw it: the Strait! 10 miles wide, 500 feet deep, it led east between high, snowy mountains. He thought it was the Northwest Passage.

At that time, Philadelphia and Boston had cobblestone streets and daily newspapers, yet the known world ended west of the Missouri River; beyond that was marked "unknown" on the maps. Another 13 years would pass before Lewis and Clark would uncover the vastness and the beauty of the American west.

A week after entering the strait that turned out to be *not* the Northwest Passage, Vancouver's ships turned south and entered a waterway the Captain named for one of his lieutenants, Peter Puget. Vancouver was stunned by what he saw.

"I could not possibly believe that any uncultivated country had ever been discovered exhibiting so rich a picture... To describe the beauties of this region, will, on some future occasion, be a very grateful task to the pen of a skillful panegyrist. The serenity of the climate, the innumerable pleasing landscapes, and the abundant fertility that unassisted nature puts forth, require only to be enriched by the industry of man with villages, mansions, cottages, and other buildings, to render it the most lovely country that can be imagined; whilst the labor of the inhabitants would be amply rewarded, in the bounties which nature seems ready to bestow on cultivation." —George Vancouver, *A Voyage of Discovery*

In order not to miss the entrance to the Northwest Passage, Vancouver followed the mainland north, exploring, charting, but always following the shore. When he arrived in Puget Sound and saw the myriad channels leading off in all directions, it was obvious to him that the task was too difficult for the cumbersome ships *Discovery* and *Chatham*. The solution lay in small boats, his 20-foot cutters, rigged to row and sail. The big boats would anchor and the small boats would set out, sometimes with Vancouver and sometimes without, charting the vast land they had discovered.

A Few Traveling Companions:
Your Author And His Various Boats

Like most fishermen, many boats carried me through northern waters. On some I was the owner, on some the crew. Some were large, steel, and very able, like the 104' steel crabber *Flood Tide*. Others, were old, wood, and downright unsafe, like the 28' *Denise* on the right

No season was without its drama, adventure, or danger, be it the frustrations of a broken engine far from any port, or a genuine life or death struggle against the dreaded buildup of ice in a storm at sea.

In 1997, I began traveling North on a number of cruise ships as well, both small and large.

Here and there around this book, I've put in observations from these cruises as well as journal entries from my other Alaska experiences.

The ill-fated Denise *and I, at Kingston, Puget Sound, WA, 1970. The engine blew up and the boat caught fire; I had to shelve my Alaska plans for that season.*

The Maggie Murphy Boys

For many young people, growing up on Puget Sound and hearing the stories of Alaska and the North from those who had been

Would you go to Alaska in this rig? These men did.

there, the itch to follow was strong. In the 1930s two teenagers, John Joseph Ryan and Ed Braddock, salvaged a derelict 26-footer from the mud flats at Tacoma, rebuilt it as best they could (thanks to the unknowing help of a nearby lumber mill), and set out up the Inside Passage. They had barely reached Seattle when one of the flaws of their vessel revealed itself.

"First of all, the pilothouse proved to be utterly uninhabitable. It had about two inches less headroom than was needed to permit either of us to stand erect while steering; the engine was right underfoot, belching fumes and heat that rose up to smother the helmsman; furthermore, there was no danger that either fumes or heat would escape because the windows had been nailed and puttied in place, sealing the pilothouse as tight as a mummy's crypt."

—John Joseph Ryan, *The Maggie Murphy*

Seattle

And the Spectacular Northwest

R ising from the shores of Puget Sound with dramatic mountain ranges both east and west, Seattle has one of the most scenic settings of any U.S. city.

It was the tall straight-grained Douglas fir trees that the first settlers came for—building sawmills on sheltered harbors and cutting lumber for the California builders following the 1849 gold rush.

The Yukon Gold Rush of 1897-98 put Seattle on the national map as the jumping-off place to the riches of The North. In the 20th century the economy grew with the building of Boeing airplanes and, most recently, the remarkable rise of Microsoft. Today the region has a diversified economy, but with high tech and services providing more and more jobs.

The mild winters allow the many outdoor-minded residents a choice that is almost unique to the northwest: either skiing or sailing on most any day from Thanksgiving to late March. Ski areas are located in the mountain passes above the city, just an hour away from downtown. Mt. Rainier, a 14,000' volcano that is deep in snow year round and flanked by glaciers, seems to loom mysteriously above the Seattle landscape, and climbing it is a rite of passage for many northwesterners.

An occasionally dreary climate in the winter makes for a vibrant arts, crafts, and writing community. It's no surprise that Starbucks Coffee started here and that this is a city of avid readers.

WHAT TO SEE: Many of Seattle's attractions are close to where you will board your ship:

The **Pike Place Market** located above the waterfront downtown is a fascinating array of kiosks and shops featuring fresh and cooked foods, crafts, live performers and much more. A number of reasonably priced restaurants are also sited here with dramatic high views.

The **Chittenden Locks** separate a connected series of fresh water lakes with the salt water of Puget Sound. In the summer, boats of all sizes transit this waterway, and its grassy banks offer pleasant viewing.

Fishermen's Terminal. Seattle is the home port for much of the Alaska fishing fleet. Close to the locks, here you'll find restaurants, a fishermen's memorial, and a fascinating variety of watercraft.

Seafood kiosk at the Pike Place market

Alaska Way runs along the waterfront where thousands of gold-hungry prospectors boarded the steamers headed up to the Yukon. Today you'll stroll past shops, boating excursion vendors, restaurants and the popular Seattle Aquarium with its Omnidome Theater. If the Mount St. Helens eruption feature is playing while you are here, don't miss it: the footage is stunning.

Museum of Flight. Located next to the original Boeing plant a few miles south of the waterfront, this is a fascinating collection of planes, with excellent presentations on aviation history. Among the highlights are a SR-71 Blackbird spy plane, and a recently retired British Airways Concorde.

The **Seattle Art Museum** located on First Avenue a few blocks south of Pike Place market, is a very attractive venue for the arts.

The **Burke Museum of History and Culture**, located in the University district has an excellent collection of northwest native art.

A 35-minute ferry ride from the waterfront takes you to Bainbridge Island, Follow the foot path to the harbor and a rental kiosk for rowboats and kayaks.

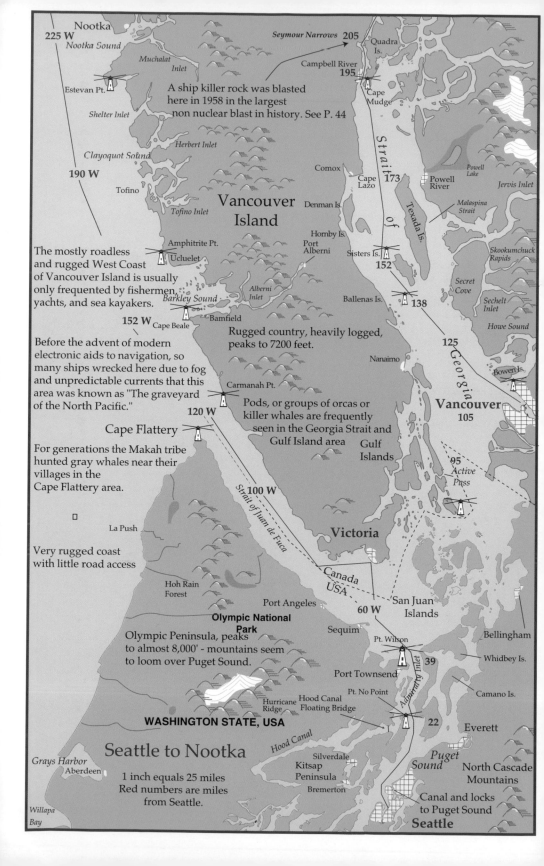

CHAPTER 1
To the Wild and Lonely Coast

Mile 0 to Mile 320W

*Seattle, May 11, 1973: The last jobs have been done, the last things
bought, the last goodbyes said. Our little boat lies still in the water
tonight, freshly painted, engine and electronics tuned, every cubby
and corner jammed full of supplies, ready for a long season.
Tonight, the roar of the traffic. Tomorrow, the stillness of The
North. Away in the morning, away for Alaska!*

— author's journal

Your ship leaves from the Seattle waterfront, the traditional beginning of the Inside Passage to Alaska. From
here, thousands of gold-hungry men embarked on a
journey to the Alaska and Klondike gold fields that changed
so many lives in 1897 and 1898. This is also **mile 0** of the
route numbering system used in my maps and books.

Look for the ferries. Puget Sound has
one of the largest ferry systems in the
world, with 24 of the green and white
double-ended vessels serving nine routes.
Busiest is the Bainbridge Island ferry to
Seattle, where 2,000 commuters and 210
cars squeeze aboard for the 35-minute
rush-hour sailings across Elliott Bay. If
you can park your car in Bainbridge and
walk on, commuting is a breeze. But if you are one of the
many drive-on commuters, you'll wait an hour or more each
morning and evening.

*A commuter ferry
heads to Bainbridge
Island from the
downtown Seattle
docks. In the distance
the Olympic Moun-
tains loom over
Puget Sound.*

The beach around the first point to the south at **mile 2** is
Alki. It was here that the Denny party, Seattle's first settlers,
slogged ashore in a rainstorm in November 1851. The women
of the party, who'd spent the previous six months struggling
with the rigors of the Oregon Trail, broke into tears when
they saw the promised land: a roofless cabin at the edge of a

gloomy forest with a rough-looking Chief Sealth and members of his Suquamish tribe waiting to greet them.

If they had looked around them they might have noticed an evergreen tree with peculiar flat needles, not seen in the East: the Douglas fir, or Oregon pine ("Doug fir" in the lumber business). It was the foundation of the Northwest's principal industry for the next century.

Less than a month later, the sailing ship *Leonesa* dropped anchor, and her skipper offered the party $1,000 cash for a load of 50-foot fir piles. The settlers sharpened their axes and an industry was born.

Puget Sound is like a northwest Chesapeake Bay: a many-armed waterway, very urban in places, rural in others, but deeper and surrounded by high mountains. The new Puget Sound is along the Seattle-Tacoma-Everett corridor: fast-growing, fast-paced, busy, noisy, even polluted in places.

When the white men arrived, seafood was the primary component of the native diet here.

The old Puget Sound of cedar bungalows and wooden boats, forests sloping to the water's edge, driftwood fires, eagles, and native settlements lingers mostly in the western and southern sound. The smell of the sea and the woods, a long log raft headed to a mill, a graceful salmon boat setting a net on a gray and drizzly summer morning, and Mount Rainier breaking suddenly through the overcast sky, dramatic and bright—these are the elements that make the Puget Sound country unusual.

Does it really rain that much here? Ironically, Seattle, with 38 inches of rain annually, gets less than New York's 43 inches or soggy Kansas City's 50 inches. It's just that it's spread out over so much of the year that it seems as if it rains a lot.

Look to the south as you leave Seattle. That brilliant white cone (seen on clear days) is Mount Rainier, the 14,300' volcano looming over Puget Sound. The remarkably symmetrical Rainier is part of a volcanic chain stretching south to California that includes Mount Baker, Mount St. Helens, Mount Adams, and Mount Hood.

Washington State has an extensive series of marine parks. A number of parks and campsites are just for the use of kayakers and other paddled or rowed boats.

These volcanoes were considered extinct until 8:18 on a Sunday morning in May 1980. After two months of throat-clearing, Mount St. Helens blew 1,300 feet of mountain and a cubic mile of ash into the atmosphere. The explosion and ensuing landslides and floods killed 57 people and knocked flat several million trees.

Look for fishing boats exiting the Hiram Chittenden Locks at the marina on the eastern shore, **mile 7**. The locks lead from Lake Washington and Lake Union, winter shelter for many of the thousand plus vessels that travel to Alaska each summer to fish for salmon, herring, crab and other species. The fresh water kills the marine growth on their bottoms and there is no tide, so access to the boats berthed here is easy.

DID YOU KNOW? Washington State has 3,026 miles of tidal shoreline, the tenth longest in the United States. Alaska is first with 31,383 miles; Florida is second with 8,426.

Over the bluff six miles east of **mile 18** is the engine that drove Puget Sound's economy during the 1960s and '70s, less so today: The Boeing Company, jet builder to the world.

Look for this new style of tugboats - they don't have propellers!
(See page 96)

Trouble with Bridges

The water depth in Puget Sound poses a particular problem to bridge builders. Had the sound been as shallow as Chesapeake Bay, for instance, no doubt there would be a bridge across the Sound. But with depths to 800 feet and distances of three miles from shore to shore, a pile-supported or suspension bridge was impossible, so floating bridges were the best solution, but they had a few problems

The first bridge to sink was the Hood Canal Floating Bridge, which did so on February 13, 1979. The bridge was designed to be opened in a storm to relieve pressure on the windward side. The opening also allowed passage of the 560-foot Trident submarines to their West Coast base at Bangor, 10 miles south. The canal was deep enough for the subs to travel submerged, but threading through the bridge's mooring cables submerged would have been too dangerous.

On that stormy February night, when the bridge tender tried to open the bridge to ease the strain, the mechanism failed to work, and as he watched in astonishment part of the floating portions of the bridge sank.

Next to go was one of the Lake Washington bridges. It lay on a key commuter link between Seattle and its rapidly growing east-side suburbs, which induced enough traffic flowing across the lake during rush hour to require a pair of four-lane bridges, the busiest route being big cross-country Interstate 90.

Imagine the consternation of east-side residents with water-view property as they looked out from their 1991 Thanksgiving dinners while a violent 60-mile-per-hour gale swept the city. A long section of spare bridge, section after section, sank as they watched.

Of course, to Puget Sound folk, collapsing bridges were not new. Although it was a suspension bridge rather than a floating bridge, the Tacoma Narrows Bridge broke up and fell into the sound on November 7, 1940, just four months after it opened.

Oops! "Galloping Gertie," AKA The Tacoma Narrows Bridge, collapses in a windstorm. On windy days the graceful bridge would oscillate so badly that cars would be bounced around. Big trucks loaded with heavy gravel were parked on the span on windy days to reduce the motion, but the bridge was no match for the violent winds that roared through this gorge. Just before it collapsed, the motion was so violent that drivers abandoned their cars and ran for their lives.

MOHAI

Port Townsend and the Forts

About two and a half hours after leaving Seattle, look for the above lighthouse at **mile 40**, just before your ship swings west into the wilder and much more rugged landscape of Juan de Fuca Strait. In the days before radar and long range aircraft provided strong coastal defenses it was big guns in narrow passes like this that kept enemy ships out. Here the geography allowed for the siting of three forts, on opposite sides of the channel, whose cannons provided a killing field of fire for any ship trying to enter Puget Sound. If you have binoculars, look just south of the lighthouse and past the beach where you'll see a wide grassy parade ground flanked by grand Victorian style buildings. These were the officers' and enlisted men's quarters at Fort Worden. If the place looks familiar, it's possible you saw it as the setting for the movie, *"Officer and a Gentleman."* Today it is a state park, and the cozy fireplace-equipped officer's quarters are available for rent and popular for area families coming for weekends or to attend some of Port Townsend's many festivals and other cultural activities.

The lighthouse at Point Wilson marks the entrance to Juan de Fuca Strait.

Below: traditional wooden watercraft at Port Townsend's annual Wooden Boat Festival in September.

For much of the 20th century, sawmills and logging provided many of the jobs in the Puget Sound area.

The town to the west at **mile 38** is Port Townsend. According to the real estate sharps in the 1880s, Port Townsend was certain to be the western terminus of the Northern Pacific Railway, which was then advancing across the plains. A lot of land was sold to speculators before the bubble burst with the announcement that Tacoma was selected instead. Look for gracious Victorian houses with ginger-bread trim on the bluff at Port Townsend.

Look for tide rips, too, which occur when the wind and the tidal current oppose one another, or when these currents accelerate in constricted passages.

Puget Sound proper ends at **mile 40**, Point Wilson. Wherever tidal currents turn a corner, as they do here, they are apt to swirl and eddy, causing the so-called tide rips. When they are opposed by a wind, these currents can produce conditions that are difficult for small craft. Native travelers in canoes held the Point Wilson tide rip with particular regard. It is reported that the natives sat very still and paddled carefully to avoid disturbing the god of tide rips and safe passages over troubled waters.

Here your ship turns west to enter **Juan de Fuca Strait**, 10 miles wide and 50 miles long. It seems big, but Captain

The First 707

Gold Cup Day, on August 7, 1955, was the highlight of the annual Seafair. Some 250,000 spectators, including members of the International Air Transport Association and the Society of Aeronautical Engineers, who were in town for a conference, stood on boats and on the shore to watch the unlimited hydroplanes race on Lake Washington.

The sound of a jet approaching low and fast from the west made the crowd look up. What they saw remained etched in memory.

The new Boeing 707 airliner, first ever built, which was being flight-tested that day, approached at 500 miles per hour in a shallow dive, right over the race course. Then, as the crowd gasped, the huge airplane pulled up smoothly into a steep climb, rolled slowly on its back and did a perfect barrel roll. Then it turned back over the crowd and did one again.

The pilot, Tex Johnston, said later that as Boeing's competitors were telling airlines the big jet was unstable, he figured a demonstration of the aircraft's capability was in order. Watching from the ground, the Boeing president, Bill Allen, probably had to take a heart pill when he saw the precious airplane on which the company had bet its future perform the unplanned maneuver.

Cook and other early explorers missed it.

To the north here are the **San Juans**, an archipelago of 172 islands, small and large. Bucolic and sleepy for most of the year, it is transformed each summer as boaters and summer folk arrive from the Puget Sound cities to the south.

The city visible 14 miles north of **mile 60 W** is **Victoria**, the British Columbia capital. It is an unusually graceful and accessible small city, its downtown within walking distance of the lake-like inner harbor. Today Victoria is elegant and genteel, but in earlier days, life there had a few rough edges:

The Boeing Aircraft Company with two huge assembly plants in Puget Sound, was the region's largest single employer for much of the 20th century. This is an early Boeing airliner on display at the Seattle Museum of Flight.

"I have witnessed scenes after sunset calculated to shock even the bluntest sensibilities. The fires of Indian tents pitched upon the beach casting a lurid glare upon the water; the loud and discordant whoopings of the natives, several of whom were usually infuriated with bad liquor; the crowds of the more debased miners strewed in vicious concert with squaws on the public highway, presented a spectacle diabolical in the extreme."
—Matthew Macfie, *Vancouver Island and British Columbia: Their History, Resources, and Prospects*, London, 1865

Victoria
Capital of British Columbia

Your ship docks just a few blocks from Victoria's inner harbor, a "don't miss" spot dominated by the Empress Hotel and the classic architecture of the buildings housing the provincial legislature. This is a city that also truly celebrates its maritime heritage—look for the brass plaques around the top of the inner harbor's sea wall across from the Empress that commemorate people like Miles and Bea Smeaton, who battled Cape Horn in their 38-footer as well as their crew John Guzwell, who circled the globe in a homemade 26-footer.

While Vancouver—just 75 miles to the NW—is a totally cosmopolitan modern city with a heavy sprinkling of Asian immigrants, Victoria seems a bit more like a taste of England. The British fondness for gardens is especially evident in the many private and public gardens and plantings that line its streets.

Originally settled when a Hudson's Bay Company trading post was established here in 1843, this city and Vancouver Island became a crown colony in 1849. Ten years later another colony was established on the mainland to support the many prospectors that had arrived with the 1858 Fraser River gold strike. Eventually the two colonies merged to form what is today British Columbia and Victoria became its administrative capital, while Vancouver became the industrial center.

Today though separated by 75 miles of water and islands, the two are intimately liked with regular ferries (Vancouver bound ferries leave from Sidney, about 20 miles NE of downtown Victoria) as well as big twin-engine floatplanes that go downtown to downtown.

Victoria's inner harbor is dominated by the Empress Hotel, above, and the Parliament, out of sight to the right.

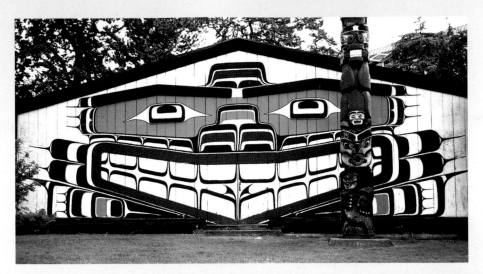

Known in Canada as First Nations, the native tribes of British Columbia have a colorful cultural heritage. This clan house is on the grounds of the Royal British Columbia Museum, a truly excellent facility located near the Empress Hotel, just off Victoria Harbor. The large totem display area is open to the street and is easy to view, even in the evening when the museum may be closed.

WHAT TO SEE: Fortunately, many of Victoria's attractions are centered around the harbor:

The **Royal British Columbia Museum** is one of the best small museums you'll ever encounter. If you want to see Northwest Native culture up close, this will be probably your best opportunity. While the tribes in British Columbia are distinct from those along the areas of Coastal Alaska that you will be traveling through, their art such as totem poles, share many of the same themes.

The **Empress Hotel** was part of a series of large and very notable resorts built by the Canadian Pacific Railway. Make a point of visiting the restored lobby, where afternoon tea is a major local event. Right behind the hotel is the glass roofed **Crystal Garden**, with its tropical plants and animals.

The **Royal London Wax Museum** is the big building on the south waterfront next to the floating aquarium, and across the harbor are the seaplane docks and the booking and boarding area for **Whale Watching** tours. There is a resident population of orcas or killer whales that often hang out in Haro Strait, between Vancouver Island and the nearby San Juan Islands. In addition, humpback whales are also sometimes seen here.

12 miles from downtown are **Butchart Gardens**, which has become one of the most visited sites in the province. What is now a stunning 50 acre showpiece had rather humble beginnings: In 1904 Jennnie Butchart, whose husband operated a cement plant near the site, got tired of staring at the ugly scar in the land that his limestone quarrying operations left. She brought in a few plants to spruce up the area, one thing led to another and now hundreds of thousands of visitors come to see her handiwork.

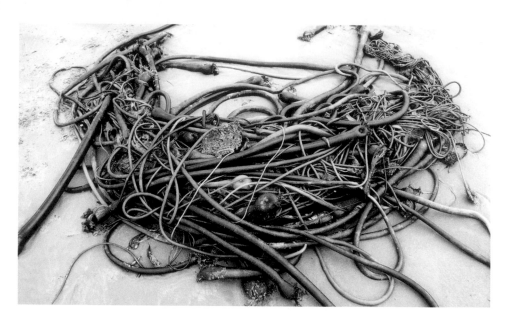

Kelp, Long Beach, Vancouver Island. Kelp is the mariner's friend. It attaches itself to rocks in shallow water and floats to the surface. As most small boat operators have learned, it is very unwise to drive through kelp.

About six hours after leaving Seattle you'll be at around mile 120, off Cape Flattery. Before the advent of modern electronic aids to navigation, this area had the nickname of "The Graveyard of the North Pacific." Don't worry, your big Princess ship has all the equipment she needs to find her way safely. But imagine yourself in November of 1915, on the crew of the big three-masted sailing ship *Carelmapu*, trying to find Juan de Fuca Strait in foggy weather. They'd been at sea almost two months and were looking forward to some R&R along Seattle's rough waterfront. For two days they tacked

A Mosquito Fleet

In the early years of this century, dozens of small steamboats, a "mosquito fleet," people said, provided transportation up and down Puget Sound and coastal British Columbia.

Before radar came along in the 1940s, the little steamboats tried to keep to their schedules by any means, fog or not. The more astute skippers felt their way along by tooting their whistles and horns and listening for the echoes off the land and for the answering cries of animals along the way.

The Lady Rose, *similar to some of the early "mosquito boats," still carries passengers and freight between Port Alberni and Bamfield on the rugged west coast of Vancouver Island.*

back and forth, hoping to find a tug to tow them into sheltered waters. But instead a strong gale came up, blowing out most of her sails, and she could only drop her anchors off the rocks and hope that they would hold.

Above: a bad place for ships - the shores of northwest Washington and Vancouver Island are rocky, often fog-shrouded, and swept by unpredictable currents.

The coastal steamer *Maquinna* spotted them, and approached carefully in the 50-foot seas, the worst the captain had ever seen. He dropped two anchors and tried to let the wind push him close enough to get a line to the doomed ship. But before he was able to, a thundering sea swept his vessel and the strain ripped his anchor winches off his deck, and he could only cut the chains and escape while he could. The next great sea swept the *Carelmapu* onto the rocks, and of the 25 on board, only five were left to stagger to shore when the tide went out.

"The coast is, in most places, low and rocky and fringed with numerous rocks and sunken dangers; a very short distance inland it rises in mountains of considerable height. When about to make the coast, it cannot be too strongly enjoined that every opportunity should be taken of ascertaining the position of the vessel, for fogs and thick weather descend on this coast at any season of the year."
- *British Columbia Pilot, Vol. 1. 7th edition, 1965*

So many ships and sailors met their end along this ironbound coast, that a trail for shipwrecked sailors was established along its most dangerous section, between Carmanah Point and Cape Beale. A number of huts were located along the trail, stocked with food and firewood, and provided with a telephone that was connected to the lighthouses at either end.

The wet climate on the western slopes of these coastal

mountains create perfect conditions for forest growth, and much of the old growth forests of British Columbia are located here. Because the land along the west coast of Vancouver Island is so rugged, there are very few roads. So logging camps were often built on floating log rafts that could be towed from inlet to inlet as areas were harvested.

"In the distance the tugboat that had come from Port Alice to tow away the company buildings and those that would follow the camp to Holberg, tugged and struggled to separate the floats from the shore, much like a dentist pulling teeth. I went back inside, angry, "What about my memories?" I may not have said exactly that, but it was the essence of what I felt at the time, for until then Spry Camp had been the sum of my experience in the world. I didn't know yet there would be other experiences of a childhood raft-life, of snaking up and down Quatsino Sound until each turn was as familiar as a neighborhood street is to a city child.

– Alan Oman, "The Day They Took Our Town Away," in *Raincoast Chronicles*

For most of the 20th century, you either worked in the forest or the sea along this coast, or businesses associated with them, such as fish canneries or sawmills. The salmon resource, especially was strong, and the companies that bought and processed the fish often loaned money to promising fishermen for boats and gear.

Most of the salmon were kings (also called 'springs' in British Columbia) and silvers or cohos. Fishermen used vessels called trollers to tow an array of hooks and lines behind them from the tall trolling poles that are lowered to 45

degrees to fish and are usually pulled into the vertical position when they enter a harbor. See P. 103

Unfortunately for the many coastal residents that depended on strong salmon runs, catches fell off dramatically starting in the 1970s. A number of factors were to blame: careless logging practices, overfishing, and the cumulative effects of a number of dams that were built along the Columbia River beginning in the 1940s.

Though no one knew it at the time, it turned out that many of the large king salmon that supported so many fishermen along the Alaska and British Columbia coasts had come from eggs laid in the many tributaries of the Columbia River, over a thousand miles from Alaska fishing grounds.

These were rugged people who took the day by day challenges of difficult lives in stride. Loggers worked long hours for small wages and often lived in very modest housing. Fishermen spent long days at sea in small boats, anchoring up at night in remote coves, far from the nearest settlement or town. Fish-buying vessels would provide food, fuel, water, and on a very

For generations salmon fishing was the bread and butter of many Vancouver Island families.

A growing awareness of the powerful beauty of the west coast of Vancouver Island has made it very popular with kayakers.

good day, a hot shower for men who might be weeks at a time without returning to home port.

The towns along the outside coast, Bamfield, Uculet, Tofino, and Nootka, were small rough outposts, connected by long and winding roads to the rest of Vancouver Island, if there were any roads at all. For generations, the old iron steamer *Maquinna* made weekly round trips between Victoria and the settlements along Vancouver Island's west coast.

As the best trees were cut and the salmon runs declined along this coast, an unexpected transformation began. Winding down the rough roads from the populated east coast of Vancouver Island came kayakers, sports fishermen, whale watchers, surfers and well-heeled Canadians seeking second homes. Today in remote inlets where a decade ago you would have found only loggers and commercial fishermen, you are more apt to find kayakers, yachts, and perhaps instead of a floating logging camp, a floating fly-in sportsfishing lodge.

While wild salmon runs were declining, the market demand for salmon remained strong, and entrepreneurs wasted no time realizing that the remote sheltered coves and clean water of this coast were perfect for salmon aquaculture. Today British Columbia-farmed salmon is shipped all over the world, and many fishermen who once operated their own boats for wild salmon, have found work with some of the many salmon farms in the area.

When your ship passes close to land, take your binoculars

and have a look into the secluded coves. If you see lines of red buoys or rectangular floating structures, it is probably an aquaculture operation.

Ships leaving Seattle in the late afternoon usually find themselves somewhere off **Nootka Island, mile 240 W** the following dawn. North of here is the most remote and little visited part of the Vancouver Island coast. By early afternoon, your ship has usually passed into the wider waters of Queen Charlotte Sound and Hecate Strait.

Surfers at Long Beach, Vancouver Island wait for the perfect wave. Even on the hottest day of summer, rare is the surfer without a wet suit in these chilly waters.

Native Culture and the Coming of the Whites

Before Cook and Vancouver, before the tide of whites that flooded into the region in the 1800s, coastal natives here had lived thousands of years in a culture that, compared to other native Americans, could only be described as idyllic. The sea and the forest provided.

There was cedar for houses, and halibut, salmon, herring, whales, candlefish (a herring-like fish harvested for its oil), clams and berries for food. They had no agriculture; they didn't need it. They were hunter-gatherers but they could gather food without the nomadic life of their Plains brothers (They might, however, move each spring to summer villages near the mouths of salmon streams.)

The coming of the white man brought something worse than the loss of their lands; it brought a plague like that which swept Europe in the Middle Ages. Who first brought smallpox and tuberculosis to the Northwest Indians? Was it a Spaniard, or a "Boston man" from Gray's ship? Captain Cook's sailmaker or Vancouver's gunner?

It mattered little; when the first sail appeared over the horizon in the 1770s, the curtain was about to be drawn on a powerful culture that had endured for centuries.

Things to Do in Vancouver

Water buses wait at the Granville Island dock for downtown-bound travelers. Below: If you do nothing else, take a walk or a horse trolley through spectacular Stanley Park.

Plan time on your trip to explore Vancouver, a particularly livable and exciting city. A vibrant mixture of races, a dramatic waterfront setting, and a dynamic arts and business community combine to make Vancouver a memorable port of call. Many of the sights are easily accessible from where your ship docks.

Within walking or short taxi distance is much of the city core with almost unlimited shopping and dining. There is also a subway/elevated rail system called the Skytrain which makes getting around fairly simple.

A few blocks east of Canada Place is Gastown, where the city was first settled, and today is an eclectic neighborhood of old warehouses made into restaurants, artist's lofts, condos, and all manner of shops. Do you have a feeling of deja vu as you walk around Gastown? You may have seen a movie filmed here: Gastown is popular with cinema producers.

Chinatown is a few more blocks to the south (consider a taxi) and its size reflects Vancouver's popularity with Asians. This is the real thing: If you don't read Chinese, make sure your menu has English as well. With the waters of Georgia Strait and the North Pacific close at hand, many restaurants feature live tanks from which patrons may select their meal.

Visitors and Vancouverites alike are indeed fortunate that its founders set aside the 1,000 or so acres that today is Stanley Park. It features restaurants, a zoo, the ubiquitous totems, but most of all a stunning waterfront setting right next to downtown. A popular walk leads through the park to a dramatic overlook at Lion's Gate Bridge, where all manner of marine traffic can be seen in the tide that pours in and out of Burrard Inlet.

Take the foot ferry to Granville Island on False Creek. Granville Island is a combination of a farmer's and craftsmen's market, with restaurants.

Within walking distance west of Granville Island is the Vancouver Maritime Museum, whose showpiece exhibit is the brave little steamer *St. Roche.* When the Canadian government decided to send the ship and her crew of Canadian Northwest Mounted Policemen from Vancouver to Newfoundland via the Northwest Passage, that is, through the Arctic ice, it was to be a voyage that made history. They steamed for seven weeks, got frozen into the ice for nine months, and then set out again once the ice freed them. Their long-awaited freedom was short-lived; the ice locked them in again after just three weeks, this time for 10 months!

If you have time, consider a flight to Victoria - float planes fly regularly from downtown. The capital of British Columbia, Victoria seems more like a bit of England than fast-paced glitzy Vancouver.

Downtown Gastown and its many galleries are just a few blocks from the big Canada Place cruise ship terminal.

The Museum of Anthropology

In the early 1900s, collectors made it their business to preserve the hauntingly beautiful, almost mysterious artwork of the coastal tribes of British Columbia. Much of what they found or purchased is housed today in a specially built hall in the Museum of Anthropology at the University of British Columbia. If you have any interest in Northwest Indian art, this is a "must" stop; the collection rivals any in the world.

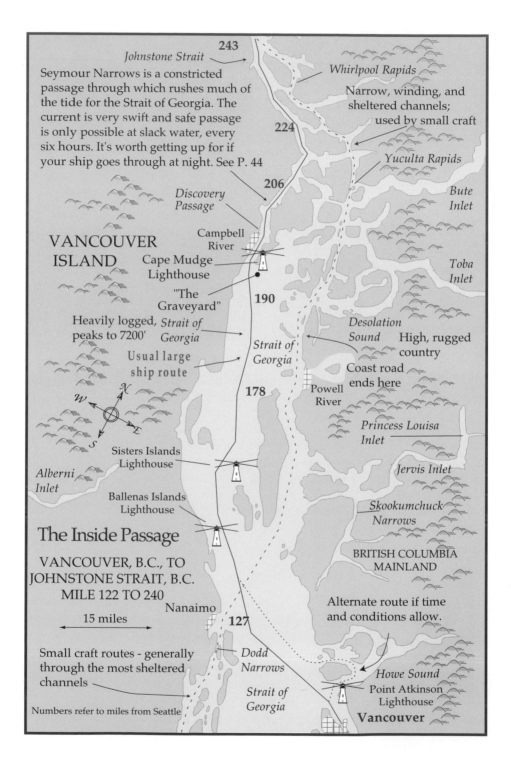

243 _Johnstone Strait_

Whirlpool Rapids

Seymour Narrows is a constricted passage through which rushes much of the tide for the Strait of Georgia. The current is very swift and safe passage is only possible at slack water, every six hours. It's worth getting up for if your ship goes through at night. See P. 44

224

Narrow, winding, and sheltered channels; used by small craft

Yuculta Rapids

206

Discovery Passage

Bute Inlet

Campbell River

VANCOUVER ISLAND

Cape Mudge Lighthouse

Toba Inlet

"The Graveyard"

190

Heavily logged, peaks to 7200'

Strait of Georgia

Strait of Georgia

Desolation Sound   High, rugged country

Usual large ship route

Coast road ends here

178

Powell River

Princess Louisa Inlet

Sisters Islands Lighthouse

Jervis Inlet

Alberni Inlet

Ballenas Islands Lighthouse

Skookumchuck Narrows

The Inside Passage

VANCOUVER, B.C., TO JOHNSTONE STRAIT, B.C. MILE 122 TO 240

BRITISH COLUMBIA MAINLAND

Alternate route if time and conditions allow.

Nanaimo

127

15 miles

Small craft routes - generally through the most sheltered channels

Dodd Narrows

Howe Sound

Point Atkinson Lighthouse

Numbers refer to miles from Seattle

Strait of Georgia

Vancouver

CHAPTER 2

The Wilderness Begins

Vancouver, B.C., Mile 95 to
Alaska Border, Mile 575W

"Tracing shining ways through fiord and sound, past forests
and waterfalls, islands and mountains and far azure headlands,
it seems as if surely we must at length reach the very paradise
of the poets, the abode of the blessed. "
　　　　　　　　　　　—John Muir, *Travels in Alaska*

V ancouver voyages begin or end amidst the bustle
　　　of commercial traffic in one of the Northwest's
　　　busiest harbors. Imagine how it was in 1792,
when British explorer George Vancouver came seeking the
Northwest Passage, that legendary passage back to the
Atlantic Ocean. Between here and Skagway, Alaska, 900
miles north, lay many inlets like this; each had to be
explored mile by mile. Most of the exploration was done
by rowing and sailing in small launches lest they miss a
narrow entrance that might lead to the Northwest Passage.
These were frustrating trips:

　　"The inlet now took a N.W. by W. direction, without any
　contraction in its width, until about five o'clock in the
　evening, when all our hopes vanished, by finding it termi-
　nate, as others had done, in swampy lowland producing a
　few maples and pines, in latitude 50 6', 236 33'."
　　　　—Captain George Vancouver, *A Voyage of Discovery*

　　Over the next three summers, the boat parties' hopes
of gaining the fame of being the first to find that elusive
passage will vanish in many such dead end inlets.

　　Much of your travel on this day will be in the Strait of
Georgia, which stretches from the cities in the south to
wilderness in the north. To the west across the strait is
Vancouver Island.

Vancouver's famous
Stanley Park will be
on the south side of
the ship as you pass
Lion's Gate Bridge.
If you look carefully,
you might get a
glimpse of the totems.

Look for:

- The milky-colored water that enters the strait to the south. It is glacial flow from the Fraser River.
- Log and chip barges: British Columbia is a legendary producer of forest products. Wood chips are moved in big high-sided barges so full they seem almost submerged.

B.C. Ferries S-class, 560' *Spirit of British Columbia,* and *Spirit of Vancouver Island.*

- Log booms: The rectangular rafts of logs towed slowly behind tugs are hard to see at night, because frequently they are marked only by dim and flickering kerosene lamps.
- Alaska-bound tugs and barges from Puget Sound, stacked high with container vans with large items, such as boats, strapped on top.
- **Orcas, or killer whales**: Puget Sound and lower British Columbia, especially Johnstone Strait and the Strait of Georgia, are home to 200 to 300 of these intriguing mammals. Attaining an adult length of 20 feet or more and a weight of three to four tons, these handsome black and white whales are easily recognized by their tall dorsal fins as they travel on the surface. They travel in groups, called pods.

B.C. Ferries C-class, 457' *Queen of Cowichan, Queen of Coquitlam, Queen of Oak Bay, Queen of Surrey.*

- Ferries: The British Columbia coast is served by a large fleet of ferries. Biggest are the 560-foot S-Class vessels such as the *Spirit of British Columbia,* which feature escalators between decks.

The $2.5 Million Herring Set

For a period in the late 1980s, the market for herring was so hot that Japanese buyers were known to fly out to the fishing sites with briefcases full of cash handcuffed to their wrists.

Canadian fisherman Don Dawson hit the jackpot in 1987, with one 970-ton set in Barkley Sound, on the west coast of Vancouver Island, worth $2.5 million. Several other vessels helped transport the catch. When Dawson's boat, the *Snow Cloud,* arrived at the Ocean Fisheries plant in Vancouver, plant officials had a case of champagne waiting.

Herring gillnetters like these harvest smaller catches, but have less expenses than the fisherman in the story who operated a seiner, a much larger boat.

Approaching or leaving Vancouver Harbor, look at the distant shore to the west. This stretch is part of the **Gulf Islands** (Canadian), which together with the **San Juan Islands** (American) to the south, form an extremely intricate and sheltered archipelago, containing rural villages, hidden beaches, quiet anchorages—all the elements of great small-boat cruising.

The store at Olga, Orcas Island, WA. The American San Juan and Canadian Gulf Islands offer a wide variety of truly excellent camping and boating opportunities.

Look to the west for smoke from the sawmill and pulp mill at **Nanaimo, mile 127.** Just south of the mills a channel leads to **Dodd Narrows,** the narrowest of the passes among the Gulf Islands, heavily used by small craft and subject to swift currents. Smart small-boat skippers heed the admonition from Sailing Directions that "no attempt should be made to pass through against the tidal stream."

I didn't heed this warning one black fall night, in a 70-footer. Foolish me:

> "**October 17, 1982, Dodd Narrows, B.C.** Went through against a big ebb in the black. Close one! Plus we were towing a gill-netter with engine problems. Fortunately I shortened the tow line before we started through. If I'd known it would be so bad I'd never have started, but once we were in, there was nothing but try and get through, swerving violently back and forth in the current. The guy we were towing had to steer his boat to stay off the rocks. After we got through I called him on the radio.
>
> " 'Oh,' he says, 'That wasn't too bad—except I bit my cigar in half..' "

JOE'S JOURNAL

Point Atkinson Lighthouse, a few miles north of Vancouver, with the dramatic mountains of Howe Sound behind.

Tips For Mariners: In Georgia Strait, if your barometer drops to 29 inches or lower with a clear sky and you notice a long swell starting from the southwest, expect bad weather in three hours.

Howe Sound: VANCOUVER DEPARTURES: After you pass under the bridge and leave the harbor, your ship may take a loop through Howe Sound, if your skipper has some time to kill waiting on the tide at Seymour Narrows. (See P.44.) After swinging to the right around Point Atkinson lighthouse, look for the large waterfront homes on the right. This is one of the most expensive neighborhoods in North America.

On the left is Bowen Island, and Snug Cove, a particularly popular spot for excursions and picnickers who would board the vessels of the Union Steamboat Company in downtown Vancouver. Today many Vancouver residents have second homes here.

If your ship cruises through Howe Sound, look for the waterfront homes on the right.

As your ship swings to the west around Bowen Island, the landscape changes substantially. Behind is a shore dotted with houses and lights, but ahead the shores are much more lonely, with fewer settlements. The steep mountains and long arms of the sound cut the road; auto travelers must ferry across the sound to continue north. This is your first taste of what most of the north coast is like: dramatic, steep, forested shores, where man is only a visitor.

Tips For Mariners: Watch at night for vessels displaying three white lights in a vertical line. These are tugs with tows—barges, log rafts, and so forth—more than 600 feet behind them. Watch out if you cross behind the tug. Some very large barges or very long rafts may be marked by the

dimmest of lights, and be traveling quite fast, able to trample the unwary mariner who strays into their path.

Evening in Howe Sound.

The end of the road. If your ship takes a loop through Howe Sound, look for the big ferry terminal in Horseshoe Bay, on your right, a few miles past the lighthouse. From here ferries travel across Georgia Strait to Nanaimo, on Vancouver Island, but also to

Approaching the Lion's Gate Bridge.

Langdale, on the mainland west side of Howe Sound, and the gateway to the so-called Sunshine Coast. Here the rain shadow of the mountains on Vancouver Island creates a much drier micro-climate than much of the British Columbia Coast, and a much more relaxed and laid back culture than in the busy Vancouver area.

40 miles north you'll take another ferry across deep Jervis Inlet. But about 30 miles north of that the road ends for good, cut off by the steep mountains in the Desolation Sound area.

The winding way north—much of the north coast consists of lonely waterways with few settlements. This is in Discovery Passage, north of Seymour Narrows, near mile 218.

There are several resident pods of orcas or killer whales in the Georgia Straits area; look for the tall dorsal fin.

Off the beaten path: **Jervis Inlet** (east of **mile 156E**), like many along the coast here, is like a fjord in Norway. For boaters used to waters where there are roads and houses along the shore, this deep winding canyon is their first real taste of the roadless, unsettled North. Near its head is Princess Louisa Inlet, dramatically scenic, the destination of thousands of small craft each year.

It's worth the trip. Mystery writer Erle Stanley Gardner said:

"There is no use describing that inlet. Perhaps an atheist could view it and remain an atheist, but I doubt it.

"There is a calm tranquility which stretches from the smooth surface of the reflecting water straight up into infinity. The deep calm of eternal silence is only disturbed by the muffled roar of throbbing waterfalls as they plunge down from sheer cliffs.

"There is no scenery in the world that can beat it. Not that I've seen the rest of the world. I don't have to. I've seen Princess Louisa Inlet."

Reached through narrow Malibu Rapids, the inlet is four miles long, with a marine park and dramatic waterfall at its head. (The rapids is one of those places vessels should traverse at slack water.) Vancouver passed the entrance in a small boat, but thought it only a creek. Don't expect a wilderness experience, though; in summer there will be many boats.

Look for the smokestack and mill at **Powell River**, east of

mile 185. In 1897, Herbert Carmichael and two other men looking for a site for a paper mill explored the mainland coast from Vancouver to Desolation Sound in a small sailboat; they looked into almost every creek. When they found Powell River falls, with 50,000 horsepower waiting to be dammed and the salt water close at hand, they knew they'd struck pay dirt. The mill they built grew to be the largest paper mill in the world.

Off the beaten track: **Desolation Sound**, mile190E: bleak, treeless, shunned by humans? "Our residence here was truly forlorn; an aweful silence pervaded the gloomy forests, whilst animated nature seemed to have deserted the neighboring country."

Vancouver really got it wrong when he named this place Desolation Sound. It was rainy, and he was no doubt discouraged by the number of dead-end inlets he had explored, and his party couldn't find any fish or game. But the place is gorgeous—one of the most popular yacht cruising grounds on the West Coast. Much of the area is protected as a British Columbia Marine Park.

The steep mountains made road building impossible along the mainland shore north of mile 188E.

The water is warm enough for swimming. This doesn't happen often in salt water at this latitude—it's unusual north of San Francisco—but a quirk of geography makes tidal currents from both ends of Vancouver Island meet here and create warmer water than any other place on the British Columbia coast, sometimes reaching almost 80 degrees F (28 C).

Gateways to The North

The land and waterways north of Seymour Narrows and Yuculta Rapids are very different from those to the south. Gone are the frieze of settlements along the shore, the necklace of lights at night. Air and water are cooler, and there are fewer pleasure craft. The land seems much wilder. This is *The North.*

No one traveling from the Strait of Georgia north to the cooler and lonelier country beyond can forget these narrow passes where the tide runs like rapids in a river. At the very place where the busy south coast ends and the wilderness begins, nature has set an obstacle, as if to warn the traveler of what lies beyond.

Along the Fisherman's Way

   While ferries and cruise ships generally take the wider and deeper channels, there are a number of alternate routes available for small craft. Your ship, for example, must transit Seymour Narrows, but many small craft will travel north along a much more narrow and winding route, further east, via Yuculta Rapids, Greene Point Rapids and Whirlpool Rapids, rejoining the "Steamer Route" near mile 241. A few highlights:

   "Slack...in the Yucultas? Nossir, don't be expecting no slack in that place. You get all that water up in Bute Inlet, see, especially after it's been raining inland, and it's too much for 'er, she just comes pouring out of there one way, and pow, she just turns around and runs hard the other way, she jes' ain't got no time for slack, see now?"

   — A local logger

   "It was thick o'fog, when we were waiting below the Yucultas fer slack, and we kept hearing something, like it was blowing, then they came up all around us— this pack o'killer whales—Jesus, there musta' been ten or twelve of them, with them big fins. Wellsir, I want to tell ya', they waited and waited just like us, and then when that tide stopped running, they timed it just right and went through along with us..."

   — A friend

From my own journals:

"**May 30, 1981, Wellbore Channel, B.C**: My crew and my wife and I had worked for weeks to get our fish-buying vessel ready for a long season. We'd left Seattle with a deck load of cargo to stow and a two-page list of jobs still to do. We'd gotten underway early, traveled late, caught slack water at Yuculta Rapids at midnight, tied to a deserted wharf at Thurlow, B.C., an hour later. We just needed to rest, to sleep for a few sweet hours, before going on: to Whirlpool and Greene Point Rapids, on and on, until we got to our cannery in Alaska, 600 miles north.

In the hour before dawn, I got up quietly, stretched my legs in the starlight, making dark footprints on the frost covered dock, past the abandoned lodge, and the rusting farm equipment. As I slipped back aboard, first light was coming to the sky above the dark hills, and the wild land all around.

The big Caterpillar engine rumbled to life. I threw the lines off the empty dock, got a coffee, and took it up to the flying bridge. We moved out into the channel; there was just the whistle of the turbo, the rush of the tide, the green smell of the woods and the rich smell of the sea."

This is from a 30-day-long, stormy and difficult trip in the fall of 1975. It seemed like that for every day we traveled, we had to wait for two or three, with the wind howling through our rigging in some lonely anchorage:

"**Oct 26, 1975, Stuart Island B.C**: Tied 5 p.m. to the dock at this closed fishing resort after difficult day. SE 30 in Johnstone Strait—right on the nose, with every third or fourth one coming right over the bow and slapping hard at the windows. Glad to finally turn off into the side channels and have the narrow slot of Whirlpool Rapids open up in the trees, leading into those winding waterways where the wind barely reached. Finally Yuculta Rapids with a big whirlpool spinning us around twice and this quiet dock where the kindly caretaker came down and opened up the showers for us—unlimited hot water—a true luxury and we soaked and let the cares of a long season in The North fade away. In the early dusk we looked out and saw the dim shapes of the islands and passages of Desolation Sound opening to the south. Tomorrow we'd be amongst the bustle of the busy south coast; the day after, Seattle: our winter lives.

"It's been a five and a half month season; you'd think we'd be glad to get off the boat. Yet the closer we get to the end, the slower we seem to go. Outside, the roar of Yuculta Rapids filled the night and the spell of The North was still very strong; we were reluctant to let it go."

Seymour Narrows Area Mile 195-208

Every six hours, at either the top or bottom of the tide, there is a brief period of slack water. It is at these periods that most vessels transit the Narrows. Sometimes, especially in the spring and fall, many vessels may be seen waiting here for slack water.

"The pilot told me that an English man-of-war started through and the tide caught him. Some fellows over on the mainland claimed they seen the boat when it first got caught in the whirl. He went around faster and faster, until he was sucked down clean out of sight. Yes, sir, they never even seen so much as a draw bucket come floating to the surface. Even the masts went down in that hole. It was just the end for every soul on board. Well, after he got done telling me about it, we waited a while, then we got the signal, and we run slow bell right through them narrows, and we never had a mite of trouble neither."

—Martha Ferguson McKeown, *The Trail Led North*

This is really worth seeing. Set your alarm, or don't go to bed if your ship goes through here at night. Start looking for swirls and current eddies near **mile 193**.

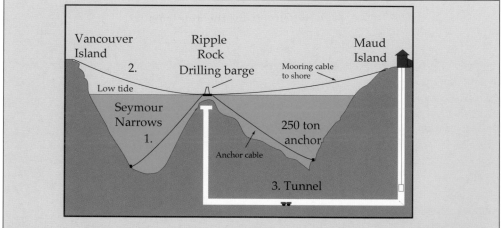

The Struggle to Blast Ripple Rock

1. 1943—Drilling attempted from barge anchored with 250-ton anchors. Soon abandoned—current caused too much motion
2. 1944—Barge moored with cables to shore; barge motion still too much.
3. 1953—Test drilling reveals feasibility of tunneling under Seymour Narrows from Maud Island. Miners excavate 3,270 feet of tunnels and shafts to place almost 3 million pounds of Nitramex 2-H dynamite. Adios Ripple Rock!

BCARS 19613

Perhaps a third of the tide in the Strait of Georgia tries to fit within the confines of Discovery Passage. The current floods from the north here, and when a big flood is opposed here by a southerly booming up the strait, small craft better watch out. The locals call this spot **The Graveyard.** The steam tug *Petrel* disappeared here on a winter night in 1952, overwhelmed by the tide rips so quickly there wasn't even time for a radio call.

Taming Seymour Narrows, Attempt Number 2, circa 1944. Drill barge is moored to thick steel cables hung across narrows. The effort was abandoned as too slow and dangerous after an accident when nine workers were lost from a capsized work skiff.

Mile 194, Cape Mudge. Quadra Island settlers had a special present in December 1927, when the Alaska-bound steamer *Northwestern* ran ashore loaded with Christmas goods. The ship was abandoned without loss of life, and the local people made sure the cargo wasn't wasted. The hardy old ship was salvaged and put back to work.

Mile 197, Campbell River and Discovery Pier. The big dock, with flags and banners, was built for sports fishermen to take advantage of the area's abundant salmon runs.

The village of **Quathiaski Cove**, on the eastern side of the channel at **mile 198**, is the site of the Kwagiulth Museum and its collection of native art.

Mile 200 to 204: Look for vessels waiting for slack water along the eastern side of the channel. During the Gold Rush years, from 1897 to about 1910, settlers on the Quadra Island shore would sometimes hear sled dogs barking on the ships waiting for the tide. If conditions allowed, they might row out for a visit and get the news from up north.

Watch out for tide rips with southerly wind and flooding tide near Cape Mudge.

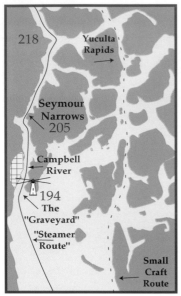

For large ships, the challenge of Seymour Narrows is twofold. You have to make almost a right angle turn, but do it at slack water—a 30-minute period that only comes every six hours.

Mile 205, Seymour Narrows: "We're going through there?" There is no other route north (except the ocean) for ships of any size. This is a famous place. The tidal currents race through this canyon at speeds of up to 15 knots (16.5 miles per hour), and safe passage is possible only at slack water, a brief period every six hours. It used to be worse.

Before 1958, Ripple Rock, a stone pinnacle beneath the surface, destroyed a ship a year. Besides the hazard the rock itself presented, its position created whirlpools and eddies strong enough to capsize small boats and shove passenger liners into the rocky shore.

What to look for: - Once your ship passes beneath the Lions Gate Bridge, it's about a 6-7 hour run up to Seymour Narrows.

However, because the tide runs so swiftly there, safe passage is only possible around the time of low or high tide, occuring every six hours, and the time changes daily.

If you're traveling in mid to late June, when days are longest, your ship might transit the narrows at twilight or dawn. But generally, northbound ships often transit the narrows in the dark of the night after midnight.

Look for the lights of a town close by on the port or left side of your ship. This is Campbell River. A little further north you'll pass a big sawmill, also on the left. Three miles north, you'll swing left at Race Point, and shortly afterwards swing right into the actual narrows. Here your ship must fit under the powerlines that span the gorge, and above the granite ridge of Ripple Shoal, all that was left after blasting Ripple Rock. It's a very dramatic spot, even at night, so consider staying up for it.

The challenge of blasting a rock out from beneath some of the most violent tidal rapids on earth delayed efforts until 1943, when work was attempted from a barge held in place with 250-ton anchors. Before the anchor cables parted from the strain, they vibrated so badly as to make work almost impossible. Anchoring the barge to bolts drilled into the shore was no better; the bolts sheared off from the strain. Next came huge cables across the narrows, but these too failed to hold the barge steady and it was given up.

A decade later, 3,270 feet of vertical and horizontal tunnels were blasted through from Maud Island. Three million pounds of dynamite were loaded into Ripple Rock, and on April 7, 1958, the largest non-nuclear blast in history turned Ripple Rock into Ripple Shoal, deep enough for almost any ship to pass over safely.

Tugs with log booms. They had to transit several rapids in the Yuculta Rapids area to get to the nearest sawmill.

Consider Vancouver's men in their small and frail sailing ships, or rowing up small waterways in longboats, without chart, engine, or tide book. They were seamen of the humblest origins; most could neither read nor write. One wonders what they thought, rowing past these islands, through these channels, wondering if the next bend in the channel would be the entrance to the Northwest Passage or a tidal maelstrom.

Johnstone Strait, which begins at mile 218, is the Route 1 of the Inside Passage. Small craft may stay in sheltered channels for a while, but at **mile 242**, they have to emerge from the back channels if they're headed north.

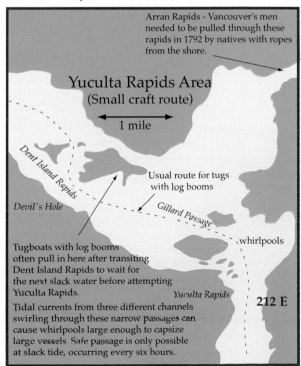

Arran Rapids - Vancouver's men needed to be pulled through these rapids in 1792 by natives with ropes from the shore.

Yuculta Rapids Area
(Small craft route)

← 1 mile →

Dent Island Rapids

Usual route for tugs with log booms

Devil's Hole

Gillard Passage

whirlpools

Tugboats with log booms often pull in here after transiting Dent Island Rapids to wait for the next slack water before attempting Yuculta Rapids.

Yuculta Rapids

212 E

Tidal currents from three different channels swirling through these narrow passages can cause whirlpools large enough to capsize large vessels. Safe passage is only possible at slack tide, occurring every six hours.

Look for:
- The salmon fleet: (see guide p. 96). You'll see gill-netters and seiners operating in these waters. Many of the fish are headed for the Fraser River, near Vancouver.
- Log barges: On inside waters logs are towed in flat rafts. To make a flat raft, you tie long, straight logs together, perhaps 60 feet long, with short lengths of chain into a rectangular perimeter, which you then fill with parallel

Self-loading log barge. Note small push boat on barge below base of crane. It will be lowered into water at destination, to push logs into position for loading.

rows of logs, strapped or bundled into groups of a half dozen or so. A tug tows the whole works to a sawmill, slowly, as all those logs make for tremendous water resistance. Today, for longer passages across open waters, the logs are moved in self-loading or self-dumping barges. The latter have ballast tanks. At the destination, the tanks on one side are filled, the barge tilts, and the logs slide off.

Many of the logs processed by mills in the Vancouver area come from inlets off Johnstone Strait and the adjoining waters.

- Floating logging camps: Look into coves where you see logging activity, and you may see one of the floating camps, long a feature of life on the north coast. The road on the mainland north of Vancouver ends east of mile 185 or so, and so much of the logging activity along this coast, especially on the mainland, or right hand side of the ship as you travel north, takes place in remote inlets and bays far from any road system. So floating communities were built on log rafts that were towed from place to place as the great forests were cut. Some of these floating communities included stores, schools, even little gardens - all built on big rafts of logs. See the quote on P. 28.
- Orcas: The so-called killer whales (actually, all they're doing is feeding, like the rest of us) are frequently seen in this area. Before 1964, when the first killer whale was captured near Saturna Island by accident—they had been trying to kill one to use as a sculptor's model—

Frans Lanting, Minden Pictures

killer whales were thought to be aggressive and dangerous. In captivity, however, the whale they named Moby Doll showed himself to be tame and docile. Unfortunately, injured in the catching, he became sick and died three months later. Since then, many orcas have been captured and sold to aquariums. The public's exposure to these gentle mammals changed our perception of their manner and intelligence. As a result, Puget Sound has become a sanctuary for orcas, and in British Columbia capturing them has been severely restricted. Today it is very difficult for aquariums to obtain orcas.

There's probably no better place to look for orcas, or killer whales, than the Johnstone Strait area. Whale watchers from all over the world come here in the summer months to observe orcas.

Did you know? Whale watchers listening with underwater microphones near **mile 235** heard what sounded like killer whales singing the tune, "It's raining, it's pouring." Researchers in other parts of Canada have reported the same experience.

The waterways that lead off to the north—Havannah Channel at **mile 253,** and Blackney and Baronet Passage at **mile 269,** open up to a whole world of islands, passages, inlets and tiny and secluded harbors, and all generally off the beaten path, without road or ferry access. This is the British Columbia north coast, where many harbors may see months pass without a visitor.

Latitude is starting to make a difference in the climate once you get north of Seymour Narrows. Even though you're only 200 miles north and west of Seattle, the weather is noticeably moister and cloudier.

The normally conservative British Columbia Pilot, a detailed book of information on aids to navigation, har-

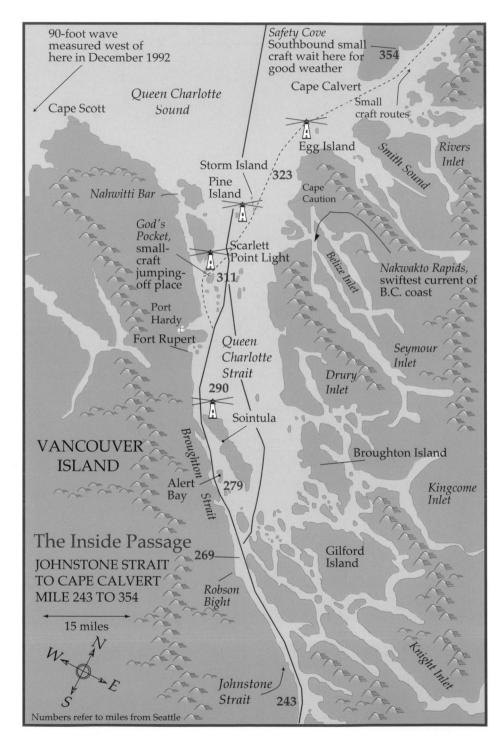

90-foot wave measured west of here in December 1992

Queen Charlotte Sound

Cape Scott

Safety Cove Southbound small craft wait here for good weather

354

Cape Calvert

Small craft routes

Egg Island

Rivers Inlet

Smith Sound

Storm Island
Pine Island

323

Nahwitti Bar

Cape Caution

God's Pocket, small-craft jumping-off place

Scarlett Point Light

311

Belize Inlet

Nakwakto Rapids, swiftest current of B.C. coast

Port Hardy

Fort Rupert

Queen Charlotte Strait

Seymour Inlet

290

Sointula

Drury Inlet

Broughton Island

VANCOUVER ISLAND

Broughton Strait

Alert Bay

279

Kingcome Inlet

The Inside Passage

JOHNSTONE STRAIT TO CAPE CALVERT MILE 243 TO 354

269

Gilford Island

Robson Bight

15 miles

N
W — *E*
S

Johnstone Strait 243

Knight Inlet

Numbers refer to miles from Seattle

bors, sea conditions and much more, uses some unusually descriptive language (for them) to describe this country:

> "Connected to the strait are several extensive inlets, the shores of which rise in almost sheer precipices to stupendous peaks, clad in perpetual snow. The inlets are very dreary and gloomy, due to their being overshadowed by the heights of the mountains and the frequent mist and rain."
> —*British Columbia Pilot, Volume I, 1965*

At the head of **Kingcome Inlet**, and two miles up the Kingcome River, past the Halliday Ranch, is the Kwakiutl village of Kingcome and the setting for a novel. (Today the name Kwakiutl is often rendered in English as Kwagiulth).

Editor's choice: *I Heard the Owl Call My Name*, by Margaret Craven, published by Doubleday, is a haunting and powerful tale of a young Catholic priest working with the Kwakiutl people. Few books describe the mystery and power of native life as well.

> "The snow lay thick on the shoulders of the Cedar-man; the limbs of the young spruce bent beneath its weight. He saw the lights of the houses go out, one by one, and the lanterns begin to flicker as the tribe came slowly, single file along the path to the church. How many times had they traveled thus through the mountain passes down from the Bering Sea?
> "He went to the door and opened it, and he stepped out

There are a number of abandoned native village sites among the islands in this vicinity. Larger ones are watched over by a caretaker in the summer months.

Life in the Remote Inlets

The mainland shore north of Vancouver is a complex of islands and winding inlets. Half a century ago, logging camps, homesteads, Indian villages and small settlements dotted this coast, served by small steamers. Settlers in the most remote places such as Kingcome Inlet might row for days to the nearest store for supplies and back again.

In December of 1895, for instance, Ernest Halliday decided to row his pregnant wife from their Kingcome Inlet homestead to be delivered by the nearest doctor, at Comox, south of Seymour Narrows, almost 120 miles away. He couldn't leave their two small children behind, so they all piled into a rowboat, along with their dog and supplies. The trip took 14 days, although much of the time was spent waiting out storms in Indian villages. The baby was fine, but Mrs. Halliday had the rest of her children delivered at home after that.

Totems, though made of rot-resistant cedar, deteriorate in the wet climate of the Pacific Northwest.

into the soft white night, the snow whispering now under the footfalls. For the first time he knew them for what they were, the people of his hand and the sheep of his pasture, and he knew how deep was his commitment to them. When the first of the tribe reached the steps, he held out his hand to greet each by name. But first he spoke to himself and he said, 'Yes, my Lord.' "

The wide cove to the south at **mile 264** is **Robson Bight**, an ecological preserve where orcas come to rub themselves against smooth rocks along the shore in the summer, for reasons not fully understood.

Your vessel may take one of several possible routes in this vicinity, depending on weather, time of day, etc. The most direct route turns north into Blackney Passage, **mile 269**, then northwest into Blackfish Sound and Queen Charlotte Sound. For cruise ships, ferries and the like, for whom a 35-knot southwest breeze is barely a distraction, this is the route of choice.

If weather and daylight permits, you may stop in front of the Kwakiutl Indian community of Alert Bay. (See P. 56.)

The traditional Inside Passage route is longer, inside the shelter of Hanson, Cormorant, and Malcolm Islands, and thence into Goletas Channel and finally Christie Passage, before entering the wide waters of Queen Charlotte Sound. For smaller craft the longer route is a sure thing: stay out of the big water as long as you can.

Editor's Choice: *The Curve of Time,* by M. Wylie Blanchet, published by Whitecap Books, is an unusually simple but powerful account of travel along the British Columbia coast in the 1920s and '30s. A widow with five children whose summer home was the 26-foot cruiser *Caprice*, Mrs. Blanchet cruised the north coast in the days when yachts were rare. Her account of an age less busy reminds us of the grace in simple lives:

Did you know?

Early English explorers spoke so often of King George, who had an unusually long reign, that they came to be known to Natives as "King George men." Most early Americans on the northwest coast hailed from Boston, so Americans came to be known as "Boston men."

Photo by Edward Dossetter, AMNH 42298

"They waited until they had each caught a shiner [a small fish easily caught by children]. 'Squeeze them,' finally ordered Jan. They squeezed them.... From the vent of each shiner came a perfectly formed silver baby. They were slim and narrow, not deep and round like their mothers. The second they were put in the water they darted to the bottom, to the weeds and safety. John kept on squeezing his, and his fish went on borning babies just as he had said. But each next baby was more transparent than the last; and they began to look like vague little ghosts with all their inner workings showing through."

Look northeast from **mile 268**: It was amongst these islands that Blanchet sought out deserted Indian villages, to "try to recapture something of a past that will soon be gone forever." We are fortunate she took those trips when she did. Although the decline and abandonment of the Kwakiutl villages had begun, the sites still were mostly intact, and they were rich with dramatic native art:

"We lifted the long bar from the great door of a community house, and stood hesitating to enter. In the old days a chief would have greeted us when we stepped inside—a sea otter robe over his shoulder, his head sprinkled with white bird down, the peace sign. He would have led us across the upper platform between the house posts, down the steps

"People-who-live-in-big-houses" was the way natives from the interior referred to coastal tribes. This is the Kwakiutl village at Hope Island, in 1881. Note use of what appear to be sawn planks, only available after the first white-operated sawmills came to the coast.

Orcas like to rub the rocks here.

Alaska Cruise Handbook **53**

into the center well of the house. Then he would have sung us a little song to let us know we were welcome.

"Sunlight and darkness; heat and cold; in and out we wandered. All the houses were the same size, the same plan, only the house posts distinguished them. Some were without wallboards, some were without roof boards—all were slowly rotting, slowly disintegrating, the remains of a stone age slowly dying."

—M. Wylie Blanchet, *The Curve of Time*

The Collectors

In a sense, it was fortuitous that collectors such as Franz Boas from the American Museum of Natural History and Johan Jacobsen from the Royal Berlin Ethnological Museum happened along in the late 1800s when the quality and availability of Northwest Indian art were at their peaks. After about 1920, many of the villages experienced the sort of decline witnessed by Blanchet and others, and it is possible much of the art would have been lost.

Those early collectors were tough. Jacobsen, for example, who bought artifacts on the West Coast of Vancouver Island and hired native paddlers to take him by canoe to Victoria, traveled in mid-November over the nastiest patches of water on the coast:

Ghost masks from Kingcome Inlet, collected by George Hunt, 1901. AMNH

"We tried to steer away from the wind, but lost control of the canoe. I must confess that this experience did not increase my respect for the local gods as we drifted like a piece of wreckage in a canoe half full of water until about three miles below Hesquiat we were tossed ashore by a thunderous wave, fortunately on a sandy beach, and lay there filled with salt water." —Johan Adrian Jacobsen, *Alaskan Voyage, 1881-1883*.

They also got *a lot* of art. So much disappeared to collectors and museums that decades later, when the Kwakiutls and other tribes wished to set up their own museums, many of the artifacts available to them were inferior to those on display elsewhere. Museums have become aware only recently that pieces in their collections are valuable parts of the tribes' cultural heritage, and some pieces are being returned.

Photo by J.B.Scott. AMNH 32734

In retrospect, it seems that Blanchet happened along just when the old houses and totems were being abandoned to nature. Another traveler four or five years later at one of the same villages noted:

> "There was not a soul there today. The large totem that I took a photo of a year or two ago is now lying on the ground and the Hoh Hoh totem that I photographed last year has now only one wing. So it goes, 'til at last they rot.
> —Beth Hill, *Upcoast Summers*

GEORGE HUNT—A FOOT IN BOTH WORLDS: Both Jacobsen and Boas relied on George Hunt, an unusual man, to guide them through the intricacies of Kwakiutl culture and the logistics of traveling and collecting in the days when there was little scheduled transportation.

Born in 1854 at Fort Rupert (south of **mile 298**) to an English father and a Tlingit noblewoman (a tribe from northern British Columbia and southern Alaska), Hunt was raised in the Kwakiutl culture, and learned much from his Kwakiutl wife:

George Hunt and wife Francine at Fort Rupert, 1930. Hunt, brought up surrounded by Kwakiutl culture, was responsible for the collection of much of the Kwakiutl art found in museums around the world.

Alaska Cruise Handbook **55**

RCBM 1889

Flour Potlatch, Alert Bay, 1908. Usually given to celebrate an important personal or tribal event, a chief's wealth was shown by his gifts. Hudson's Bay blankets were a favorite gift.

*Your vessel may take a slow pass by **Alert Bay**. Get your binoculars and go out on your balcony, or up on deck. Those really tall things behind town that look like overgrown phone poles are actually really tall totems!*

"Sometimes while we are sleeping my wife would start up and sing her PExEla (shaman) songs. Then while she stop singing she would talk to the spirit and she seems to get answer back. Next time spirit comes to her I will write what she says to it."

— *Chiefly Feasts: The Enduring Kwakiutl Potlatch,*
edited by Aldona Jonaitis

First an assistant to passing collectors, Hunt soon became a collector himself, organizing the Kwakiutl display at the 1893 World's Fair in Chicago, with 17 tribesmen demonstrating their crafts. Many Kwakiutl artifacts in museums throughout the world were collected by Hunt.

Alert Bay, at **mile 279**, is one of the centers of the Kwakiutl tribe. The town used to be across the channel at the mouth of the Nimpkish River, where the salmon were plentiful. The tribe moved to its present site when the whites opened a cannery there in 1870. The crew of the *Maggie Murphy* stopped there for gas in the spring of 1938; the town wasn't what they expected:

"That night we stopped at the Indian village of Alert Bay at the southwest approach to dangerous Queen Charlotte Sound. This village was a distinct disappointment to us, for the Indians were walking the plank main street in business suits, the shops were modern, and there wasn't a tepee in sight. The only touch of native color was a prominent burial ground where each grave was marked with a totem pole, but the poles were just cedar boards on which faces had been painted, rather than carved."

They did, however, get good advice about the next leg of the trip from the guy at the gas dock:

"Remember this one thing. Get across before noon. In the morning the sound is usually calm, but in the afternoon the northwest wind comes up and it gets too bumpy for a little boat out there."

—John Joseph Ryan,
The Maggie Murphy

Sointula, on Malcolm Island, north of **mile 282**, is a very different sort of settlement. The island was settled in the early 1900s by the Kalevan Kansa Colonization Company, a Finnish immigrant group seeking to establish an agrarian utopian community. Unfortunately, with few nearby markets for their produce, their dreams died and many settlers moved away. Today Sointula is a tidy village of Finnish farmers and fishermen.

Look for the evidence of winter storms. After mile 290 the land is much more exposed to the wind because the high mountain ridge of Vancouver Island no longer provides protection from North Pacific gales. The trees closest to the shore are bent and twisted, conveying a clear sense of the wilder land and seas that lie ahead.

Mile 297: Fort Rupert lies on the south side of the cove. This was Potlatch Central, as the presence of the Hudson's Bay Company trading post allowed natives to purchase potlatch gifts in large quantities.

Painted canoe and totems at Stanley Park, Vancouver. Chiefs were often buried with their canoes and other possessions.

Salmon boats waiting in God's Pocket for a chance to sneak across Queen Charlotte Sound without getting beat up too badly.

For small craft, the trick to crossing 'The Queen's Pond' is to start early—set the alarm for 3 a.m., sniff the weather, and if it's a 'chance', get going!

God's Pocket, mile 309: Any afternoon in late May or early June—the boats start arriving and keep coming until well after the northern latitude dusk. They are Canadian fishing boats bound for the northern fisheries and American salmon seiners and gill-netters. Some are friends who perhaps haven't seen each other since the previous season. The anchorage is small, vessels raft up and the crews visit their neighbors as they put their boats in order, tie down loose gear, and get ready for the trip across the sound.

This small harbor, which is on the west side of Hurst Island in Christie Passage, is the traditional jumping-off place for the 40 breezy miles across Queen Charlotte Sound. On fall evenings the scene is apt to be different. Boats get beat up at that time of year, and the ones that slide in as the early dusk falls might have antennas snapped off, perhaps a window broken.

It is also the site of God's Pocket Resort, established in 1986 after its owners, who were cruising the area by sailboat, noticed its gorgeous location and good fishing. Don't want to cook after a breezy trip across The Queen's Pond? Tie up and stop in for a nice steak or halibut dinner. It wasn't like this in the old days!

TIPS FOR MARINERS: Harbor too full to anchor? Try going across to the narrow gut east of the Lucan Islands. The bottom's hard and a southeast wind will whistle through it, but there are no choppy seas, and it's a lot better than being outside

in the windy black.

Seventeen miles west, exposed to the full fury of storms sweeping off the North Pacific, Nahwitti Bar guards the passage to the west coast of Vancouver Island.

Just... how... bad does it get out there? In late November of 1993, the Canadian Coast Guard measured the highest sea ever recorded off the British Columbia coast. Fifty miles west of God's Pocket near Triangle Island, the sea was 93 feet high—nine stories tall.

After many, many passages across this crooked patch of water in all manner of workboats, I traveled across on one of the big Alaska cruise ships, in September 1997. It was a cloudless day, suspiciously so, the kind of day a mariner in a small boat, ever tuned to the slightest weather nuance might call a "weather breeder." But the weather Gods kept smiling, and I spent an extremely pleasant half hour or so in the big outdoor hot tub on deck 12. There was a bit of a swell from some weather system far out in the Pacific, and the water and I sloshed slowly back and forth lazily, as I looked out at those places: Scarlett Point, God's Pocket, Cape Caution, Safety Cove - that we had truly struggled to get to. That afternoon was very pleasant, but I wasn't fooled; I knew that in a few weeks the big lows would start tracking up the coast, and even the largest ships would have to travel with caution.

If you're on a cruise ship, don't worry about that: the ships stay in the sheltered waters of the Inside Passage. And besides, in November your cruise ship is in the

Why they call it God's Pocket–when you finally arrive safely. Most Inside Passage travelers have a tale or two about Queen Charlotte Sound. Even though you try to pick your weather and leave early, sometimes a weather change catches you a long ways from shelter and you have to just slow down, hang on, and hope your boat can take it.

Alaska Cruise Handbook **59**

During the big Alaska salmon boom of the 1970s and 1980s, many small fishing boats like these would head up to Alaska via the Inside Passage in April and May, put in a long season, and head south again in September or October.

Caribbean. But I wouldn't try it in my fishing boat. Sometimes in fall and winter, small craft would wait for weeks for enough of a break in the weather to sneak across Queen Charlotte Sound.

Crossing Queen Charlotte Sound: Consider the names along this route: God's Pocket, Storm Islands, Cape Caution, Safety Cove– they tell a lot about mariners' experiences here. The worst part about this crossing is it is so exposed to winds from any direction. The tides flowing out of the inlets, the bottom contours, and other features create tide rips far from land. If you are in a small boat, leave early. The fellow at Alert Bay in 1938 who said that had it right: mariners set their alarms for 3 o'clock, get up, sniff the weather, and if "it's a chance," start across. Most who cross Queen Charlotte Sound have stories of rough seas to tell.

The *Maggie Murphy* boys squeaked across (the wind came up, but not until they were almost at Safety Cove), but they had other problems:

Feared by small craft sailors, the seas in Queen Charlotte Sound hardly affect cruise ships.

"Since leaving Tacoma we hadn't managed to warm even a can of soup on our camp stove. Each morning it dribbled gasoline all over its chin, then burst into flames two feet high when the match was applied. This called for vigorous action with the fire extinguisher. When we did succeed in starting it, the contraption would give off almost as many fumes as the engine, but nowhere near as much heat. The stove finally drove us to discovering the only convenient means of cooking on the boat. When the engine was running, we merely placed a can of beans on the exhaust manifold, and within an hour, the meal was piping hot and ready to serve."

— John Joseph Ryan, *The Maggie Murphy*

On The Queen"'s Pond

JOE'S JOURNAL

"**October 24, 1975, Lucan Islands, B.C.** Started out at 4 a.m. at Bella Bella, on as peaceful and still a morning as you could ask for and ended up in the black of a windy night with violent squalls and lashing rains battering the boat in a tiny and constricted anchorage.

Slipped away at four and ran those dark channels until daylight. Queen Charlotte Sound started out as flat as I had ever seen it, but by lonely and windswept Egg Island, we were alone, bucking into a light SE chop and the other boats were lost in the murk ahead and behind.

An hour later we were in the thick of it—the wind a steady 35, and the sea a dirty 8' chop, and every now and then I'd have to chop the throttle and let a big one slide by. Found a piece of sheltered water about the size of a house lot in the lee of Storm Islands, to lay for a few minutes while I pumped the bilge, tightened the lashings on the deck cargo, and checked things in the engine room. Just then channel 16 came on with an emergency storm warning for the north coast: SE winds to 60 knots: Thanks guys... Then there was nothing for it but cross our fingers and head out for the dirtiest kind of afternoon. Once in a tide rip, about all we could do for half an hour was idle and let the seas slide under, pitching heavily.

Lightly loaded as we were, I couldn't lay the course to Pine Island, without putting us in the trough of the waves, so we had to quarter up [run at an angle to the seas], find a moment between waves to make our turn, and then run down again. We reached Pine Island at 3 p.m. and didn't the lights in the lightkeeper's house look cozy with the sea ripping up and the wild

night coming on! Made the turn and then it was right on the nose for 12 long miles. I reduced to two thirds speed and still had to slow for the big ones not to break out a window! Even at Scarlett Point it was blowing so badly we couldn't make the turn, but had to run way over into the lee of the shore and then quarter back up to God's Pocket, and we were glad to be in, you bet!

But it wasn't over—for the anchorage was crowded with no more room. Just then my steering wheel went loose on my shaft but we were

able to tie alongside a Canadian troller to make emergency repairs. Too much swell to stay long—chewed through a 3/4 inch bow line in just a few minutes.

The Canadian introduced himself, "Nelson" —maybe 50, heavy set with wool pants and shirt. As we were tying up, he asked my girlfriend if it was just the two of us, and when she said "yes," he shook his head and said we were braver than he was. Said the best anchorage was right around the corner—just snuggle right up into the trees. Fixed at last and away, the light failing fast, the whole bay feather white and the wind blowing the tops off of everything. The anchorage was tiny and the wind howled through the trees, but there was no sea and we had a candlelit dinner with the wild world outside. That was a close one and we were glad to get through it."

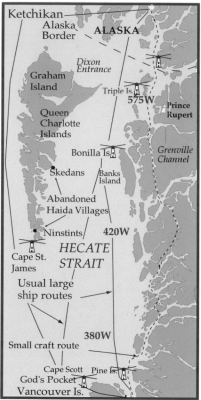

Map labels:
Ketchikan
Alaska Border
ALASKA
Dixon Entrance
Graham Island
Triple Is.
575W
Prince Rupert
Queen Charlotte Islands
Bonilla Is.
Grenville Channel
Skedans
Banks Island
Abandoned Haida Villages
Ninstints
420W
Cape St. James
HECATE STRAIT
Usual large ship routes
380W
Small craft route
Cape Scott   Pine Is.
God's Pocket
Vancouver Is.

Routes: Hecate Strait or Inside?

The right angle turn and blind corner at Boat Bluff, **mile 439,** is very difficult for large cruise ships to negotiate, and so most large ships take a somewhat more westerly route via Hecate Strait, or occasionally into the scenic, narrower waters of Laredo Sound, Caamano Sound, Principe Channel and on to the Alaska border near mile 600. (See map.)

The other problem at Boat Bluff is other boats—it's a blind corner where encountering another vessel in the wrong spot could be awkward, if not dangerous. Today, with all large ships monitoring VHF radio channel 16, vessels routinely announce their position as they enter constricted passages: "Alaska ferry *Columbia* approaching Boat Bluff light southbound. Northbound traffic please advise".

Southbound Travelers: If weather and other factors permit, your ship may travel a more easterly route today, via Milbanke Sound, Seaforth Channel, past the **native village of Bella Bella at mile 400,** and into Lama Passage and Fitzhugh Sound. This route, particularly the winding leg through Lama Passage, is typical of the 'fisherman's way'—the route small craft take to and from Alaska.

Distance saved? Actually, it doesn't matter much. The distance from Pine Island to Tree Point (the first lighthouse in Southeast Alaska) is almost exactly the same whether you follow the narrowest passages of the traditional Inside Passage, or go straight up Hecate Strait.

The whole east side of Hecate Strait is a maze of islands, channels, and rock piles with hardly any permanent settlements, and is frequented mostly by Canadian salmon trollers.

Look for commercial and sports salmon trollers near mile 380W at Hakai Passage. You may also see the larger vessels that carry and house sports-fishermen in this area. These are essentially **floating sportsfishing lodges,** allowing sportsfishermen access to good fishing, without the expense of maintaining a shore based lodge. This way, when the fish

Cruise ships may take one of several routes in these waters.

MOHAI

move, the whole lodge can move with them.

Some of the very best fishing requires threading your way, towing hooks and lures, through a maze of underwater peaks and valleys. It is challenging; being off course by 50 feet can mean having your fishing gear torn off on the rocks. The successful fishermen know the shapes of the underwater landscape by heart. When the fish are running, when you're flying the trolling gear just off the walls of some unseen canyon below you, and your poles vibrate with the hits of the big kings—it's an exhilarating experience.

New York writer Edith Iglauer came to this coast when she married Canadian fisherman John Daly in 1974. It was a different life than any she had known before:

> "We trolled back and forth in a half circle, with the sounder plunging to sixty fathoms and leaping up to twenty, then dropping to thirty and then—hold your breath—rising to ten for a single flash before the (engine) roared as John revved up and swiftly moved away from jagged underwater peaks...
>
> "I alternately looked ahead and watched John maneuver in and out among the rocks and pull in fish, in a sunset that threw a glow across the mountains, across the water, across John's face, setting off a fiery gleam from his sunglasses. He...gave me a radiant smile...and grabbed the wheel to turn into the pounding waves.
>
> "I leaned over and shouted, 'Don't you ever get scared?' " 'I love it!' he shouted back. 'I've been steer-

Steamer Mariposa, *ashore in Lama Pass in October 1915. Such groundings were not uncommon along the Inside Passage in the days before radar. These passengers were picked up by the next northbound vessel. The ship was refloated, patched up and put back to work.*

ing this edge for thirty-five years and I love every minute of it!' "

—Edith Iglauer, *Fishing With John*

Northbound voyages transit Hecate Strait in the late evening, and sometime around 2 a.m. you may feel your ship slowing, as she pauses near **Triple Island, mile 575W**, to disembark the Canadian pilot, who has helped your deck officers guide your ship through these many and intricate passages. The **Alaska border** is just 25 miles ahead.

It was near here, on a wintry march afternoon in 1971 that we had a very close call in our brand new steel 106' crab

A Close Call

"**March 2, 1971**: At around 3, alone in the wheelhouse on my afternoon watch I noticed an odd, blotchy-looking target on our radar screen. There was supposed to be no land where it showed *something*, and after I fiddled with the controls to make sure that it was really there, I woke our skipper.

He quickly scanned the chart and radar, pulled the throttle back to an idle, then stepped to the intercom, "Johnny, flood both crab tanks...quick as you can." We had been running with our huge crab tanks, or holds, empty. Filling them lowered our center of gravity, increasing our stability in heavy seas.

Sensing something was happening, the rest of the crew filed into the big pilothouse, peering forward into the early and snowy dusk.

For a long while there was nothing but the march of the big, grey-bearded seas past in the thickly falling snow. But then there was a lightening in the snow ahead and we all peered forward intently, trying to get a glimpse of whatever it was that the radar was seeing ahead of us.

Then, just for the briefest moment we saw it, glimpsed through the gloom and as quickly gone — heavy breakers, covering the entire area ahead of us.

"Damn...hang on, guys." Our skipper swiveled to look behind us, throttled up to a third, and pushed the steering lever all the way to starboard. As we swung into our turn, our boat dropped suddenly, at the same time rolling sickeningly to port for what seemed like a very long moment as a huge sea plowed into us. Time seemed to stand still. I heard dishes crashing, a strident alarm bell ranging, and then only slowly did we come around, and tilt back to an even keel, and finally the alarm stopped ringing.

Our skipper stood at the chart, shaking his head.

"Lookit this...breaking here, in a hundred feet of water...breaking, fer crissake...I heard about it once, but I didn't really believe it until just now..."

boat. We were running before a strong southerly gale, unaware that in certain winter conditions, the entire north end of Hecate Strait could become a tidal maelstrom in which no small or medium-sized vessel could live.

The fastest route to Alaska for most cruise ships is directly up Hecate Straits. The shores are wild and uninhabited, visited in summer by fishermen, loggers, and the occasional passing yacht. In winter, except for the few hardy souls trying to create a fishing lodge out of the old cannery at **Butedale, mile 473,** they are totally deserted.

If conditions are right, you may glimpse land to the west in the distance, at around **mile 455W** .

The combination of the heavy southerly gale and a flooding tide from the north was producing breaking seas in deep water, seas that we'd be foolish to risk, even in our brand new and very rugged 106-footer.

For an hour, in that wild wasteland of snow and white water, we sought a way through, for the little gully of deeper water that might not be breaking. But if it were there, we couldn't find it. With the coming of the dark, the wind came on stronger still, and it was no place to be.

At the dock in Seattle our brand-new steel king crab boat looked as if it could handle any weather. But when the wind blew against the tide in upper Hecate Straits we found ourselves in a fight for our lives.

We headed east, to find a way to the sheltered waterways of the Inside Passage, through a maze of islands.

We had no detailed chart, only the hazy memory of the mate, from a trip through several decades earlier.

Snow and black enveloped us. Our radar could barely penetrate it. Three false starts led only to dead ends with the sea beating violently on three sided narrowing cul-de-sacs. Once there was not even room to turn around and we had to back out, ever so carefully, and no one spoke and the tension in the pilothouse was very thick.

The fourth channel opened up to another, the sea died away, the water stayed deep, and long after midnight, we found our way into the calm waters of the Inside Passage.

These are the **Queen Charlotte Islands**: five large islands and many smaller ones separated by intricate waterways. They were settled by Haida Indians, who suffered the same ravages of disease and alcoholism as their coastal brothers. Logging and fishing employs most island residents.

Soaking away the cares of a long season at the remote Bishop Bay Hot Springs. That's your author soaping himself up in the outside pool while the crew looks on from the big hot pool inside the building.

Kayakers, campers, and travelers seeking a quieter vacation pace have found it in the Charlottes. Boating guides stress the remoteness of the coast and the importance of carrying adequate survival equipment and leaving a travel plan with a friend ashore.

From 1910 to 1941, a whaling station operated at Rose Inlet, about 35 miles west of **mile 420W**, taking hundreds of the blue, sperm, finback, and humpback whales each year. These boats operated in one of the most rugged parts of the northwest coast, in all sorts of weather, without the navigational electronics we take for granted today.

Thirty miles west of **mile 480W** is Skedans, the site of a large Haida village, now abandoned, but with many remaining totems and other artifacts. The Haida watchmen guide visitors who come by boat from Sandspit or Moresby Camp.

There are many abandoned Haida villages among the Queen Charlottes. Right is Skidegate, circa 1881

AMNH Dossetter 42204

Alaska Cruise Highlights

Gulf of Alaska Cruise
September 6-13, 1997

Tracy Arm morning

"Tracing shining ways through fiord and sound, past forests
and waterfalls, islands and mountains and far azure headlands,
it seems as if surely we must at length reach the very paradise
of the poets, the abode of the blessed."
— John Muir, *Travels in Alaska*

Day 1 Vancouver and the Winding Way North

Points of particular interest:

1. **Gulf Islands:** sheltered waterways, popular recreation area.
2. **Yuculta Rapids:** small craft route; even whales wait for slack water here.
3. **Desolation Sound:** roadless, semi-wilderness marine park.
4. **The Graveyard**, site of a particularly nasty tide rip when a flooding tide is opposed by a strong southerly wind.
5. **Seymour Narrows:** a gorge with swift currents; a legendary place. Safe passage is only possible at slack water, every six hours.

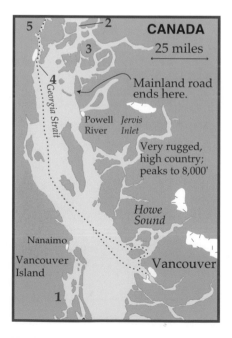

Clockwise from upper left: First Nations settlement, Desolation Sound. Troller at Sara Point, Desolation Sound. The steep mountains in this area dashed the hopes of railroad men who had hoped to bridge the narrow channels to Vancouver Island. Georgia Strait from a cove in the Gulf Islands. Workboat, Johnstone Strait. Abandoned cannery, Redonda Bay. The coast used to be dotted with tiny settlements.

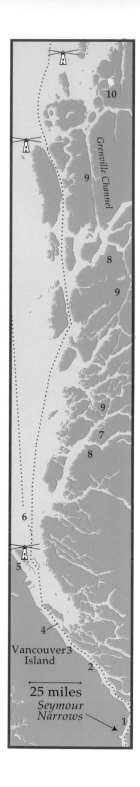

Day 2   The Wilderness Begins:
Up the British Columbia Coast

Points of particular interest:
1. **Routes:** ships use Seymour Narrows, small craft prefer sheltered channels further east.
2. **Johnstone Strait and orcas:** this is one of the best places in the world to see these big black and white killer whales. Look for their tall distinctive dorsal fin, and white puff of vapor as they exhale. See photo. Below.
3. **Mile 264** - Robson Bight: orcas like to rub their backs against the rocks here.
4. **Alert Bay:** native village, look for the really tall totem poles.
5. **Mile 309** - God's Pocket: northbound small craft would wait in this tiny cove for good traveling weather.
6. **Queen Charlotte Sound:** can be rough; small craft hurry across.
7. **Namu Cannery.** Famous killer whale Namu captured near here, became aquarium star.
8. **The lonely north coast:** few settlements.
9. **'The Northern Canyons':** small craft route, too narrow for large ships.
10. **Prince Rupert,** regional center, connected by rail to interior British Columbia.

Clockwise from above: In the steep sided inlets of the Inside Passage, floating homes were often tied together to create whole floating communities. For generations salmon fishing, and logging were the mainstay industries along the coast. Salmon gill-netters like this worked the British Columbia and Alaska coasts. Johnstone Straits is particularly popular with orcas or killer whales. Naturalists and photographers from all over the world come each summer to study and photograph these whales.

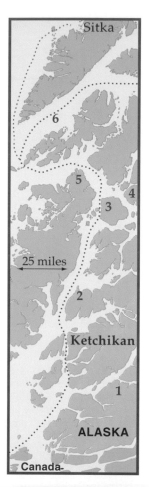

Day 3 Islands Without Number: Ketchikan and Southeast Alaska

Points of particular interest:

1. Misty Fjords National Monument.
2. Myers Chuck, **Mile 626**: roadless settlement. Look for small fishing craft.
3. Snow Passage, **mile 720**: look for whales.
4. Entrance to Wrangell Narrows, constricted shallow passage to Petersburg and points north.
5. Point Baker, **mile 745**: my island homestead was in the cove just behind the island with the light on it. Look for whales near the little island.
6. Chatham Straits, many bays with abandoned salmon, herring, or whale processing plants.

Clockwise from above: Mainland mountains, Frederick Sound. My neighbor, Flea, a hand-troller at Point Baker, 1974. Tlingit Totem, Ketchikan. This pole is a recarve, a replica of an older pole, lost to the effects of weather. Salmon tenders {fish-buying vessels} and seiners at Inian Islands. Abandoned settlement, Killisnoo Island.

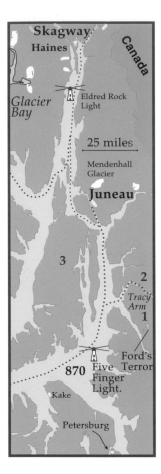

Day 4   Juneau, & Day 5   Skagway

Points of particular interest:
1. **Ford's Terror:** <u>very</u> narrow entrance leads to spectacular remote basin.
2. **Tracy Arm** - long fjord with glaciers.
3. **Admiralty Island National Monument.**

Clockwise from above: A tug tows a long raft of logs through the winding passages of Wrangell Narrows near Petersburg. A restored train waits for passengers near Skagway. Gallery at Port Chilkoot, near Haines. Known for a nearby fall and winter concentration of bald eagles, Haines is connected to the Alaska Highway. Skagway, tucked into the folds of a river gorge, at the head of a long fjord, is rich with the history of those who passed through, headed to the Klondike in the Gold Rush. The first ice, from Tracy Arm or Le Conte Bay is sometimes seen in the vicinity of mile 870.

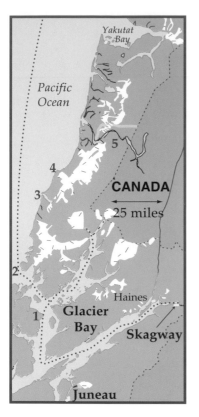

Day 6 Into The Ice: Glacier Bay and the Outside Coast

Points of particular interest:
1. **Point Adolphus, mile 1000**: hump-back whales often congregate here.
2. **Cape Spencer**, end of Inside Passage.
3. **Lituya Bay**: a 1958 earthquake made a tidal wave 1800 feet high.
4. **Lonely and remote coast**; no towns.
5. **Alsek** – Tatshenshini Rivers – popular with kayakers. After your trip a float-plane flies you back to civilization.

Clockwise from upper right: Into the icy chambers: this is entering Johns Hopkins Inlet. Vessels must proceed very carefully to avoice ice damage to their propellors. At times the ice is so thick that vessels cannot safely enter the inlet. Up inside John Hopkins Inlet - try and find a place to view the glacier where you can listen for the cracks and booms of the glacier as it calves. Have your binoculars ready! Cruise ship at Hubbard Glacier gives a sense of scale - some of the faces of these glaciers are 300-400 feet high, with building-sized pieces occasionally falling off. Also look for icebergs that calve from under water and bob to the surface. Glacier Bay vista.

Day 7 Prince William Sound:
A Jewel in Alaska's Crown

Points of particular interest:
1. **College Fjord** with many active glaciers.
2. **Bligh Reef**, site of *Exxon Valdez* oil spill.
3. **Alaska pipeline to Prudhoe Bay**.

Clockwise from upper right: Harvard Glacier calves, creating a splash almost reaching to the top of its 300-foot high face. For almost 70 years, square-rigged sailing ships served the canneries here. The 150-foot spruce trees of College Fjord give a clear sense of the massive size of Wellesley Glacier. Early morning, cruise ship off Cape St. Elias, Gulf of Alaska. The outside waters along this part of the coast are subject to bitterly cold winds in winter. Such winds can build up dangerously heavy loads of ice on vessels large and small.

Alaska Cruise Handbook **79**

Interior Alaska
Scrapbook

Clockwise from upper right: Gold dredge - these big rigs would work gravel beds on rivers. A fish wheel on the Tanana River near Fairbanks. The Trans Alaska Pipeline. Floatplanes along the Chena River. Riverboats like this were the main transportation throughout interior Alaska for much of the last century. This is bear country; follow a few simple rules to stay out of trouble. See P. 268.

"THREE FRIENDS" DREDGE ON SOLOMON RIVER, ALASKA.

After the hordes of prospectors with their simple gold pans and sluices had combed the rivers of Alaska, there was still a lot of gold, but in the form of dust and gold flakes distributed among millions of tons of river gravel. Enter the gold dredges, like the Three Sisters Dredge on the Solomon River in the above photo. Often steam powered, they would process hundreds of tons a day of river bed a day, leaving behind neat rows of processed gravel. Would such machines be allowed to work with today's stricter regulations? Probably not.

Icy Strait from Inian Cove

Today the land and the waterways in Alaska are much as the original explorers found them. This is not by chance. The history of Alaska, especially in the 20th century has been a tug-of-war between those who wished to develop and change the landscape and those who wished to preserve it.

We are fortunate that people like John Muir, Adolf and Margaret Murie, and many others successfully championed the cause that wilderness should exist for its own merit. Due to these efforts, a vast area of National Parks, preserves, and forests were created to preserve the heritage and beauty of Alaska and The North, forever, hopefully.

Portion of the 1930s Hansen Handbook, a compilation of courses, distances, sketches, and so forth, that allowed mariners to travel the Inside Passage without having to carry a complete and expensive set of charts.

214

	Seattle to Ketchikan Via Active Pass and Inside		Port or Stbd. Beam	Di
	Twilight Pt.		S	1
	Walker (Camp) Id. Lt. (26 ft. 4 mi.) Fl. W. Visible 310° to 168°.		S	1

Navigation: Then and Now

Before radar, depth sounders, radios, and all the other electronic goodies we take for granted today, a trip to Alaska was very challenging. Now machines like the handheld unit one below, which displays your position on an electronic chart make life a lot easier for navigators. Nevertheless, each year the rugged coast claims its toll of careless mariners.

GPS (Global Positioning System) handheld chart plotter— wouldn't the old timers have loved this puppy!

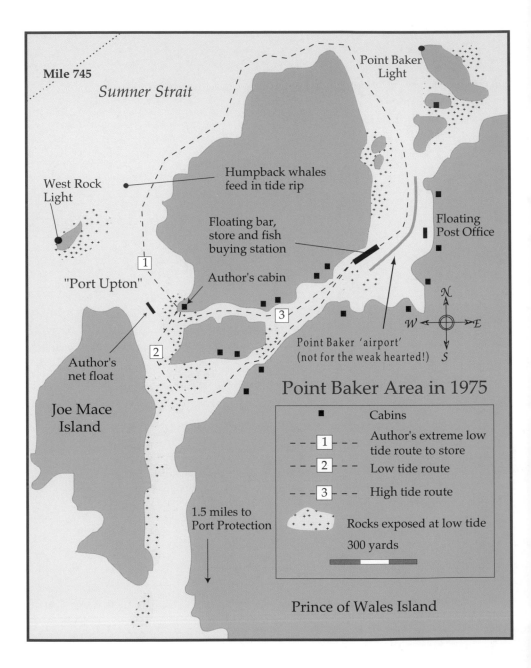

Mile 745

Sumner Strait

Point Baker
Light

West Rock
Light

Humpback whales
feed in tide rip

Floating bar,
store and fish
buying station

Floating
Post Office

"Port Upton"

1

Author's cabin

3

2

N

W   E

S

Author's
net float

Point Baker 'airport'
(not for the weak hearted!)

Joe Mace
Island

Point Baker Area in 1975

■   Cabins

– – 1 – – – Author's extreme low
tide route to store

– – 2 – – – Low tide route

– – 3 – – – High tide route

Rocks exposed at low tide

1.5 miles to
Port Protection

300 yards

Prince of Wales Island

CHAPTER 3

Life in a Roadless Community

Point Baker, Mile 745

I magine, cheap waterfront land and good fishing close at hand. This was the situation at the remote and roadless communities of Point Baker and nearby Port Protection (south of **mile** 745) in the early 1970s. A person could get an acre-sized waterfront lot on a sheltered cove, with the right to harvest a substantial amount of timber each year from the adjacent forest to use for lumber. So if you couldn't afford store-bought lumber, you could build your house from the nearby trees and make enough cash fishing salmon from an outboard skiff to support a family.

A floating store/bar/fish-buyer at Point Baker served the needs of the hundred or so souls settled around these two coves on the edge of the vast woods. The mail and freight boat came once a week, supplemented by the occasional floatplane. Families with gill-netters or trollers tried to make a trip to town—Wrangell or Petersburg, each about 40 miles away, a long day's round trip—every few months to stock up on supplies a little cheaper.

A waterfront home with a place to tie up your boat is a lifelong dream of many commercial fishermen. Inexpensive land allowed fishermen here to achieve those dreams.

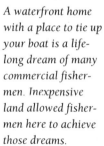

Puddle jumper, or hand trolling skiff, near Point Baker, 1974.

Point Baker from the air: with limited take-off space and tide rips at the harbor entrance, it was a particular challenge for floatplane pilots.

Strangers should use these narrow channels on a rising tide.

Behind the shore was the forest—thick, almost impenetrable. For the most part walking was so difficult everyone traveled by outboard skiffs or "puddle jumpers." At Point Baker, especially, one's traveling decisions were dictated by the tide. Have a whiskey warmup some snowy winter afternoon with your groceries at the store? Stay too late and the trip home might be a nightmare: wading along the shallow channel, towing your skiff behind you, lifting, scraping it over the thin places, picking your way with the flashlight through the snow, and hoping your batteries last until you make it home.

When I arrived here with my former wife on our 32-foot gill-netter in the spring of 1972, the flavor of the place was compelling. The older residents welcomed younger blood, and the salmon fishing in Sumner Strait was great. We found part of an island, on a private cove, with a gorgeous western exposure and view, for $17,000, 10 percent down and 10 years to pay.

After the season, in our houseboat on Seattle's Lake Union, we set to making plans for a cabin on our newly-purchased land in Point Baker. As our money dwindled, so did the size of our new-home-to-be until whatever roof we could get over our heads for fifteen hundred bucks would have to be it. We settled on a 16-by-20-

foot box with a half loft, 480-square-feet, total, tiny.

With tight-fisted determination, we scoured garage sales and discount building suppliers. At a second-hand store we found a big diesel oil range for $35; at another, all our windows and doors for $175. In my tiny floating shop I prefabbed a Formica kitchen counter top, complete with sink and drawers. We got plywood, nails, and shingles, all on deep discount, and purchased a 16-foot cedar skiff with a 10-horsepower 1958 Evinrude outboard. Tool by tool, fitting by fitting, we packed all the supplies and extras aboard my 32-foot gill-net vessel and skiff to tow north.

The weather gods granted us an easy trip, and shortly after arriving in Point Baker, the mail boat arrived with our pickup truck-sized bundle of lumber from the small sawmill in Wrangell, and our first major logistics problem.

The plan had been to tow the tightly strapped bundle of lumber through the narrow back channel to our secluded cove and house site. But when the mail boat's crane lowered the bundle of lumber into the water, it was so green and dense, it wouldn't even float. It was what was locally called, "pond dried."

So we had to set it temporarily on the dock and then

Retired salmon troller, living aboard boat at Point Baker dock.

Author and "smiley" or jargon for very large king salmon.

Our front window, 1975. For a commercial fisherman, few things are more satisfying than looking out your window and seeing your boat laying peacefully at anchor below your house.

haul it in our skiff, load by load, to our cove.

In the two weeks before the salmon season began we struggled: the wood was so wet it splashed when your hammer missed the nail. My one and only hand saw bent on the first beam we cut. It rained every day; every night we would take the skiff back to our boat at the Point Baker dock, heat up something quick, and fall, exhausted, shivering, into our sleeping bags.

And we created something exquisite: out of every window was the water. As we ate at the driftwood table, we could see eagles swooping low over the cove. There were curious seals, and most marvelous of all, a pair of humpbacks that hung out in the tide rips by West Rock, off the mouth of our cove. On still nights, we could hear the sigh-like breathing of the whales as they surfaced and exchanged fresh air for stale. When

Getting in the Firewood, Southeast Alaska Style

At Point Baker on a breezy winter morning, the CB radios crackle from cabin to cabin: good firewood logs have been spotted in the ebbing tide pouring around the tip of the island. Within minutes a handful of skiffs and small fishing craft set out across the mile or so of crooked water between the harbor and the logs. As each arrives, they stop alongside the closest large log, hammer in a big steel staple, attach a tow line, and begin the long, slow tow back to the harbor. The first to arrive latch onto really huge logs, 60 feet long by four feet in diameter, *four cords of firewood in a single log.* Hauled up on the beach at high tide, such a find would be enough for most of the winter for the smaller cabins.

the first snow came one November evening, the fire in the wood stove crackled cheerily, our kerosene lamp shone out on the vast and wild world beyond the windows, and it was magic.

Evening at "Port Upton"

Many of the new young people who arrived in the 1970s couldn't afford the price of an outboard and fell back on the traditional puddle jumper, whose origins were in the 1930s and '40s, when so-called hand trollers (they didn't have engine-operated equipment to haul in the lines) were spread all over Southeast Alaska.

The power plant in the 1970s-vintage Port Protection-to-Point Baker puddle jumper was usually an air-cooled Briggs & Stratton one-cylinder gasoline engine, turning a propeller through a homemade reduction gear of belts and pulleys. Such engines could be ordered through the Sears catalog and delivered by the mailboat.

With such a craft, sporting two fresh-cut-from-the-woods trolling poles, a young fisherman or woman could catch perhaps $6,000 to $8,000 worth of fish in the summer, with very little overhead.

Nicknamed "Flea," this local skiff fisherman would take newcomers under his wing and show them the tricks of trolling for salmon.

A young entrepreneur brought in a portable sawmill and the building boom was on.

THANKSGIVING AT PORT PROTECTION: In the fall of 1973, a good fishing season behind us and excited to be in our new, if small, cabin, we went by outboard to one

Point Baker Scrapbook

Above left: Salmon net repair with dog. Above right: Float construction at "Port Upton." Left: Point Baker, with a community dock and store, was popular with fishing families. Above: The Point Baker Airport— not for the faint hearted. Opposite page: large halibut and friend, at the Point Baker fish-buyer.

First snow, Port Protection.

of the three or four Thanksgiving dinners being held around the cove at Port Protection.

We arrived to a Norman Rockwell scene: The harbor was still, the daylight was dying, snow was falling, and kerosene lamps burned cheerily in homes along the water's edge. Tying our skiff to a big moored firewood log, we walked up the beach and went inside a big three-room cabin with an attached shop. My wife went in to help the other women, and I stayed in the shop with the men. The woodstove was hot, the rum was good and we talked about the hunting and the fishing.

But when we were all called in to sit down, my former wife and I learned a new Thanksgiving tradition. It was a big group and a small table, but it wasn't a problem. The men sat down side by side at the table, decorated for the occasion and heaped high with food. The women just sat wherever they could: on the sofas or cross-legged on the floor.

In summer, with daylight that lasted from four in the morning until after eleven at night, the focus was fishing: making enough to make it through the long winter. But when the season was over and the days got shorter, there was time for the kind of relaxed visiting that is a highlight of life in such places.

The center for much of the activity in these two

At the Point Baker Bar

Being a rough-and-tumble sort of place, the Point Baker Bar didn't offer the wide selection of drinks to which some of the newcomers in town were accustomed. Once in 1972 two gill-net vessels freshly arrived from Seattle tied up to the bar to celebrate their trip.

Bartender: "What'll it be, fellas?"

Newly-arrived fisherman to wife: "What d'ya think, honey, you wanna Manhattan?"

Bartender: "Hey guys, we got whiskey and water, whiskey and Coke, and whiskey and Tang. What's it gonna be?"

The Point Baker Floating Bar

communities was the floating bar and store in the harbor at Point Baker. Built on a raft of logs, one of the most tedious problems for fishermen drinking in Alaska's harbor towns was avoided: *The Ramp.*

The tides in the region are huge: In a six-hour period the water level might vary 20 feet. Imagine: you come in tired from a fishing trip at high tide, tie up your boat at one of Ketchikan's many marina-style floats, walk across the nearly horizontal ramp to the shore to, say, the Fo'c's'le Bar. There, surrounded by acquaintances, you relive and celebrate many fishing experiences. Six hours later, your vision

Troller's home, Port Protection

blurred and equilibrium unsteady, you head back, only to discover that the tide is way down, and the ramp is almost vertical.

At Point Baker you could tie your boat right up to the bar, with no ramp to negotiate. Not only that, it was less than half a mile from the fishing grounds, and it sold groceries and hardware and bought fish.

Seeking greener pastures, I sold my cabin at Point Baker in the mid-1980s and built a new boat for the remote salmon fishery in Bristol Bay, Alaska, 1,000 miles west. Bleak, austere, remote, with violent tidal currents and few good harbors, Bristol Bay was the opposite of Southeast Alaska. The fishing was a competitive frenzy I'd never experienced before, but there were friends to guide me and the shorter season allowed us more time at home with our families and children.

Yet to a man (Alaska law allows salmon fishermen to fish only a single region), we all missed the wooded waterways and the secluded harbors we'd left behind.

Unloading salmon, Bristol Bay, Bering Sea, 1993. That's your author's new boat on the left. Below: King Crab and friend, Bering Sea, 1971

Alaska Commercial Fishing

Blessed with a rich resource, good management, and some 30,000 miles of coastline, Alaska has the richest fisheries of any state.

The first boom was in salmon, before the turn of the century, when entrepreneurs from California, Oregon, and Washington learned of the tremendous profits to be had off the salmon runs in remote Alaskan rivers. For decades dozens of square-rigged sailing ships left San Francisco every spring, loaded with workers, fishermen, and supplies for the Alaska canneries, to return again in the fall heavily laden with canned salmon.

One of the more remarkable fisheries' booms occurred in the mid-1970s and early 1980s, when herds of large king crab roamed the floor of the Bering Sea and North Pacific Ocean around the Aleutian Islands. Using huge pots (up to 7'x7'x3' in size, and weighing 600 pounds empty), a group of remarkably tough vessels and equally tough crews fished this area, infamous for its rotten weather and heavy seas. The money made by top crab boats and crews became part of Northwest legend, but the toll was heavy. Many good vessels and talented crews were lost at sea.

The most recent boom has been for cod and pollock, particularly in the Bering Sea, using large "factory trawlers".

Today Alaskan fishermen are continually challenged by changing markets, many regulations, and the natural vagaries of wild fish stocks. But generally speaking, thanks to progressive management, they have a strong resource to work with and their industry remains strong.

What You'll Catch

At most stops in Southeast Alaska, charter boats are available to take parties sportfishing. Typically these boats are modern, comfortable cruisers, able to take parties of up to six. Depending on the season and where the "bite" is, vessels may run an hour or more to get on the fish.

Most fishermen like to target on king and silver salmon. Kings, running in size up to 60 pounds and larger, are caught from May through August with the best fishing generally in the first half of the season. Silvers run smaller, typically 6 to 10 pounds, and are available from mid-June through September. Pink salmon are smaller still, 3 to 5 pounds, but run in great numbers, beginning in mid-June.

"Will I catch a fish?" If you just want a king and won't settle for anything less, the answer might be "Maybe." But especially in July and August when the silver and pink runs are strong, many people easily catch their limit (six fish per person). If for some reason, the salmon aren't running that particular day, many skippers will shift over to target on tasty lingcod, rockfish or halibut, so rarely would you come back empty-handed.

"What if I'm not very experienced?" Don't worry—there are a lot of fish in Alaska, and charter skippers are quick teachers. Many people who have never fished before catch their limit.

"What's it like?" As much as anything else, going out on a charter boat for a day is a chance to get out and see, close and at first hand, some of the most abundant marine life and most dramatic scenery in the world. Whales, dolphins, seals, and eagles are all common sights to the charter fisherman. Bring your camera! Many skippers also give an informative tour on the way out to the grounds.

"What do I do with the fish?" In most towns, services are available to freeze, store and ship your fish. Some cruise ships are able to freeze fish as well, and most will happily cook and serve a passenger's fish. Typical prices run from $100 to $150 (U.S.) per person for a day's outing.

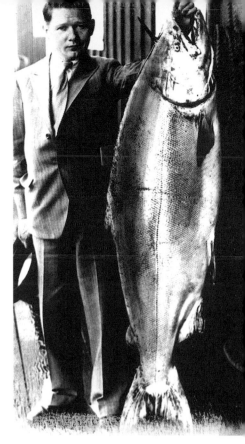

There are still a lot of big salmon in Alaska. However, the really huge king salmon that were caught regularly early in the 1900s became scarce after the construction of the big dams on the Columbia River in the 1930s and 1940s. These fish apparently fed regularly along the Alaska coasts on their way back to Oregon from the North Pacific Ocean
CRMM 1970.291E

Traveler's Guide to Work Boats

TUG. Size: 40 to 150 feet. Range: all waters. Distinguishing features: High bow, low deck aft with tow winch behind deckhouse. Gear: none. Crew: 3 to 8. History: Many supplies arrive in Alaska by barge and tug, especially in Southeast Alaska. During the rush to get pipeline and drilling supplies to Prudhoe Bay in 1975, tugs were chartered from as far away as Louisiana.

SELF-LOADING LOG BARGE. Size: 200 to 400 feet. Range: Puget Sound to Southeast Alaska. Distinguishing features: Twin cranes on tall wide supporting structures. Gear: none. Crew: 2 to 4. History: For long distances or rough water, towing logs in traditional rafts is unsuitable. These barges and their cousin, the self-dumping barge (ballast tanks flooded so that logs slide off) are used to reduce losses on these routes.

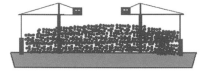

WOOD-CHIP BARGE. Size: 200 to 300 feet. Range: Puget Sound to Southeast Alaska. Distinguishing features: High-sided barges deeply loaded with chips heaped and spilling over. Gear: none. Crew: none. History: A generation ago all sawmills had sawdust burners. Today environmental regulations and the demand for chips for paper making and chemical production have changed this waste into a valuable product.

TRACTOR TUG. Size: 100 to 160 feet. Range: Puget Sound. Distinguishing features: Pilothouse is more amidships than other tugs. Gear: none. Crew: 4 to 6. History: This unusual tug doesn't have a propeller. Rotating vertical fins beneath the vessel propel it and allow it to move sideways or to turn in its own length. Used frequently for oil tanker escort duty in Puget Sound.

HALIBUT SCHOONER. Size: 60 to 100 feet. Range: Washington coast to Bering Sea. Distinguishing features: Two masts, setting chute, baiting shack on stern. Gear: longline for halibut or black cod. Crew: 5 to 8. History: Some of these fine vessels were built in the 1920s or earlier. They fish by setting strings of baited hooks in deep water.

KING CRABBER. Size: 80 to 160 feet or more. Range: Bering Sea and Aleutian Islands, occasionally in Southeast Alaska. Distinguishing features: articulating cranes for moving pots. Gear: large metal pots (up to 8-by-8-by-3 feet) fished in deep water for king crab. Crew: 4 to 6. History: in the early 1980s some crewmen made $100,000 in a three-month season. Today fewer crab mean harder times.

POWER SCOW. Size: 70 to 100 feet. Range: throughout Alaska. Distinguishing features: Boxy shape, pilothouse and living quarters aft, twin booms. Gear: used as salmon tenders. Crew: 3 to 7. History: Many were built for World War II Aleutian Campaign. Popular for their shallow draft and large capacity. One, the *Balaena*, even has room below decks for a salt water hot tub.

PURSE SEINER. Size: 35 to 58 feet. Range: throughout Alaska. Distinguishing features: Round power block hung on boom, carries or tows large skiff. Gear: encircling net. Crew: 3 to 7. History: Used for herring in spring, salmon in summer. Many vessels built to Alaska-limit rule: 58 feet maximum overall length.

Traveler's Guide to Work Boats

SALMON TROLLER. Size: 30 to 50 feet. Range: northern California to Yakutat, Alaska. Distinguishing features: tall trolling poles. Gear: lures and baits. Crew: 1 to 2. History: In the 1980s, Alaska established two different troll licenses. Power trollers have mechanical gurdies or winches to raise and lower the lines. Hand trollers, which display HT plaques, must crank lines up and down by hand.

SALMON GILL-NETTER. Size: 28 to 45 feet. Range: Columbia River to Bristol Bay, Alaska. Distinguishing features: Net drum or reel mounted in stern with vertical rollers aft. Gear: surface drift gill net, 16 feet deep by 900 to 1,200 feet long. Crew: 1 to 4. History: Many gill-netters bring their families for the season, especially in Southeast Alaska.

DRUM SEINER. Size: 50 to 75 feet. Range: Puget Sound to northern British Columbia. Distinguishing features: Large steel drum or reel mounted aft, sometimes recessed; large skiff towed astern or aboard. Gear: encircling net. Crew: 4 to 7. History: Prohibited in Alaska. In British Columbia, fishermen may not have engines in skiff.

SCHOONER-STYLE TENDER (HOUSE AFT). Size: 60 to 100 feet. Range: throughout British Columbia and Alaska. Distinguishing features: Carries no fishing gear; usually displays fish company identifying sign, such as "Icicle Seafoods." Gear: none. Crew: 2 to 5. History: Vessels vary; some date to the 1920s, when they were built to service fish traps (outlawed in 1958).

FLOATER (FLOATING PROCESSOR). Size: 150 to 600 feet. Range: Gulf of Alaska and Bering Sea. Occasionally seen in Southeast Alaska. Distinguishing features: Cluttered superstructures with cranes, housing trailers, and so forth. Sometimes has vessels unloading alongside. Gear: none. Crew: 20 to 200 or more. History: Much Alaska fishing occurs remote from town-based processing plants. Floating processors can move from fishery to fishery.

FACTORY TRAWLER. Size: 120 to 400 feet. Range: Bering Sea and Aleutian Islands. Distinguishing features: High sides, large gantry and net reel aft. Gear: trawl nets for cod and pollock. Crew: 20 to 150. History: Before the mid-1980s, foreign factory trawlers dominated the Bering Sea. Today, American-owned vessels have displaced the foreign fleets.

HOUSE-FORWARD TENDER. Size: 50 to 100 feet. Range: throughout Alaska. Distinguishing features: No fishing gear, but has weighing or pumping equipment aboard as well as fish company sign. Gear: none. Crew: 3 to 5. History: During the July peak of the salmon season, hundreds of tenders of all sorts work the waters of Alaska. Look for "CASH" signs, signifying buyers who don't have their own fleets.

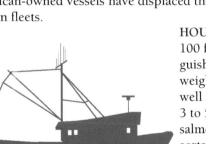

HOUSE-AFT CRABBER. Size: 80 to 200 feet. Range: Bering Sea and Aleutians. Occasionally in Southeast Alaska as tenders. Distinguishing features: Tall house aft with deck forward and articulated cranes for handling crab pots. Gear: large metal pots (up to 8-by-8-by-3 feet) fished in deep water for king crab. Crew: 4 to 8 or more. History: Popular design allows skipper to see crew working; evolved from halibut schooners.

Halibut Longlining

A traditional halibut schooner. Some of these boats, built in the early 1900s are still operating today.

Iron men in wooden ships were the mainstays of the halibut fishery. For generations, fishermen of Norwegian descent set out from northwest ports in graceful halibut schooners for long trips, sometimes almost to Siberia. Baiting and hand coiling miles of gear set out along the bottom, hauling it back, and cleaning the fish as they came aboard made for 18- and 20-hour days on deck. The stamina of these men was legendary along the waterfront.

In the early 1990s the joke in the fishing business was that "all you need to be a halibut fisherman is a few free weekends." By 1994 the halibut season had been reduced to a few 12- to 48-hour "openings," or periods vessels were allowed to fish. This wasn't because of a shortage of fish, but rather that a huge fleet was taking the quota.

It was a poor system. The catch, coming all at once, overwhelmed processors, and gear tangled on the grounds. Finally in 1995, fishermen were given quota shares according to their catch history, and were allowed to fish whenever it was convenient for them.

The northwest halibut resource is strong. On occasion, during a 24-hour or 48-hour opening, vessels have caught more than 50,000 pounds. Today fishermen receive $1.50 and more a pound for their catch. Several species of cod are also targeted by longline fishermen.

LONGLINER'S DICTIONARY:
BECKET: a short piece of line knotted into the ground line, into which the gangion is attached.
CHICKEN: small halibut.
CIRCLE HOOK: efficient style introduced in 1980s.
GANGION (pronounced ganyon): leader between ground line and hook.
SKATE: unit of longline gear, usually 300 fathoms long (1,800 feet) with hooks every 21 feet.
SNAP GEAR: system using friction snaps to attach leaders to ground line.
STRING: 10 skates tied end-to-end, with anchors and buoys at either end.
WHALE: very large halibut.

Purse Seining

Each spring thousands of college-age young men walk the docks of Puget Sound ports seeking their ideal summer job—a crew job on an Alaska-bound purse seiner. The lucky ones begin work in late May or early June—painting and readying the graceful 58-footers, overhauling and building their expensive nets, and sailing north.

Seining is a complicated operation requiring coordination between the seiner, the large skiff, and a four- or five-man crew.

Purse seining for salmon in Chatham Strait. These vessels use a very large skiff to help work the net. When these boats are traveling, they usually pull the big skiff up onto the stern of the vessel.

"Let 'er go!" cries the skipper and the crew pulls the pin on a shackle, releasing the skiff, which begins towing the net off the seiner's stern. The seiner then makes a wide curving turn, typically "hooking" the net off a point, to catch fish traveling with the tide.

At the appropriate time the skiff will circle back, passing the end of the net to the larger vessel. Next the crew winches in both ends of the purse line, pulling up the net's bottom and transforming it into a sort of basket from which there is no escape. As the net is hauled aboard with the power block, the basket becomes smaller, until the fish can be easily dipped aboard.

In the late 1980s, when fish prices were booming, a crewman might make $10,000 to $20,000 in a good season on a top boat.

Salmon purse seiners catch primarily pink and chum salmon

PURSE SEINER'S DICTIONARY:
BUNT: the end of the net where the fish become concentrated.
HUNG UP: net hung on object or snagged on bottom.
MONEY FISH: sockeye salmon, much more valuable than pink salmon.
POWER BLOCK: hydraulically operated, boom-mounted pulley or sheave which pulls the net from the water, to stack on deck. When it was introduced, it revolutionized seining.
WATER HAUL: a no-fish set.

Made of very fine nylon, gill-nets must be repaired frequently.

Salmon Gill-netting

Imagine taking your family commercial fishing in Alaska in a nicely fitted-out 40-footer—gill-netting three or four days a week and having the rest of the time to explore, sports-fish, beachcomb, and so forth. This is what many men do, fishing with the simplest of nets—a floating vertical wall that has meshes sized to snag just behind the gills of traveling fish. A gill-netter will roll the net off his drum into the water in a likely spot, wait for a few minutes to several hours, and then wind it back onto the drum, standing in the stern and stopping the drum to "pick" fish as they appear.

Although the gear looks simple, fishing it in the tides of the region is tricky. The best fishermen know where to set their nets at each stage of the tide.

To fish for salmon commercially in Alaska you must buy a "limited entry permit" from someone who wants to leave the fishery. In the boom years of the late 1980s permit prices ranged from about $65,000 for a Southeast Alaska gill-net permit to $350,000 or so for a False Pass (Alaska Peninsula) gill-net permit. Today, due to low fish prices, permits are much cheaper.

GILL-NETTER'S DICTIONARY:
A FRONT ROW SEAT: setting your net right on the district boundary just as the fish are coming in with the tide.
BACKLASH: when a net snags and rips as it comes off the reel.
GETTING LACED OR CORKED: having another fisherman set his net too close to yours.
GETTING TRASHED OR KELPED UP: getting a net full of kelp or driftwood.
HITS: fish visibly hitting and becoming gilled in the net.
SOAKER: keeping one's net in the water for several hours or more.

Salmon Trolling

More than any other Alaskan fishery, salmon trolling is an art. The fisherman must choose among many styles and colors of lures or bait for the one just right for the particular time of day, depth of water, color of sky, and other factors.

Identified by their tall trolling poles, vertical for traveling, lowered to 45 degrees for fishing, these ubiquitous craft use hooks and lines to catch king, silver, sockeye, chum, and pink salmon. Some of the larger boats are "freezer trollers," able to make longer trips, not limited by how long their ice lasts. Most boats, however, make trips of up to a week and deliver a premium-quality iced fish. Most trollers use small power-operated drums to haul in their lines. Some smaller vessels, displaying "HT" signs, may use only hand power for this task.

Although net-fishing vessels are restricted to certain areas, trollers pretty much have the entire region to choose from when their season is open.

The troller's life is solitary, at times even spiritual. These fishermen, especially those who fish offshore, become much more separated from the cares of the land than their net-fishing brethren.

TROLLER'S DICTIONARY:
BIG SCORE: good catch.
FAIRWEATHER GROUND: popular offshore trolling area northwest of Cape Spencer.
FLASHER: a large (to 12 inches long) rectangular, shiny, metallic device to attract fish.
HOOTCHIE: plastic squid lure, available in many colors.
SKUNK DAY: no fish.
SMILIE: very large king salmon.

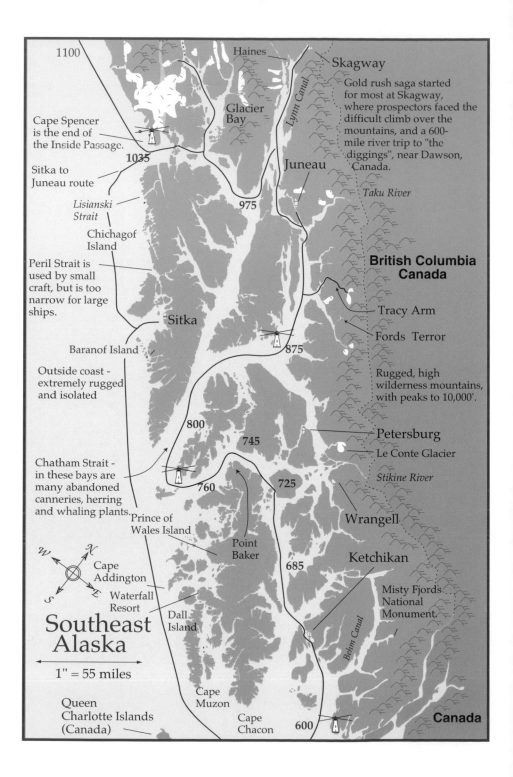

1100

Cape Spencer is the end of the Inside Passage.

Haines

Skagway

Glacier Bay

1035

Sitka to Juneau route

Gold rush saga started for most at Skagway, where prospectors faced the difficult climb over the mountains, and a 600-mile river trip to "the diggings", near Dawson, Canada.

Lynn Canal

Juneau

Lisianski Strait

Chichagof Island

975

Taku River

Peril Strait is used by small craft, but is too narrow for large ships.

British Columbia Canada

Sitka

Baranof Island

Tracy Arm

875

Fords Terror

Outside coast - extremely rugged and isolated

Rugged, high wilderness mountains, with peaks to 10,000'.

800

745

Petersburg

Le Conte Glacier

Chatham Strait - in these bays are many abandoned canneries, herring and whaling plants.

760

725

Stikine River

Prince of Wales Island

Wrangell

Point Baker

Ketchikan

685

W *N* *E* *S*

Cape Addington

Waterfall Resort

Dall Island

Misty Fjords National Monument

Southeast Alaska

1" = 55 miles

Behm Canal

Queen Charlotte Islands (Canada)

Cape Muzon

Cape Chacon

600

Canada

CHAPTER 4

Islands Without Number

Alaska Border, Mile 600,
to Juneau, Mile 930

"So we came to Alaska, on a wild and lost afternoon, caught in a tide race off a nameless point, in failing light, far from any help. The heavy westerly swell, the dirty southwest chop, and the push of the tide on top made it all I could do just to keep way on the boat, throttling over the big ones and then diving deep into the troughs. The seas came from all directions, and even at dead slow, waves slapped at the windows, sagging-in the thick glass".

—Joe Upton, *Alaska Blues*

T he United States border is at **mile 599.** There are no flags, nor duty-free shopping here. The border runs across windy Dixon Entrance, a place where small craft hurry to cross. It's not as wide as Queen Charlotte Sound, but the tidal currents pouring out of all those deep inlets, when opposed by the southwest breeze, can get ugly. The passage, "So we came to Alaska," which opens this chapter, describes a crossing of the tide rips near the border.

Look for the high ridge of snow-covered peaks to the east. They effectively seal off Southeast Alaska from any land connection, except in the very north at Haines and Skagway, and tiny Hyder, far up Portland Canal.

Study the map carefully here. This region to the east, with many winding inlets that all had to be explored, was very difficult for Vancouver and his men.

Look for salmon gill-netters, typically fishing Sunday noon through Wednesday noon. If the weather

A man in a boat could travel for weeks here and never find a town. This part of Alaska is mostly a forested wilderness with hundreds of islands. This is a humpback whale blowing in the narrow waters of Kootznahoo Inlet.

The entire lower mainland here is part of the Misty Fjords National Monument

Herring skiffs on an April morning at Kah Shakes Cove, south of Ketchikan. In the 1980s herring roe was a prized commodity in Japan, and the fishery was a boom for northwest fishermen.

JOE'S JOURNAL

is calm, you may also see fish packers (they're larger) making their rounds among the fleet, buying fish. Many vessels remain the summer here, remote from any town or cannery, getting water, groceries, fuel, and supplies from the tenders, or fish packers, that service the fleet. The nets they use here are 1,800 feet long by 30 feet deep; a good day might be 2,000 pounds (400 fish) of red salmon or 5,000 pounds of pink salmon.

Emily Jane, **July, 1981**: Garnet Point Days: each Saturday night my wife and I and our engineer would leave the Icicle Seafoods Cannery in Petersburg in our 75' fish buying vessel or "tender" *Emily Jane* for the 15 hour run down to Garnet Point, just north of the Canadian border. Our fleet - a group of 10 gill-net vessels that spent much of their summers in that remote area would be waiting for the mail, groceries, and other supplies that we had brought out from town for them.

Their "fishing period" - usually 3 or 4 days - began Sunday at noon - and the boats would spread out, setting their floating gill-nets for migrating salmon. Each evening they would come into the protected cove where we were waiting, to unload, get ice, water, or fuel, and visit for a bit before anchoring up for the night.

If fishing was heavy, we'd be up some nights until 1 a.m. or later, but it was a schedule that gave us days to

explore. On a beach below rotting totems in the forest we found tiny colored glass trading beads that had been cast into the waters when the Tlingit natives set off in their large canoes on trading or hunting voyages.

If you traveled through here in April, you'd be right in the middle of one of Alaska's stranger activities — the herring sac roe fishery, occasionally known as "Kazunoko madness" (kazunoko is the Japanese name for salted herring roe).

Fishermen use strange craft called herring skiffs (which may be 35' long and carry 60,000 pounds of herring) to gill-net for herring about to spawn. (See photo on P. 106.) Many times the fishermen will wait, anchored up, while the authorities and fish buyers monitor the 'ripeness' of the herring, which should be harvested just before they are ready to spawn. Sometimes the waiting can go on for weeks...

Tree Point Light at **mile 607** is the first in Alaskan waters. Before it was automated in the 1970s, the crews lived in four beautifully crafted houses set in the woods near the cove south of the light. One house was barged to Ketchikan after the families left.

This part of Alaska is a long narrow strip of mainland and islands nestled against British Columbia. The U.S. - Canada border runs along the tops of the highest peaks in the coast range, like these behind a Petersburg salmon cannery.

If it's clear, set your alarm for just before dawn, get up and go topside— this is truly spectacular country!

A small excursion vessel noses slowly into Punchbowl Cove, in Misty Fjords National Monument. The scenery here is particularly grand. A flightseeing trip to Misty can be spectacular.

Towns that disappeared - Anyox, British Columbia, just across the border was a thriving copper smelter in the 1920s, and is now abandoned.

The southernmost part of Alaska is part of the Misty Fjords National Monument, the centerpiece of which is the canyon-like Boca de Quadra area, to the east at **mile 625.** Also dramatically beautiful are Rudyerd Bay and Walker Cove, 30 miles farther north.

Several excursions from Ketchikan visit Misty Fjords.

The Boca is 50 miles of steep-sided fjords and side channels, whose sides quickly rise to two- and three-thousand-foot peaks. Aside from the ubiquitous cannery ruins and a lodge on the shore of Mink Bay, the land is wilderness, visited mostly in summer by people seeking its natural beauty by floatplane and excursion boats, and in winter by shrimp and crab fishermen.

The Boca is also the proposed site for the largest open- pit molybdenum mine in the world.

"Here?" you ask, "here in this gorgeous National Monument, an open-pit mine?"

The same question was asked by hundreds of fishermen who were concerned about the effects of toxic mine tailings on nearby salmon and crab stocks.

In the late 1970s, when Southeast Alaska's two key industries, forest products and fishing, were in a cyclic downturn, the mine promised employment to the region. Eventually, to the astonishment of most of its opponents, the mine received all the necessary permits for construction.

Then, to the surprise of almost all, the project faded away without being built, the victim, apparently, of the end of the cold war. (Molybdenum is a key ingredient in steel alloys, particularly those used in aircraft and mis-

sile parts.) Today, all that is left of the grand plans so widely proclaimed is a dock on Smeaton Bay and a road that is slowly being taken over by the forest.

The two-mile-wide channel extending to the northeast at around **mile 630** is **Behm Canal**, named by Vancouver and charted by his small-boat crews, rowing into and out of each inlet and bay. Halfway up the canal he remarked on a rock that from a distance looked like the sail of a ship.

"On the base of this singular rock, which, from its resemblance to the lighthouse rock off Plymouth, I called the New Eddystone [Rock], we stopped to breakfast, and whilst were thus engaged, three small canoes, with about a dozen of the natives, landed and approached us unarmed, and with the utmost good humor, accepted such presents as were offered to them."

—George Vancouver, *A Voyage of Discovery*

Before the invention of the chain saw, small groups of men called handloggers worked to cut the monster trees is places where gravity would side them down into the saltwater.
UW 17617

The large island to the west, from **mile 628** to **mile 645**, is **Annette Island, a reservation for the Tsimshian tribe**. Most of the Tsimshians lived in Metlakatla, Canada, across from Prince Rupert, where they thrived under the supervision of their pastor, a Mr. William Duncan. A dispute with authorities in 1887 led Mr. Duncan, along with most of the tribe, to move across to their present home on Annette Island, where they built a village, also named Metlakatla.

Today Metlakatla, supported by its own sawmill and salmon cannery, is a tidy and successful native community. It was to this cannery that I came as a lad of 19, and worked as an engineer aboard a fish-packing vessel.

When early travelers in a power boat stole a totem from a native village here, the outraged natives followed to Seattle by canoe!

Before the Ketchikan airport was built across from town on Gravina Island in the 1970s the airport was near Metlakatla. Travelers flew in and out of Ketchikan in converted navy patrol bombers or PBYs. Taking off from Tongass Narrows in front of Ketchikan, they flew 20 miles to Annette Island, lowered their wheels and landed to meet their connections.

The thunder of floatplanes taking off is a regular part of daily life in Ketchikan year-round. Many of the smaller communities around this part of Alaska have no roads and depend on floatplanes for much of their needs. This is an Otter, one of the largest single engine planes in Alaska.

West and north of Behm Canal, starting at **mile 630**, is **Revillagigedo Island** ("Re-VEE-a gi-gay-do," known locally as Revilla). Penetrated by long, deep inlets, it is heavily logged in places close to the shore, though for the most part it remains a roadless wilderness. Spread along the eastern shore of Tongass Narrows is the city of **Ketchikan**, beginning at Mountain Point, **mile 645**.

Pennock Island is across from where your ship docks. Take your binoculars and inspect the homes along the shore. These are essentially little Alaska homesteads, very popular with fishermen. Without roads, most Pennock residents do their shopping by outboard skiff.

Look for totem poles and a big native lodge, partially hidden by trees, on the right, near **mile 647**. This is

Cash Buyers

When I was a young engineer on a fish-buying vessel, one of my jobs was watching out for cash buyers. Our fishermen, like many, owed money to the cannery for nets, food and so forth, a debt that was repaid during the season.

Cash buyers, working for canneries or freezer plants without their own loyal fleets, would cruise the grounds, paying cash, giving out free beer to those who sold them fish and asking no questions about who owed what to the cannery. If one of our fishermen had a particularly good catch and happened to be near a cash buyer, and we weren't around, it would be to his advantage to sell part of his catch for cash and the rest to us.

So our tactic would always be to anchor near the cash buyers, so our fishermen couldn't deliver their fish to a cash buyer without our seeing them.

the native village of **Saxman**.

The big salmon canneries are just south of town at **mile 649**. The largest boats are tenders, mother ships to the smaller purse seiners and gill-netters. The big containers, or vans, stacked on the dock are filled with frozen or canned salmon as the season progresses.

Entrepreneurial blood flows through the veins of many Alaskans. Before Southeast Alaska had weekly barge service from Seattle, people like Captain Niels Thomsen, who had a small freight boat running regularly from Seattle to Ketchikan and other Alaskan towns, kept groceries on the store shelves. Thomsen started his business on a shoestring with the help of Ketchikan investors:

> "Most of my stockholders lived by Mountain Point, and I really wanted to impress them, so I'd made a dummy radar antenna out of wood, with a pipe coming down into the pilothouse. Every time I came past Mountain Point, I had my son cranking on that pipe to make the antenna go around. This was back in the early 1950s when radar was really expensive. 'Boy,' those guys must have thought, 'Radar! Well, old Cap Thomsen must really be doing well.'"

Look for brooms tied in the upper rigging of purse seine salmon vessels. A sign of very good fishing, a broom means a vessel has caught at least 100,000 fish. When prices were good in the late 1980s—50 cents a pound for pink salmon—that translated to $200,000 or

Native lodge at Saxman Village, mile 647. There are excursions to this village from Ketchikan. Want to stretch your legs? It's about a 45-minute walk going right from the dock.

There are several large canneries in the vicinity of mile 649. These large vessels are fish buyers; smaller vessels are gillnetters.

Alaska Cruise Handbook **111**

Kayakers below Creek St. boardwalk

Ketchikan is also known as the Salmon Capital of the World so if you want to try for one of Alaska's legendary big fish, go for it here!

Ketchikan

A Saturday afternoon in summer, 1951: the steam whistle at The Great Atlantic and Pacific Tea Company's Sunny Point salmon cannery echoes across Tongass Narrows as hundreds of workers stretch their tired muscles, start to clean up, and fan out to the bars and eateries that line the waterfront. Out in the channel floatplanes start to land, big twin-engine Grumman Geese, and the slow, lumbering Stinsons, bringing in loggers from Prince of Wales Island and Tsimshian Indians from the village of Metlakatla. As the sun slants toward the northwest, the fishing boats begin arriving from the outer districts, Dixon Entrance in the south and Clarence Strait to the north: big 60- and 80-footers loaded with salmon for canning and fishermen in for a night on the town.

At Big Dolly Arthur's and the other brothels along the boardwalk at Creek Street, the ladies finish their makeup and wait for their first customers. At the police station downtown, the boys in blue check their nightsticks and their pistols before heading out; Saturday night is always busy.

Almost half a century later, Ketchikan is still *ALASKA* in capital letters: all the rough-and-tumble elements that make this region what it is still ebb and flow through the streets and harbors of this town.

Second largest of only nine towns in an area larger than many states, Ketchikan is the economic center of lower Southeast Alaska. A narrow strip of a town along the steep western side of Revillagigedo Island, its few miles of roads aren't connected to anywhere else.

WHAT TO DO: The historical sights celebrate, in some fashion, Tsimshian and Tlingit culture, logging, or fishing. At the minimum, take the walking tour around downtown, and make the trip to one of the totem pole centers. The Creek Street Historical District, the Tongass Historical Museum, and the Thomas Basin Boat Harbor, as well as good shopping, are all within an easy walk of each other.

Just to the right of where your ship docks is Thomas Basin, a boat harbor. A stroll here is a good chance to see some of the Alaska fishing fleet up close.

A particularly good hike is up the Deer Mountain Trail that starts just a mile from downtown. At the top of the three-mile ascent is a dramatic view of the waterways and islands around Ketchikan.

FISHING: If catching a salmon is high on your list of things to do on your Alaska cruise, Ketchikan might be a good bet. Strong hatchery silver, and abundant pink and king salmon runs make for good fishing. If you really want to go after those big halibut, probably Sitka, being right on the ocean, would be better. Remember—as well as a fishing trip it's a chance to cruise along a real working waterfront and see some of Alaska's sea and bird life up close. Bring your camera.

Tip: If you go out sportsfishing, consider having your catch smoked at one of the local smokeries like Silver Lining Seafoods. Most will smoke, hold, and ship your fish to you after you return home.

Horse cart driver and friend with hat

Totem pole carver at Saxman Village, a few miles south from the cruise ship docks

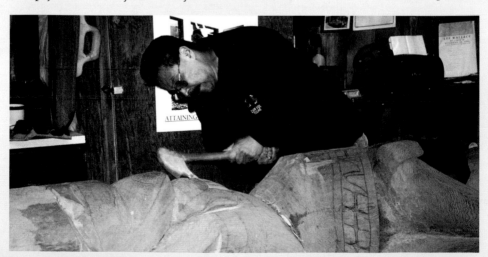

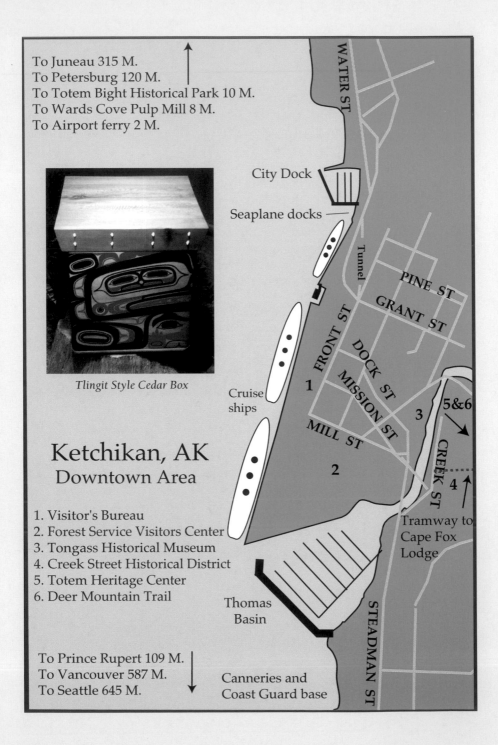

To Juneau 315 M.
To Petersburg 120 M.
To Totem Bight Historical Park 10 M.
To Wards Cove Pulp Mill 8 M.
To Airport ferry 2 M.

WATER ST

City Dock

Seaplane docks

Tunnel

PINE ST

GRANT ST

FRONT ST

DOCK ST

MISSION ST

Cruise ships

1

3

5&6

MILL ST

2

CREEK ST

4

Tramway to
Cape Fox
Lodge

Tlingit Style Cedar Box

Ketchikan, AK
Downtown Area

1. Visitor's Bureau
2. Forest Service Visitors Center
3. Tongass Historical Museum
4. Creek Street Historical District
5. Totem Heritage Center
6. Deer Mountain Trail

Thomas
Basin

STEADMAN ST

To Prince Rupert 109 M.
To Vancouver 587 M.
To Seattle 645 M.

Canneries and
Coast Guard base

Don't Miss Creek St.

An easy walk from the cruise ship docks is the Creek Street Historical District, a unique over-the-water boardwalk setting for shops, restaurants and sightseeing.

In Ketchikan's not-so-long-ago rough and tumble days, this is the place where the men and the fish came to spawn. Off the main drag and out of sight, but convenient to visiting fishermen, loggers and natives, this was a busy brothel community.

Cleaned up in the 1950s, the flavor of the place remains unique in the region.

A sampling of the many interesting shops:

Poker Creek Gold: this is a jewelry shop and mini gold mining museum all rolled into one. High marks for creativity and visitor-friendly environment.

Soho Coho Gallery: Ray Troll's eclectic art has become a northwest regional icon. This gallery is a "must" stop. From T-shirts to sculpture, from Ray and other artists, it's all here.

Parnassus Books: great books and gifts. Grab a chair and browse while you enjoy the view from her upstairs location.

Hungry? Downstairs are the Star Cafe and the Good Fortune Restaurant (Mandarin, Chinese, and Szechwan) to sit and enjoy something hot.

A tramway operates from Creek to the Cape Fox Lodge, located on a bluff with great views.

The shops and galleries of Creek St. are built along a salmon stream. In earlier days, this was Ketchikan's red light district. It's a short walk from the docks. In the background is the tramway to the Cape Fox Lodge.

Fish Traps and Creek Robbers

Brailing a fish trap, circa 1940. Such devices, mostly owned by Seattle fishing companies, were banned shortly after Alaska became a state in 1958. *Tongass Historical Society.*

If there were one burr under Alaskans' saddles, spurring the push for statehood (1959), it was the fish traps. Made of netting and hung from big, floating log frames or from piles driven in shallow water, the traps caught salmon and held them alive until a trap tender could take them to a cannery.

Each trap had a watchman. Trap robbers or fish pirates would approach the trap at night and threaten or, more commonly, pay off the watchman and make off with whatever fish they could load. Few Alaskans frowned on this, feeling that the Seattle-owned canneries were stealing their resource to start with. It all depended on the watchman:

> "The cannery told me it wasn't worth getting shot over a few fish, so if pirates came, I was to let them have what they wanted. But I decided no pirate was taking fish when I was watching, so the first one that came, sneaking around in a big boat with no lights on one night, I got my rifle and shot out his pilothouse windows, and I didn't have no trouble after that."
>
> —A fish trap watchman

"Crick robbing" is illegally fishing in closed areas, typically the mouths of creeks or rivers where spawning fish congregate. Today, "Fish cops" patrol in float-planes, and seasonal workers camp on some creeks and count fish, keeping poachers out.

Salmon purse seiners are identified by a big net piled on the stern and a large work skiff that is either towed, or pulled aboard.

more, but when the price plummeted a few years later to 10 or 15 cents, a one-broom season meant barely breaking even.

Ketchikan was known as the Salmon Capital of the World, from the 1930s and '40s when 11 canneries operated here and in nearby inlets. Today, two big canneries and several small freezer plants operate in town and the resource is strong again after a prolonged slump in the 1970s. You may have heard that salmon are scarce, even in danger of extinction, in northwest states. Not in Alaska. The 1994 statewide catch of 194 million salmon was the largest in Alaska's history. So please, eat plenty!

On a weekend, perhaps a hundred of the graceful 58-

SOUTH TONGASS AVE ROADKILL, KETCHIKAN, AK

foot "limit seiners" (Alaska limits the length of salmon seiners to 58 feet) might be tied up along the wharves of Ketchikan, the young crews "uptown" for whatever entertainment they might find. On Sunday they'll leave, dispersed to hundreds of coves and bays for the week's fishing.

A whimsical sculpture by Ray Troll, a well-known Ketchikan area artist. Ray's gallery is located on Creek Street.

Look east for the big pulp mill in **Wards Cove at mile 654**. This is the Ketchikan Pulp Company, the engine that has driven the local and regional economy since it was built in 1954. Trees cut throughout lower southeastern Alaska were towed here to become "dissolving pulp," a product used in the manufacture of cellulose-based products such as rayon and cellophane. In recent years concerns about the impact of logging on salmon steams reduced the amount of timber available for harvest and the mill closed in 1997.

The deeply indented land to the west at Guard Islands, **mile 660**, is **Prince of Wales Island**, the third largest island in the United States. From these shores and others like it come the fish and the logs that are the mainstays of the region's economy.

The closing of this mill was a major blow to the Ketchikan economy.

The wide channel to the northeast at Guard Islands is **Behm Canal**. It narrows to less than a half-mile wide at Behm Narrows and continues east and south, putting Ketchikan on an island.

Sixteen miles up the canal is **Traitors Cove**, where Vancouver had his closest brush with death. Low on food, circumnavigating Revillagigedo Island in the launch and the yawl boat, his boat was nearly overwhelmed by the natives before the other boat could get close enough to aid them. Vancouver attributed their behavior to bitter trading experiences with other Europeans, the natives exchanging the best they had for goods that turned out to be made shoddily.

Twelve miles farther north is **Yes Bay**, where a hand-logger in 1925 almost knocked an airplane out of the sky with a tree. The huge cliff-top spruce W.II. Jackson had just cut was toppling toward the water far below when he spotted a Fish and Wildlife floatplane almost directly beneath the falling tree, flying low along

Heard in Ketchikan:
Tourist to child: "How long has it been raining?"
Child: "I don't know; I'm only five."
(*Ketchikan is also known as the Rain Capital of the World!*)

the beach looking for fish pirates. It was a close call.

North from Ketchikan the Inside Passage goes up **Clarence Strait**, where Vancouver checked every significant side channel to make sure none was the strait he sought. When the wind blows against the tide, especially in the fall, this can be a difficult stretch of water for small craft:

A boater's nightmare: dangerous logs, known as deadheads, perhaps 70 feet long and weighing several tons, are the scourge of mariners in these waters.

JOE'S JOURNAL

"October 26, 1974, Ratz Harbor, Clarence Strait, Alaska. Third day blown into this narrow gut of a bay, waiting for weather good enough to travel. This morning squally, but the wind eased by noon, so set off to the south. Got only eight miles before being turned around by violent squall and rips. Lucky to make it back to the harbor to lick our wounds without getting a window busted out by the seas. Grub locker so low had to trade booze to beach loggers for frozen pork chops and instant spuds."

Land: So how come there's no one living along that great waterfront? The irony of Southeast, and indeed most of Alaska, is that there is so little land to buy. The reason is most of it belongs to the federal government and is protected in some way—national forests, national monuments and the like. Entrepreneurs who wished to use the bays of the region as sites for sportsfishing lodges, but were unable to buy the land, have built floating lodges which they moor in sheltered bays. They fly in the customers by floatplane.

A few residents have also built floating homes: houses on log rafts, moored between tiny islands or in sheltered nooks in remote bays.

Headed for Sitka via the outside coast? See end of this chapter for route and Sitka information.

Thorne Bay, west of mile 680, used to be the largest logging camp (it was a floating camp) in Alaska and the source of most of the logs for the Ketchikan mills.

Meyers Chuck, hidden in a crack in the eastern shore at about **mile 686**, is one of a handful of roadless fishing communities scattered throughout the region. In the late 1930s, the crew of the *Maggie Murphy* stopped here, still looking for the fishing bonanza they had come so far for:

Float Home Tales

Land to buy is so scarce in this region that some enterprising folks build their houses on floating log rafts. Of course, living like this entails a few wrinkles that wouldn't occur to land dwellers. For one family with growing kids, sometimes the house just doesn't seem big enough. So when the kids have cabin fever, this mother just sends them out to fish in the outhouse!

Another time, the husband noticed one of his big hundred pound propane bottles was leaking, and he was unable to fix it. Concerned that the leaking gas would be ignited by the nearby fish smoker, he disconnected and rolled it into the cove, thinking he'd let it drift out a bit with the tide, and shoot a hole in it so as to let it sink harmlessly to the bottom. But, by accident, his first shot instead knocked the valve off, and, propelled by the escaping gas, the propane bottle began moving rapidly like a torpedo in a circle back toward the float home.

Now the man really had a problem—as his horrified wife and children watched, the propane bottle gathered speed and straightened its course into a beeline right for them.

Letting his rifle rest on the porthole opening in the door to steady his aim, he tried to get a bead on the speeding bottle, but each time he was ready to shoot, the propane bottle would submerge and travel along just under the surface, impossible to hit with the rifle! Finally, when it was about 20 yards away, it surfaced just long enough for him to get a clear shot, blowing a hole in its side and it quickly sank!

In places like Myers Chuck, where there is a settlement next to good fishing, fishermen such as these can make a good living fishing from an open skiff.

"We found a feud raging in the harbor that was as ancient and fierce as that waged between picnickers and ants. The most tedious chore the cabin dweller knows is keeping up a supply of firewood. In Alaska, stoves burn continuously for nine months of the year, and they consume prodigious amounts of fuel. All this fuel must be obtained by felling trees and chopping them into cordwood.

"Where fishermen are living on boats, the problem is even more acute. While most boats have oil stoves, many still have old fashioned wood burners, and the owners must make frequent trips ashore in search of fuel. In Meyers Chuck, the fishermen who lived in boats piled their stove wood on the float alongside the point where they habitually docked at night.

"Once Ed and I watched a fisherman creep out of his boat and approach a nearby woodpile. He gazed furtively about to see if anyone was watching, then lifted the canvas, deftly grabbed a slab of wood, and dashed back to his boat. A few minutes later we heard him chopping, and it wasn't long before clouds of smoke were bellowing from his stove pipe.

"When the owner of the firewood came to dock, he took inventory of his woodpile and promptly missed one piece.

"Gathering firewood is the god-awfulest job in this country!' he roared, 'A man that'll steal it ought to be strung up like a cattle rustler.'"

—John Joseph Ryan, *The Maggie Murphy*

Humpback whales are frequently seen in the vicinity of Snow Pass, mile 720.

The chuck has a really narrow entrance, perhaps 30 yards wide. Before radar, the mail and freight boat operators would pick their way into the harbor in thick or snowy weather by tooting their horn and listening for the echoes off the steep rocks on either side of the entrance.

The narrow passage your ship transits around **mile 720 is Snow Passage.**

Look for humpback whales feeding in this area. These 40- to 50-foot mammals seem especially to like the tide rips in Snow Passage.

If you're really fortunate and have strong binoculars, you may be able to observe bubble net feeding, a method used by humpback whales to herd fish into compact, easy-to-eat schools. The whales circle beneath the herring, exhaling slowly. The circle of bubbles serves to contain or herd the fish, and the humpbacks then surface in the middle, with their mouths open.

Often when we traveled through the Snow Pass area, Dall porpoises would often play in front of our bow. Our dog would get especially excited!

Whale stories: Do orcas (killer whales) take revenge? In British Columbia they tell the story of a logger who, sighting an orca below him as he was falling a tree, dropped it on the whale for sport. Onlookers said the whale appeared to be hurt but swam away. Later that day, the logger got in an outboard to motor across the inlet. Halfway across, a killer whale struck and capsized the boat, and the logger drowned.

Inuit Eskimos on Alaska's North Slope tell a similar tale. A whaler harpooned an orca instead of his usual quarry, the much larger bowhead. After that, whenever he would go down to his skin boat, orcas would be waiting for him, and he was afraid to go out. He finally had to give up fishing and whaling.

Off the Beaten Track—the village of **Wrangell** is 24 miles east of Snow Pass. The

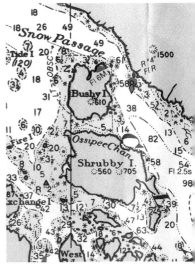

Northbound Travelers: about 2-3 hours after leaving Ketchikan, you will transit Snow Passage. The tidal currents run swiftly here, often stirring up tasty herring for humpback whales and other mammals. Get your binoculars and get up on deck. Even though your ship probably has a naturalist aboard, you might see a whale that they miss.

Window at abandoned cannery, Washington Bay.

muddy water sometimes seen near here is from the Stikine River, six miles north of town. Before 1900, eager hordes from three different gold rushes ebbed and flowed through this town to board steamboats headed up-river. The Stikine Strike occurred in 1861, followed by the Cassiar Strike in 1873, and the Yukon Strike in 1897; for a while Wrangell was the busiest spot in the new Alaska territory. But when John Muir arrived by steamer from Portland in 1879, the town was between rushes and it was life in the slow lane:

"The most inhospitable place at first sight I had ever seen. The little steamer that had been my home in the wonderful trip through the archipelago, after taking the mail, departed on her return to Portland, and as I watched her gliding out of sight in the dismal blurring rain, I felt strangely lonesome... There was nothing like a tavern or lodging-house in the village, nor could I find any place in the stumpy, rocky, boggy, ground about it that looked dry enough to camp on until I could find a way into the wilderness to begin my studies."

— John Muir, *Travels in Alaska*

John Muir in Alaska

This well-known naturalist came to Alaska in 1879, just 12 years after the territory was purchased from Russia.

Muir didn't have Gore-Tex waterproof clothing, nylon tents, Kevlar canoes or Coleman camp stoves. Yet in his five trips to Alaska, he made journey after journey that many of today's outdoors people wouldn't attempt. And he wrote—glorious prose, some of the best ever written about Alaska.

"Of all the thousands of camp-fires I have elsewhere built none was just like this one, rejoicing in triumphant strength and beauty in the heart of the rain-laden gale. It was wonderful—the illumined rain and clouds mingled together and the trees glowing against the jet background, the colors of the mossy, lichened trunks with sparkling streams pouring down the furrowed bark, and the grey bearded old patriarchs bowing low and chanting in passionate worship."

— John Muir, *Travels in Alaska*

Visited by few cruise ships, **Wrangell** has a slower pace. Visitors can expect to be greeted by children selling garnets (a dark-red stone) gleaned from a ledge in the **Stikine River**, five miles north of town. A half-mile walk south of the dock in Wrangell Harbor is Shakes Island, with impressive totems and a large replica Tlingit lodge.

If you look to the north from about mile 725, you might get a glimpse of the entrance to **Wrangell Narrows**. All Vancouver found was a muddy slough in September of 1793; but industrious fishermen and loggers, aided by Coast Guard and Corps of Engineers dredges, have dug out the thin spots and put in 65 buoys and markers to create a 20-mile shortcut between Sumner Strait and Frederick Sound. The scenery is dramatic, like a river through the woods, and the route knocks 90 miles off the run to Juneau, but it's too narrow for large ships.

The Alaska state ferries take this route, generally going through when the tide is high. At night or in fog, their skippers are doubly challenged, as not only does the tidal current run hard, but in places it runs obliquely across the dredged channel.

Tight quarters in Wrangell Narrows— note how the tug has shortened the towline so the barge is right behind him. When these boys come through, you want to give them plenty of room!

Wrangell Narrows is too shallow and constricted for most cruise ships.

Small section of Wrangell Narrows: when it's black and foggy this is no place for the faint of heart, especially when a big ferry or tug is headed the other way and taking up the whole channel!

Consider this foggy meeting between a big ferry and a 70-foot fish packer:

"I hate to go through them narrows in the black and the fog, but the cannery wanted the fish, so we had to go. Then right in the narrowest place, the radio blasts in my ear: 'This is the Alaska ferry *Matanuska,* southbound at marker 16. Northbound traffic please advise.' The *Matanuska*? Just a mile ahead, and him with the tide pushing him on? I called him right back, and mister, I could hear the tension in that man's voice. '*Matanuska* back. Yeah... I see you on my radar... but you'd better pull over and let us by... it's pretty damn tight here.' We were right below Burnt Island Reef, and I could see his target on the radar getting bigger and bigger all the time. So I just slowed down and pulled over into the shallows. I'd rather put 'er ashore on a mud bank than get T-boned by a 400-foot ferry!

"I slowed right down until I was just idling into the current, and looked out into the black, trying to see him. You know how it is with that radar: when something gets really close, it just disappears into the sea clutter in the middle of the screen and you can't really tell exactly where it is. Well, the ferry did that and I was just bracing myself to hit either the shore or him, when I saw him— just a glimpse of a row of portholes rushing by fast in the night, the big tide pushing him on, and then he was gone. Man, I don't know how them fellows do it, but I know I wouldn't have liked to been him that night."

—An Alaskan tender skipper

You can imagine how rapidly the tide runs through a narrow channel like this. At Petersburg, a fishing community at the north end of the narrows, the tide can rush past

Petersburg

Also known as Little Norway for the heritage of its residents and spectacular setting, this is a town that fishing built. Originally shipping their fish south with ice from nearby Le Conte Glacier, Petersburg fishermen have created a waterfront with three canneries and several custom processing facilities. In recent years these fishermen have expanded their operations into the crab and salmon fisheries of the Bering Sea and western Alaska.

the wharves at up to 6 mph! When you make a landing with a boat, the trick is to get the lines all tied to the dock before you take the engine out of gear. Landing a big fish packer loaded with several hundred thousand pounds of fish into a berth with no room on either side can be a real challenge with the tide running—once you're committed, there's no second chance!

Wrangell Narrows with Petersburg canneries on right. The mountains in the background rise up to 10,000 feet and are a climbing destination.

Look for the Sumner Strait salmon gill-net fleet from **mile 740** to about **mile 743**, typically fishing from Sunday noon to Thursday noon. The fish come from the west here, and the trick is to set your net back from the district boundary at Point Baker, so that the ebbing current carries you to the line, then stops, just as the tide turns. This gives you a front row seat, with no room for another boat to set legally between you and the incoming fish.

It was this strongly flowing tidal current that caused Captain Johnny O'Brien's luck to run out in the black of a November night in 1917. The *Mariposa* was one of the finest steamers on the Alaska run, but while Dynamite Johnny caught a nap in his stateroom as a pilot steered, the strong current set her off course and onto Mariposa Reef, **mile 745**, where parts of her still remain.

Gill-net vessels are identified by a large drum or reel, usually mounted behind the cabin.

Tricks of the old time fish buyers

The great thing about the Icicle Seafoods cannery in Petersburg is that it's right next to the grocery store. When you get your groceries, usually two or three carts'-worth, you just roll the carts right out onto the dock, over to the big boom mounted electric hoist, and then lower the whole full shopping cart right down to the deck of your boat! It sure beats carrying them one bag at a time all the way down a 30-foot steel ladder dripping with slimy fish guts.

First snow at my Point Baker cabin, 1975. Situated close to a tide rip where herring and whales often congregate, on still nights in the summer, we could lay in our beds and hear whales blowing.

Watch for humpback whales at Point Baker, mile 745, usually in close to the shore, west of the point. Typically a pair remains here for most of the summer, feeding on herring in the tide rips. In the 1960s, a particular whale got to be known as Ma Baker. Local lore has it that she once surfaced under one of the puddle jumpers, or small fishing skiffs, lifting the surprised fishermen and his boat completely clear of the water for a moment.

Point Baker and the nearby community of Port Protection are two roadless fishing communities. It was here that we built our little island homestead. See Chapter 3.

This bay was the occasion of one of Vancouver's closest calls. Late on the afternoon of September 8, 1793, while exploring and charting Sumner Strait, a storm was seen approaching the area. It was at last light that Lieutenant Broughton in the *Chatham* saw the entrance to what looked like a cove and signalled Vancouver to follow him into the bay, south of **mile 745**. It was just in time:

"We had scarcely furled the sails, when the wind shifting to the S.E., the threatened storm from that quarter began to blow, and continued with increasing violence during the whole night; we had, however, very providentially reached an anchorage that completely sheltered us from its fury, and most probably from imminent danger, if not from total destruction. Grateful for such an asylum, I named it Port Protection."

—Captain George Vancouver, *A Voyage of Discovery*

Look north as you pass Port Protection — the land seems to knit together at the head of the distant bay. Actually there are two separate major islands, Kudu Island on the west and Kupreanof Island to the east. Between them is **Keku Strait**, known locally as **Rocky Pass**, a popular shortcut for small craft before the Coast Guard removed the navigational markers in the late 1970s as not cost-effective.

Near Rocky Pass in August, 1794, Lieutenant Johnstone, exploring in Vancouver's small boats, was approached by several canoes, with natives who apparently wanted to trade:

"One of the canoes now advanced before the rest, in which a chief stood in the middle of it, plucking the white

feathers from the rump of an eagle and blowing them into the air, accompanied by songs and other expressions, which were received as tokens of peace and friendship."
—Capt. George Vancouver, *A Voyage of Discovery*

The sea provides. Many residents in Alaska's small coastal communities are dependent on strong fish resources and good fish prices.

However, ever since the near-disastrous struggle with natives at Traitors Cove the previous summer, Vancouver's men were wary of situations in which they were outnumbered. So they wisely declined the invitation to stop and kept on rowing.

Hole in the Wall, east of **mile 751**, is one of Southeast Alaska's special places. A channel, so narrow that trollers must use care if their poles are down, leads to a tranquil and lake-like basin where deer and bear may be seen along the shore.

An hour or so past Point Baker, the vessel track turns sharply northward again at **Cape Decision Light**, **mile 773** and into **Chatham Strait**.

Look for dramatic **Helm Point**, a conspicuous headland on Coronation Island, 10 miles south. Rising sheer from the sea to a thousand feet, it is the nesting place for thousands of sea birds.

The bays of Coronation Island have a bad reputation among fishermen for williwaws: violent, unpredictable gusts of wind.

Seeking a place to anchor, a salmon trolling vessel transits the narrow entrance to Hole-in-the-Wall, west of Point Baker.

"Fishermen are not certain what causes the williwaws. They only know that on peaceful summer evenings, when the sea is calm and boats are resting at anchor, a dull roaring noise is sometimes heard in the harbors of Coronation Island. The noise gains steadily in volume, and suddenly, with terrifying force and swiftness, a blast of wind sweeps down off the rocky hills, scattering boats like bowling pins."
—John Joseph Ryan, *The Maggie Murphy*

MOHAI 15329

Sperm whale, Port Armstrong, circa 1940. Today protected by law, several species of whales frequent Alaskan waters.

For much of this century, **Chatham Strait** was a beehive of activity. Between the salmon plants, the herring plants, and the whaling stations, almost every bay in this canyon-like region was home to some sort of commercial activity. Then the herring and the whales disappeared, and refrigerated tenders allowed consolidation of the salmon canneries into towns like Petersburg and Ketchikan.

For many of the plant operators, who were headquartered in Seattle, the decision to close a plant came in the wintertime, when just a caretaker remained in the remote Chatham Strait bay. Sometimes it was easier to abandon the plant than to send up a vessel and a crew to bring out the supplies. The plants were in reality whole little towns, with well-built houses for the managers and their families, bunkhouses and mess halls, warehouses, workshops, powerhouses, and so forth. When they were no longer needed, the owners just walked away, leaving

The Trapper's Tale

Some fishermen supplement their winter income by trapping, for mink and marten, traveling in their small craft to remote bays. It can be difficult in unexpected ways:

"Our boat was fiberglass and didn't have any insulation on the hull up where we slept, so some mornings when we woke up, my hair would be frozen to the condensation on the side of the hull. John would have to get up first, get the stove going to heat some water to get my hair out of the ice..."

the warehouses full of supplies. Word that the company in a particular bay had "jerked their watchman" was notice that it was free pickings, and the region's fishermen and trappers were quick to make sure nothing was wasted.

For the small craft traveler, it is almost spooky to travel in Chatham Strait, to anchor and go ashore and wander through the ruins, rarely encountering another traveler.

Port Alexander is another popular spot for hand trollers or skiff fishermen.

In a cove on Baranof Island, west of **mile 792, is Port Alexander**. With a good harbor, a settlement, a fish buyer and a store, and good fishing at Cape Ommaney (west of mile 786), it's a popular spot in summer. In its heyday, the 1920s and 1930s, it was Alaska with a capital A, as the *Maggie Murphy* boys noted:

> "It became the number one trolling port in the territory, a wide-open, carefree, money-kissed little place that old-timers still recall with nostalgia."
> —John Joseph Ryan, *The Maggie Murphy*

When they walked into town, they were halted by an elderly man who told them, "Boys, it's illegal to walk on the streets of Port Alexander sober."

In those days, many trollers worked out of open boats, some without motors, rowing as they towed their lines through the water. A little tent city sprang up south of the dock each summer. By the late 1940s the

Getting in the winter's meat, Southeast Alaska style

UW Thwaites 0098-1

A Hand-troller's Life

"Port Alexander, June 1975: Visited Amy and Scott in their little cabin today. With a garden in back and his beautiful 14-foot hand-trolling skiff in front, they've come a long ways since the last time I heard about them.

"That was last year, and she was very pregnant. They were squatting at a tumble-down cannery in Pillar Bay and trying to make a living hand-trolling from his small open boat.. There was a fish buyer there, but when he needed medicine or groceries the fish buyer didn't have, he'd take that little skiff of his all the way across the strait to Port Alexander. Those are big waters and he told me once that old engine pounding away was the only thing between him and a cold and wild sea.

Scott's hand troller

"Now, with a fat baby nursing, a garden planted, a pile of firewood outside, good fishing here, and friends all around, it looks as if he's about got 'er licked."

Almost every bay in Chatham Strait had at one time some sort of cannery, saltery, or fish processing facility. All are now abandoned, as refrigerated fish-transport vessels have allowed the plants to move to the towns where operating is less expensive.

party was over, the great runs rapidly diminishing as the newly-built dams on the Columbia River, 1,200 miles south, prevented the big kings from reaching their spawning grounds.

At **Port Conclusion**, three miles north of Port Alexander, Vancouver anxiously awaited the four overdue cutters and yawl boats that were filling in the last blank places on his chart in August, 1794. Finally the boats hove safely into sight during a rainstorm on the 19th.

Then with grog for all hands, and cheers ringing from ship to ship in a remote cove halfway around the world from England, there ended one of the most remarkable feats of navigation and exploration in modern times. In three summers of exploring and charting this unknown coast, through persistent fogs, swift currents and occasional thick ice— losing just one man to bad shellfish— Vancouver had disproved the ages-old notion of a Northwest Passage back to the Atlantic. In doing so, he charted, explored, described and named much of the Northwest coast. It was nothing less than a stunning achievement. He was 38 years old.

To the west at **mile 800 is Port Walter**, the wettest place on the United States mainland, with 240 inches of rain a year. Hidden at the head of the bay is the narrow entrance to **Big Port Walter**, an unusually steep-sided basin containing the village-like ruins of a herring plant.

One wonders about the spirits of the winter caretaker, with the sun gone over the mountain on October 15, not to appear again for four or five months, and the inner basin frozen eight to ten feet thick.

Bay of Pillars, east of mile 813, and **Washington Bay**, east of mile 820, both contained substantial herring or salmon processing plants in their day. In a visit to Washington Bay in 1975, the buildings were intact, but the forest was growing up around them.

Likewise, Tyee, at the southern tip of Admiralty Island, was a major salmon cannery in the 1940s, the brightest lights for miles around. Today it is a small fishing lodge.

Look southeast from around **mile 845** to the head of the island-choked bay and to Rocky Pass, the narrow back channel to Sumner Strait. It was this narrow channel ("we paddled on through the midst of the innumerable islands") from which John Muir, an evangelist companion, and a group of native paddlers emerged on the morning of October 19, 1879. The natives dreaded the crossing of Frederick Sound to Point Gardner at the southern tip of Admiralty Island:

In calm waters, vessels may tie together for more convivial traveling. My boat, in the middle, is a good example of a troller/gillnetter combination. The net reel is located in the middle, while on either side are the gurdies or small winches used to haul the fishing lines in and out.

Traveling like this is great for partying in the boat with the biggest cabin, but tide rips or the wakes of large boats passing can break the lines holding the boats together. So you have to be watchful!

"Toyatte said he had not slept a single night thinking of it, and after we rounded Cape Gardner and the comparatively smooth Chatham Strait, they all rejoiced, laughing and chatting like frolicsome children."

John Muir, *Travels in Alaska*

The village visible to the southeast from mile 845 is **Kake**, a Tlingit village supported by a cannery and logging on native land. Locals use narrow Rocky Pass frequently as a short cut to Sumner Strait. According to one story they were astounded a few years back, to see a tug towing a big barge emerging from the constricted passage. No one could remember such a big vessel or barge coming through the pass before. The skipper stepped out and hailed those on shore.

Most of the coves along this part of the coast used to be home to sawmills, salmon canneries, herring plants or whaling stations. Refrigerated transport vessels allowed the canneries to move to places like Ketchikan or Petersburg. This is the settlement of Tenakee Springs.

"Say," the rough-looking man said, waving a hand back toward Rocky Pass, "that Wrangell Narrows ain't nothing like the chart." He stopped and looked over at the village on the shore, "And I thought Petersburg was larger than this." He was 40 miles west of where he thought he was!

"**June 5, 1974**: Underway at 5 from Kake, on yet another gem of a morning. Across the channel, looming eerily over the trees and water, pink in the rosy dawn, towered Baranof Island, 30 miles away. Then we were in Rocky Pass, weaving in and out of the flats and rocks, in the very shadow of the trees—twice my trolling poles knocked branches down on deck. There was a warm smell to the air, the alders and birch bright green on the shore. We even saw Mr. Bear today, clamming on a beach, scooping up a paw full, and smacking one big paw down to smash the clam, then putting the whole mess up to his mouth.

The landscape in these inlets that penetrates deep into the mainland wilderness is spectacular.

Fords Terror Journal

About 20 miles southeast of mile 900, hidden in a fold in the hills, is the remote and little-visited inlet called Fords Terror. We explored it one weekend between fishing periods in 1973. The memory is etched in my mind still today:

"September 5, 1973: Just at one, traveling dead slow, with little water under us, we passed the rapids in the creek-like entrance to Fords Terror. Hardly spoke a word for the next mile, so overpowering was the scenery. The channel was barely a hundred feet wide. To the north a sheer rock wall rose out of the water a thousand feet before sloping back out of sight. We passed a waterfall, with at least a hundred-foot clear drop into the trees. The gorge opened up to a basin perhaps one-mile-by-three, and we dropped the anchor, rowed ashore, and walked, until our boat was just a dot on the far shore.

"The sun went over the mountain at 4:30, and the evening came early and chill. At dusk, flight after flight of ducks came in low and fast, to settle on the water near the shore with a rush of many wings and soft callings.

"The night was chilly, with northern lights again. Stood out on deck and watched, until the cold drove us in. Yesterday and today, the places we visited make us feel tiny indeed.

"September 6, 1973: First frost! The stove went out in the night, and we woke to find the dog nestled in between us. To go out onto the frosty deck on such a morning, with the still glassy basin around, and the dark forests and frozen hills above—words can't tell it, pictures can't show it.

"Our cup seems pretty full just now."

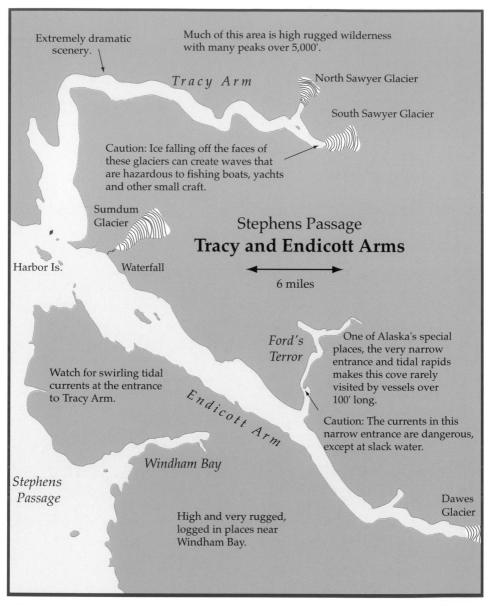

Extremely dramatic scenery.

Much of this area is high rugged wilderness with many peaks over 5,000'.

Tracy Arm

North Sawyer Glacier

South Sawyer Glacier

Caution: Ice falling off the faces of these glaciers can create waves that are hazardous to fishing boats, yachts and other small craft.

Sumdum Glacier

Stephens Passage
Tracy and Endicott Arms

← → 6 miles

Harbor Is.

Waterfall

Ford's Terror

One of Alaska's special places, the very narrow entrance and tidal rapids makes this cove rarely visited by vessels over 100' long.

Watch for swirling tidal currents at the entrance to Tracy Arm.

Endicott Arm

Caution: The currents in this narrow entrance are dangerous, except at slack water.

Windham Bay

Stephens Passage

Dawes Glacier

High and very rugged, logged in places near Windham Bay.

"*Tracy Arm*, the north arm of Holkam Bay, takes a general northerly direction for 9 miles, then turns eastward 13 miles to its head, where two large glaciers, North and South Sawyer discharge into salt water. The arm is often clogged by small icebergs for several miles and great care is needed in navigating the ice field. At times **South Sawyer Glacier** is very active, huge blocks of ice falling off its face into very deep water."

— *U. S. Coast Pilot, Volume 8, 1969*

"The day was so fair we stopped at a long-deserted cabin in a small sheltered bight on Sumner Island for lunch. We lay on a grassy knoll and got pleasingly sunburned for the first time in two years, with the wind in the trees, and the cries of the gulls in our ears. When the sun grew cool and dropped in the sky, we were on our way to cover the last miles to Point Baker, where we tied up after five weeks away.

"On the flats behind our cabin, the grass was green, the garden had sprouted, and the flowers were all out. With the gill-net season opening in this district in two weeks, a float to build, and a net to hang, we'll just stay here.

"So ended our Chatham Straits troll trip. We fished a lot of country; we hardly made a dime. Yet I'd do it again in a minute. That lonely canyon cast a spell on us. We fished for days, went in and out of a dozen bays, and in all that time, hardly saw another boat."

Tracy Arm is truly a canyon. Look for long horizontal scratches or striations made by the millions of tons of moving ice.

Start looking for ice at Turnabout Island, mile 856. This is the southern limit of drift ice from the glaciers in Tracy Arm, east of **mile 900**, and Le Conte Glacier, east of Petersburg. On occasion Le Conte Glacier puts out tremendous amounts of ice, some of which may find its way into Wrangell Narrows.

Five Finger Light, at **mile 870**, was the first manned lighthouse in Alaska and the last one automated, in 1983. Compared to other coastal areas, Alaska has relatively few lighthouses because of the difficulty of building and supplying such structures in remote areas. Wherever possible the Coast Guard relies on buoys and untended lights for navigational aids.

Victrola in abandoned fox farm, Harbor Is., east of mile 900.

Look for humpback whales throughout Frederick Sound and Stephens Passage. Much larger than orcas, up to 50 feet long, humpbacks sometimes breach—leap completely clear of the water—a good trick for a 30-ton creature.

John Muir passed this way by canoe:

> "Around noon we rounded Cape Fanshaw, scudding swiftly before a fine breeze, to the delight of our Indians, who had now only to steer and chat. Here we overtook two Hoona Indians and their families on their way home from Fort Wrangell. They had exchanged five sea otter skins, worth about a hundred dollars apiece, and a considerable number of fur-seal, land-otter, martin, beaver, and other furs and skins, $800 worth, for a new canoe valued at 80 dollars, some flour, tobacco, blankets, and a few barrels of molasses for the manufacture of whiskey. The blankets were not to wear, but to keep as money, for the almighty dollar of these tribes is a Hudson's Bay Blanket."

—John Muir, *Travels in Alaska*

The two canoes began to race each other, continuing until after dark. The water was "firing": exhibiting phosphorescence, showing each stroke of oar or paddle and the wakes of the canoes as shining tracks in the black. They headed for a well-known salmon stream to camp, and could see the schools of fish glowing in the water. Muir and his traveling companion set up their tent against the steady rain. The Hoona natives, two families, simply took their rest on the wet ground: "Our Hoona neighbors were asleep in the morning at sunrise, lying in a row, wet and limp like dead salmon."

On the shore of **Harbor Island**, which guards the entrance to Tracy Arm, west of **mile 900**, is an abandoned homestead and fox farm These were common on small Southeastern Alaska islands in the 1940s and 1950s. Typically fed salmon in season, the foxes were a problem to feed when the fish weren't running.

> "When we were low on fox food, Dad would send my brother and me over to Point Astley, where there were lots of seals and sea lions. We'd shoot those big sea lions, and

Courtesy of Steve Snapp

Glacier Bay vs. Tracy Arm

Glacier Bay is a National Park with many rules regarding access for vessels of all sizes. Tracy Arm, however, is not, which means that vessels may visit freely. Also the distance from the entrance to the actual ice face is much less: around 23 miles for Tracy Arm, and about 55 in Glacier Bay For this reason, it is popular with yachts, fishing craft as well as cruise ships. Endicott Arm with Dawes Glacier is an excellent alternate glacier viewing destination as well.

then we had to cut the carcasses into pieces with a two-man saw to load into the skiff. God, it was a mess."

—A fox farmer

All the land to the west here, from **mile 870**, all the way almost to Juneau, is **Admiralty Island**. Much of the island is part of the Admiralty Island National Monument. This island is the only one in Southeast Alaska where one is apt to encounter brown bears.

Tracy Arm: Traveling up Tracy Arm (the entrance is five miles northeast of **mile 900**) is like going back through geologic history. The fjord's dramatic walls lose their vegetation until they become bare shining rock, shaped and ground smooth by the ice. In many places the mountains plunge vertically into the water, which is more than a thousand feet deep.

Muir was genuinely moved by the power and the beauty of the glaciers, and he was able to communicate some of this enthusiasm to his companions. Once, when they had paddled most of an afternoon up Tracy Arm, frustrated with the narrow and ice-choked channel, they turned yet another corner and found what he had come to seek, the glacier itself. While Muir stood in the canoe, sketching the glacier, several huge icebergs calved off, thundering into the water of the narrow fjord. "The ice mountain is well disposed toward you," one of the native paddlers said to Muir, "He is firing his big guns to welcome you."

One of the most impressive things about glaciers is the noise. You have millions of tons of ice being pushed forward through a frequently twisting channel, and it is an impressively noisy process.

The inlet to the east at **mile 914** is **Port Snettisham**, at the head of which is a dam supplying power to Juneau. The sides of the inlet are so steep the power lines had to be strung by helicopter.

Taku Inlet is the wide channel leading northeast at **mile 929**; it is the mouth of the Taku River. Vancouver's Lieutenant Joseph Whidbey and his party faced sleet, rain and thick ice as they traced the continental boundary here in early August, 1794; they went only 13 miles before being stopped by the ice.

Juneau is at the head of 10-mile-long Gastineau Channel. Surrounded by land, and tucked into the mainland shore, winters here are a lot colder than Ketchikan or Sitka.

Had the settlement of Alaska proceeded at the same time as, say, Boston, or Philadelphia, five thousand miles to the east and south, it is unlikely that anyone would have chosen Juneau for a town site. According to Vancouver, Gastineau Channel was impassable because of the ice, and his men passed through in August.

Indeed, the conclusion that the climate was substantially colder in the late 1700s than it is today is inescapable.

Today the glaciers in the Juneau area have retreated substantially back from the salt water.

In remote Steamboat Bay, a steam winch waits for workers who will never return.

Whale Watching
Scrapbook

Once hunted for oil and bone, today the whales of the northwest coast are recognized as being unusually intelligent, gentle creatures. The most common whales you are apt to see here are orcas, or killer whales, and humpbacks. From a distance, whales are apt to be spotted by the distinctive white spout, as they exhale when surfacing.

I have been amazed at the narrow channels that whales sometimes manage to swim in and out of. The whale above has swum into the very narrow and tide swept waters of Kootznahoo Inlet, by the native village of Angoon, on Admiralty Island. There were a lot of herring in the narrow inlet that evening, and I think the humpback had followed them inside, with the incoming tide. Eventually the tide turned and the current ran the other way, carrying whale and herring back out into the wide waters of Chatham Strait.

These two humpbacks usually hung out right in front of our cove, "Port Upton," in the 1970's. Local legend had it that once one came up underneath one of the local fishing skiffs, lifting it completely out of the water!

There were always a couple of whales that hung out in the tide rip at Point Baker, **mile 745**. That's the place where the incoming tide from the ocean boils around the point and is always a popular spot for the whales favorite, schools of herring. There is a small cove just inside the point, and it was there that we built our cabin in 1973. (See Chapter 3) The whales were there all summer and into the fall, and on still nights, when the wind wasn't blowing or the tide running hard, and if we had a window open, we could hear the sigh-like breathing of the humpbacks.

One quiet night during the fishing season when the harbor at Point Baker was full of salmon commercial trollers and gillnetters, we had just come in to tie up and sleep for a few hours, and as I was coming down the dock from walking our dog, I was startled by a humpback blowing right next to the dock, in the midst of all those boats!

Another time my parents, on left, had come for a visit. The green boat was a funky craft I had fixed up

with a Briggs and Stratton inboard engine. It wasn't very dependable, but my parents wanted to go out and catch a salmon out by the point, so away they went. I was working on my net at our float, and when I heard what sounded like yells from out by the point, I assumed that Mom and Dad were excited about hooking into a big salmon.

But when they finally made it back in, I learned that they were yelling for a very different reason: the engine had died, they couldn't start it, and suddenly found themselves right next to two very curious humpbacks, surfacing right next to the boat!

HUMPBACKS

C ommonly seen throughout British Columbia and Alaska in summer, they migrate south and west in the winter, frequently to Hawaii. Adults are up to 50 feet long and 40 tons in weight. Distinguishing marks are white throat and belly, and knobs and bumps on head and flippers. Gregarious, they frequently are seen in groups, sometimes using a technique called bubble feeding to herd and feed on herring or other small fish. Their most dramatic behavior is breaching, or jumping clear out of the water. A 30- or 40-ton whale hitting the water makes a huge splash which may be seen at long distances. They seem to congregate particularly at places where the current runs rapidly around a point. Traditional places for seeing whales are Clarence Straits, north of Ketchikan, Snow Pass, **mile 725**, Point Baker, **mile 745**, Frederick Sound, Stephens Passage, Point Adolphus, **mile 1000**, and Glacier Bay.

While the above spots are good places to look, whales are basically where you find them. Fortunately when they breathe, they blow water vapor into the air as well, creating a "spout" that can be seen for several miles, if the water is calm. So the best way to look for whales is to always have your binoculars with you and to get into the habit of scanning the horizon when you are out on deck. Your ship will probably have a naturalist on board, but that doesn't necessarily mean that every whale sighting will be announced.

On the opposite page top are five humpbacks feeding on herring near Point Adolphus, **mile 1000**, directly south of the entrance to Glacier Bay.

Whale watching boats, ships, etc, are required to stay at least 50 yards from whales. In this case, our ship, the big *Dawn Princess,* stopped carefully fairly distant from the whales. I went outside on the promenade deck to get as close as I could. Then to our amazement and delight, all five whales turned and came right over to our stopped ship, and blew so close to where I was standing that I could hear their nasal trumpeting and smell their very foul breath!

Two really good spots for whale watching are Sitka Sound, and Lynn Canal, west of Juneau. In both cities whale watching excursions are offered. In the spring of 2004, I went on a salmon fishing charter offered out of Sitka and got way more than I expected. First we got our fish - some nice kings - within the first 45 minutes. But then the real excitement - about a mile away two humpbacks were working together. One was wildly banging the surface violently with its tail. For I while I didn't understand. Then with no warning the other whale breached - came vertically almost totally out of the water

with its mouth open and blowing water out of both sides. This happened three times before I grasped what was happening - the first whale was stunning a school of herring with its tail, and his partner would shoot up mouth open, through the school and up into the air gobbling up fish on the way!

ORCAS

Easily recognized by their tall black tails, orcas are seen throughout the Alaska cruise area. The best places to look for them are in western Johnstone Strait, where they seem to congregate to feed on salmon in the summer. They usually show up there in July and stay until the last salmon run passes through, usually in September. Whale watchers from all around the world come here in the summer to set up tents on remote islands and travel the strait in small craft with cameras and

Frans Lanting, Minden Pictures

tape recorders equipped with underwater microphones to gather all the data they can. Vancouver departing ships usually pass this area around 6 in the morning after departing, and Vancouver arriving ships usually pass here in late afternoon or early evening the day before arriving.

While not posing a threat to humans, these whales can be extremely aggressive. Once when my wife and I were watching some seal pups at a remote island beach near the Alaska border, a large orca drove onto the beach on the shoulder of a big wave, snapped up the nearest seal pup with a single bite, and caught the next wave to wriggle back into the water.

Orcas usually travel in family groups called pods, and researchers have identified many members from distinctive patterns on their tails.

BELUGAS

Nicknamed sea canaries for their extensive vocalising, these small (to 20') whales are usually found along the shores of the Bering Sea and Arctic Oceans. However, they frequently stray as far south as Cook Inlet and Turnagain Arm during the summer, and can often be seen chasing schools of salmon.

These whales particularly like shallow rivers and strandings when the tide goes out are not uncommon.

Salmon fishermen who work the shallow rivers of Bristol Bay on the eastern

shore of the Bering Sea are often surprised by belugas rubbing gently against the hulls of their boats as the big gentle mammals explore the river bottoms.

In recent years belugas have discovered, to the dismay of commercial salmon fishermen, that if they lie waiting among the channels in the shallow estuary of the Kvichak River, they can feast on the young sockeye salmon fingerlings by the thousands as the fish leave the river and head out to the ocean

On the left, somewhere along the bleak Arctic coast a stranded beluga waits for the tide to come in and free him.

Belugas have learned to rest quietly when they are stranded and waiting for the tide, so as not to attract the attention of bears, man and other predators.

Flip Nicklin, Minden Pictures

Juneau

"The Glory Hole" was the nickname for the cavernous entrance to the gold mine across Gastineau Channel from Juneau. In those days, at the turn of the century, men were cheap and safety regulations were few. Sometimes a miner a week went to glory—in a cave-in or an accident in the pit and the miles of tunnels that led off it.

Just as it did for the territory, gold put Juneau on the map. But the fine gold in the creeks that Joe Juneau and Richard Harris found in 1880 played out, to be replaced by a very different enterprise: industrial-style hard-rock mining.

Juneau waterfront: built on the side of a mountain. There is an aerial tramway that operates from the cruise ship terminal. There are great views at the top and for the fit, there is a winding trail that eventually leads back downtown.

The gold at Juneau was embedded in rock, which had to be drilled, blasted, and transported to one of the noisiest contraptions of the industrial age: the stamp mill. This crude device crushed the ore-bearing rock into pieces small enough for chemical removal of the gold to be effective. The Treadwell mill at Juneau was the largest in the world, with 960 stamp machines crushing 5,000 tons of ore a day.

Today, the mines are gone and city, state, and federal governments now provide half the jobs in Juneau. Cosmopolitan, yet surrounded by wilderness, Juneau is a town where you can come out of an espresso shop and encounter a bear rummaging through a garbage can.

There are many things to do around town; these are some of the editor's choices:

- •GO SEE THE ICEFIELDS: In the mountains behind town is the dramatic Juneau Icefield and nearby Mendenhall Glacier. To see the glaciers by air is a remarkable experience, allowing the traveler to comprehend more easily the geology and the dynamics that produce the region's glaciers. If small airplanes are not

Mendenhall: The Glacier Next Door

Just a half hour drive from downtown Juneau is Mendenhall Glacier. Slowly retreating into the mountains, the glacier calves small icebergs into the lake which is also the headwaters of Mendenhall Creek, a popular rafting location. The charm of Mendenhall is that you can walk almost up to the edge of grounded icebergs, or kayak, canoe, or raft safely around them. Most Juneau bus tours include Mendenhall.

Floatplanes at Juneau. The glaciers and icefields behind town are spectacular, and flightseeing is available both on float planes and by helicopter. Some of the helicopter tours land on top of the glaciers.

for you, take the coach tour to Mendenhall Glacier, 14 miles from downtown; the visitors' center at the glacier has a comprehensive display on glaciology.

•RAFT THE MENDENHALL RIVER: Mendenhall River raft excursions begin on Mendenhall Lake, with great views of the glacier, and follow the Mendenhall River, with a snack of smoked salmon, reindeer sausage, cheese and a beverage along the way. The guides provide rain gear, life jackets and boots. Total trip time, including travel to and from downtown, is three and a half hours.

Usually there are a number of whales that stay year-round near Juneau, making for dependable whale watching.

•TAKE THE TRAM - Just completed in 1997, this cable car
runs from the docks to near the top of Mt. Roberts.
Visitors may hike, shop, have a meal, and watch a film
presentation on Tlingit culture. Terrific views!

•FLY-IN TO A SALMON BAKE: The Taku Glacier Lodge,
built in 1929 on the Taku River—17 miles northeast of
Juneau, offers a unique tour. Floatplanes pick up guests
downtown for a flight over the glaciers and up the Taku
River valley to the lodge for a baked salmon lunch.

•WALK AROUND THE TOWN: Like most Southeast
Alaska towns, Juneau is small enough to know quickly:
just grab a walking-tour map and hit the trail. The neo-
colonial place with a totem pole out front is the governor's
mansion. Don't pass a stop at the Alaska State Museum.
And make time for shopping for crafts and gifts around
Seward and South Franklin streets.

Hit the Galleries!
A selection of
museum-quality
art is available in
Juneau galleries.

Cape Addington:
"That's an evil place,
and we gave it plenty
of room in order to
stay clear of the tide
race, but even so, it
was a wild hour
before we were
around."

Outside Waters to Sitka

Vessels traveling to and from Sitka to San Francisco travel the outside of **Prince of Wales Island**, the third largest island in the United States. Close to the mill at Ketchikan, the island has been heavily logged.

Your vessel will be paralleling the outside coast of Alaska. This land is particularly wild and rugged, especially near the shore where winter storms have stripped the forest to bare rock. If you see light, it will be from anchored fishing vessels; there are several native settlements, but they are on the inside, protected channels.

The area between **Cape Addington, mile 700W**, and **Cape Bartolome, mile 685W** is a favorite spot for trollers seeking king salmon. Before the seasons were limited in the late 1970s, outside trolling opened on April 15, and many small vessels would beat their way up the coast from Puget Sound to be there for it.

It was, as they say, a tough berth. Trollers anchored for the night at Steamboat Bay on Noyes Island and then headed out through the tide rips at Cape Ulitka to the outside. Consider these excerpts from my 1974 log:

JOE'S JOURNAL

"**April 29. Steamboat Bay cannery**. Day came at 3 A.M. with violent squalls heeling us over at the float. Pulled on oil skin and ran a long bow line out to the float, then back in the sack for some good winks with the eerie whine of the wind loud around us.

"**April 30.** Headed out to Cape Ulitka, where the ocean pours around the point and meets the outgoing tide. That's a dirty spot; we almost turned around right there. The swells on the outside were 15 feet high, mean and ominous in the early morning light with a wind chop on top.

"If you only see Cape Addington once, it should be on such a day. The wind was coming on hard and running against the tide, and the cape, a long rocky arm, was almost lost in the mists as the heavy seas beat against its rocky sides. That's an evil place, and we gave it plenty of room in order to stay clear of the tide race, but even so, it was a wild hour before we were around. Once, on top of a big one, I took a long look around. To the south, the water was white and the sky was dark. A quarter-mile away, another troller labored through the rip, but beyond that we were alone. There was nothing but the sky and the troubled sea.

"**May 9. At anchor, Paloma Pass.** Today the seas drove white around the point and beat on the rocks off our stern, but in the lee we were secure, our world bounded by the dark shores and the racing clouds above. Neither on this island nor most of the islands around is there any sign of man. Saw one boat yesterday, none today; tried to get music on the radio but there was only the hiss of static."

Behind Suemez Island, northeast of mile 680W, is Waterfall Resort, better known to generations of salmon fishermen and travelers as Waterfall Cannery. It was the showpiece of the southeastern Alaska salmon industry in the 1940s and 1950s. Supporting a fleet of boats and several hundred cannery workers as well as a full-time gardener, it canned fish caught in fish traps, including a trap at Cape Addington.

Craig, Klawock, and Hydaburg native villages are on the remote west coast of Prince of Wales Island.

Cape Ommaney, mile 750W, is the southernmost tip of Baranof Island. In the heyday of **Port Alexander, mile 795**, the big Columbia River king salmon fed in the tide rips at the cape, creating a fishery that was the stuff of Alaska legends.

The outside coast here is deeply indented with almost three dozen different bays between the cape and Sitka. But except for **Goddard Hot Springs, mile 790W**, there are no settlements along this shore. If you see lights at night it is probably anchored fishing vessels.

If it's a clear night you may see Mt. Edgecumbe, an inactive volcano at **mile 815W**, on your way to Sitka.

Sitka

When Juneau was woods and snow and Ketchikan was a summer village of the Tlingit people, Sitka residents enjoyed theater, fine wines, and all the riches that the sea otter trade provided her Russian residents.

It was a trade based on the sometimes unwilling participation of the native people. In the Aleutian Islands, for example, the *promyshlenniki*, as the Russian fur traders were called, had no qualms about destroying whole villages if the Aleut residents didn't quickly obey them.

At Sitka, the proud Tlingit people cared little for the Russians, and in 1802 they destroyed the first Russian outpost, north of the present town site. Two years later the Russians returned with three ships and many Aleut mercenaries in kayak-like bidarka boats. Finally routing the Tlingits, the Russians reestablished Sitka on the site of the Tlingit village, Shee Atika.

For much of its Russian history, Sitka's leader was Aleksandr Baranov, who established schools for the Tlingits and made Sitka the trading capital of the northwest coast.

Fortunately for the Americans, the Russians' enlightenment didn't extend to conserving the valuable fur resource, for once the sea otter had been slaughtered almost to extinction, financial reverses made the Russians willing to sell Alaska to the United States for $7.2 million, about 2 cents an acre, which they did in 1867.

Today, having missed the booms and busts of the gold rush, Sitka, way out on the ocean side of Baranof

Island, is the cultural center of Southeastern Alaska. Yet Sitka offers more than museums and vistas; there are many things to do:

- GO FISHING: If you have any inclination to try for a salmon or halibut, Sitka is an excellent place to go out on one of the charter vessels. The city's unique position on the outside coast and the strong runs of king and silver salmon make the chances of getting a fish here very high. Such a trip is also an opportunity to see close-up the dramatic coast of Alaska and its sea life and wildlife.

Russian Orthodox Cathedral—the influence of the Russians is very strong in Sitka.

- JET BOATS: Advances in vessel design and propulsion have made an unusual experience available at Sitka: the high-speed jet boats. Propelled by water jets (essentially large pumps) rather than conventional propellers, these impressive craft allow passengers to travel quickly to places such as Salisbury Sound, 25 miles north of town. The abundant wildlife populations make it likely you'll see a whale, bear, or sea otter (today protected by federal law).

The Alaska Pioneer's Home, many of whose residents once fished these waters, dominates the Sitka waterfront.

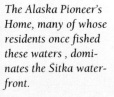

Halibut fishing vessel and anchored cruise ship. With no docks large enough for large cruise ships, passengers come ashore by tender.

•THE SHELDON JACKSON MUSEUM: In his travels through the state as education agent, Dr. Jackson acquired a remarkable collection of native art and historical artifacts. Even if you have seen other such displays, you will find this collection unusually complete and worth seeing. The Aleut and Eskimo exhibits are particularly fascinating, with material such as rain gear made of walrus intestines.

•ALASKA RAPTOR REHABILITATION CENTER: A place where injured hawks, falcons, owls, and eagles (mostly eagles) are cared for, this volunteer-run facility lets visitors view the dramatic birds close-up.

Sitka is known as the arts and cultural center of Southeast Alaska. This young woman plays her fiddle at the dock to welcome visitors.

•SITKA NATIONAL HISTORICAL PARK: If you didn't get to Totem Bight or Saxman at Ketchikan and want to get a good view of totem poles, this is a close-to-downtown opportunity to do so. Set among trees in a dramatic walk along the shore, the 15 totems are "recarves" of poles collected from Prince of Wales Island at the turn of the century. Cedar totems have a life of about 100 years outside exposed to the elements.

•THE RUSSIAN BISHOP'S HOUSE AND ST. MICHAEL'S CATHEDRAL: Both downtown, these are culturally rich elements of Sitka's Russian period. The Bishop's House is the original 1842 structure; the cathedral is a replica of the one destroyed by fire in 1966 (much of the artwork was saved).

MUSEUM RAVE: "Do the Sheldon Jackson Museum! I had absolutely no idea of the intricacy of the native cultures. The sleds, the skin boats, the kayaks—it just makes one very humble to realize how well they were able to get around before we created our gasoline-powered world. They made everything—one of the neatest things on display was an Eskimo woman's tool case made out of fish skin."

Sitka is also known for its excellent salmon fishing.

— A Sitka visitor

Christine Cox

Skagway, Winter 1897

For some, the challenge of the north—the cold, the difficult conditions, was simply too much:

"It was a real cold night. We walked along in the snow and we come to a fellow setting on the back of a Yukon sled. Yep, he was setting there in the middle of the road talking to hisself. His head was down on his hands. He looked plumb played out. He never seen us; he just went on talking to hisself. Over and over he'd say: "It's hell. Yes; multiply it by ten and then multiply that by ten, and that ain't half as bad as this is. Yes, it's hell..."

—Martha Ferguson McKeown, *The Trail Led North*

Christine Cox

John Muir and Dog, Brady Glacier, 1880

"...He looked up along the row of notched steps I had made, as if fixing them in his mind, then with a nervous spring he whizzed up and passed me out on the level ice and ran and cried and rolled about fairly hysterical in the sudden revulsion from the depth of despair to triumphant joy."

— John Muir, *Travels in Alaska*

See story on page 190.

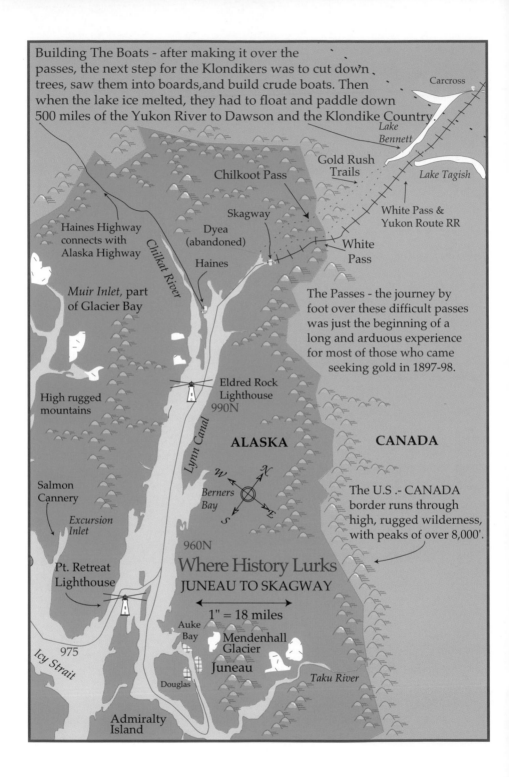

Building The Boats - after making it over the passes, the next step for the Klondikers was to cut down trees, saw them into boards, and build crude boats. Then when the lake ice melted, they had to float and paddle down 500 miles of the Yukon River to Dawson and the Klondike Country.

Carcross

Lake Bennett

Gold Rush Trails

Lake Tagish

Chilkoot Pass

White Pass & Yukon Route RR

Skagway

Dyea (abandoned)

White Pass

Haines Highway connects with Alaska Highway

Haines

Chilkat River

Muir Inlet, part of Glacier Bay

The Passes - the journey by foot over these difficult passes was just the beginning of a long and arduous experience for most of those who came seeking gold in 1897-98.

Eldred Rock Lighthouse 990N

High rugged mountains

Lynn Canal

ALASKA　　**CANADA**

Salmon Cannery

Berners Bay

The U.S.- CANADA border runs through high, rugged wilderness, with peaks of over 8,000'.

Excursion Inlet

Pt. Retreat Lighthouse

960N

Where History Lurks

JUNEAU TO SKAGWAY

1" = 18 miles

Icy Strait 975

Auke Bay

Mendenhall Glacier

Juneau

Taku River

Douglas

Admiralty Island

CHAPTER 5

Where History Lurks

Juneau, Mile 930, to Glacier Bay,
Mile 1000, via Skagway

"We came to a place where the water was covered with boards and stuff. But there wasn't a soul left living to call to us for help. Seemed like, just standing at the rail and looking at little boards that had once been a ship and straining our eyes to see folks that weren't there no more, and then looking at them high mountains around Lynn Canal and thinking we had to go over them and on beyond before we even got to the gold country, quieted us all down. Somehow we didn't feel the same way we'd been feeling on the trip up. That country up there didn't look cordial. It made you feel like cutting out the horseplay and saying a prayer for the fellows who wasn't there no more, and for the rest of us who didn't know what was ahead, neither."

—Martha Ferguson McKeown, *The Trail Led North*

The 1898-99 Klondike Gold Rush still casts a huge shadow over this part of Alaska.

For the human throng bound for Skagway and the Klondike in the Gold Rush years, the last 100 miles, from Juneau to Skagway, were somber ones. The mountains rise steeply from the water here and seem to funnel the wind. Moreover, there is something about this landscape that humbles a person. Salmon fishermen bound north in their 30- to 40-foot gill-netters have a word for the vista north: "Looking up at the Big Lynn." Working these waters was often a challenge for small fishing boats as the mountains walls tended to funnel the winds and the seas, especially in the fall.

The mountains on either side of Lynn Canal form a natural wind tunnel.

The steep sided fjords of this part of Alaska are very different from the Ketchikan and Juneau area. This is the dock in Skagway where the trains come right down to the cruise ships.

There is a major sea lion rookery on Benjamin Island, east of mile 967N.

Storm-bound mariners anchored in Auke Bay would row ashore and hike out to Point Lena, **mile 956**, for their weather report — row after smoking row of gray-bearded seas, as another weather system funneled up or down the narrow canyon between these mountain walls.

The bottom is littered here with the pieces of two of the finest steamers to travel north, both belonging to the Canadian Pacific Railroad. First was the *Princess Sophia*. At around 1 a.m. on October 24, 1918, the gold miners and the crews from the 10 Yukon River paddle-wheelers aboard the *Sophia* were probably still celebrating. They'd left Skagway a few hours earlier, the rivers freezing up, their season over, the bright lights ahead.

Upstairs in the pilothouse, the atmosphere was more subdued, the captain anxious. He'd seen Eldred Rock Light, **mile 994**, at midnight through the snow but navigation on such a night relied on something called "time and compass." The skipper would calculate from the engine revolutions how fast his vessel was traveling. Taking his course line from the chart and making allowances for the wind and the tidal currents, he would steer until his time ran out, that is, when he should be at the next point of reference.

On that bitter night in 1918, with blowing snow and limited visibility, the next checkpoint after Eldred Rock was Sentinel Island Light, 28 miles away. Over such a distance, a steering error of one degree would put the vessel a half-mile off course.

Sometime around 2 a.m., as her skipper was groping

through the snow and trying to see the Sentinel Island Light, the *Sophia* drove her whole length ashore on Vanderbilt Reef. Fortunately the rocks cradled her, and there was no need to try and launch lifeboats on such a rotten night.

By first light a rescue fleet was standing by: the *Cedar, King and Winge, Estebeth, Elsinore*, and others. But as the *Sophia* seemed to be resting securely on the rock, it was decided to wait until better weather to evacuate the passengers and crew.

It proved to be a tragic mistake. In the late afternoon, the northerly began to blow with renewed fury, and the rescue fleet was forced to seek shelter in a nearby harbor. Darkness came with driving snow and bitter wind, and the vessels had to set anchor watches to make sure they weren't dragging.

Roaring down the canal, the wind caught the *Sophia*'s high exposed stern, driving her off the reef, ripping open her bottom, and sending her into the deep water beyond. There was time for one desperate radio call: "For God's sake come! We are sinking." In the morning only her masts were above water, her 343 passengers and crew drowned in the northwest coast's worst maritime disaster.

Glacier Bay lies beyond the high mountains on the west side of the canal.

Princess May, *on Sentinel Island, mile 966N, in 1910. She was lucky— there were no injuries, and she was refloated with little damage.*

MOHAI

Eldred Rock Light, mile 990N. Painting by Ann Upton, author's collection.

Thirty-four years later, miscalculation of a course change drove the graceful *Princess Kathleen* ashore at Lena Point, **mile 956**. Her passengers were more fortunate. They climbed down ladders to the rocky beach and watched the favorite of all the Alaska-run steamers slide off the rocks and disappear into deep water.

At mile 990N, your ship passes to the east of **Eldred Rock,** an unusual octagonal lighthouse, reminiscent of Russian architecture. Here, on a morning in 1908 the light keepers were astonished to find part of the hull of the *Clara Nevada* that had been lost with 100 souls on a winter night a decade earlier. The seaweed-draped hull, still containing the bones of many victims, had been lifted from the canal floor and deposited on the rock by the storm the night before.

Look for glaciers in the valleys on both sides here. Since Vancouver's time, these small rivers of ice have receded substantially.

JOE'S JOURNAL

"**September 24, 1972, Twin Coves, Lynn Canal.** Beach picnic tonight, with four other gill-netter families in here, our boats laying in the cove before us, the glaciers seeming to hang, glowing over us in the high latitude dusk. In the stillness after supper as we sat around the fire, there was a noise like thunder, and we looked up and saw house-size pieces of ice tumbling from Rainbow Glacier into the trees below."

Look carefully at the vegetation along the shores here. The spruce, cedar and hemlock are joined by deciduous trees as the effect of latitude and the cold mainland land mass that surrounds the canal makes itself felt. Like in Juneau, the climate here is much more severe, much less moderated by the sea, than in Ketchikan or Sitka.

Northwest of **Seduction Point at mile 1,002N,** (Vancouver named it after the natives had tried to lead his Lieutenant Joseph Whidbey into a trap,) is Chilkat Inlet, the last hurrah each season for salmon gill-netters. Into this narrow and steep-sided bay hundreds of thousands of chum salmon return each fall. As many as 450 vessels, each deploying a 900-foot-long net, will crowd into its barely six-square-mile area in a chaotic and competitive high-stakes frenzy. Along with the crowds, the fishermen have to fight the weather, for snow comes early to these northern fjords.

Each year salmon gill-netters flock to Chilkat Inlet to catch valuable chum and red salmon.

"It came on hard, snow and wind, while we were still fishing. They hadn't yet pulled the floats for the winter in Cannery Cove, and the storm broke them all up. The smart guys quit fishing right with the first of the snow and headed for Haines, but we stayed until the fishing period was over. By that time it must have been blowing seventy out in the canal, and the fish buyers were huddled with us in two little coves. We were the last boat at the *Emily Jane*, our fish buyer, and the cannery was calling on the radio telling him to head on down to Petersburg, storm or not. They weren't none too eager to go, and when they picked up the anchor and disappeared into the snow and the black, I wasn't sure I'd ever see him again."
—A Lynn Canal salmon fisherman

Until recently a cannery near Haines processed salmon caught here.

Salmon that make it past the fishing fleet spawn each fall in the lower reaches of the Chilkat River, where thousands of bald eagles await their arrival. Look for eagles along the west side of the canal, especially in the fall. Possibly the largest concentration anywhere occurs around the shallow mouth of the Chilkat River, as the eagles feed on the dead salmon.

Haines and Port Chilkoot

The spot that looks like a New England village at mile 1012N is Fort William H. Seward, sometimes known as Port Chilkoot. Decommissioned after World War II, it was purchased sight unseen by five veterans and their families to pursue their dream of a planned community. Now part of the city of Haines, just to the north, the fort offers a variety of cultural activities.

Haines, until a highway was recently completed out of Skagway, was the only place in southeastern Alaska with a road that went anywhere (it connected to the Alaska Highway). Today it is rich with Tlingit culture and is especially known for the dramatic fall migration of bald eagles that feed on Chilkat River salmon.

Totem poles under construction at Port Chilkoot

The Last Easy Miles

The Grand Adventure begins—the Excelsior *departs San Francisco, loaded with gold seekers, 1897.*

For the tens of thousands who came north during the Gold Rush years, upper Lynn Canal represented the last easy miles of their journey to the diggings.

As you enter Taiya Inlet at **mile 1,014N** from Seattle, imagine yourself at the crowded rail of a ship like the *Queen* or the *Victoria* in the fall of '97, jostling for your place with hundreds of other Klondikers, looking out through a snow squall, trying to get a glimpse of what lay ahead. There is but an hour or two before you must put on your pack, get the boxes and sacks of your "outfit" (a year's worth of supplies) ready to unload, and step out into the wind and the cold and whatever fate had in store for you.

Selling supplies brought a major boom to Seattle merchants.

Much of the United States was gripped in a depression at that time. Perhaps you were a farmer from the Dakotas; you had left your family to try for fortune in the North. You had bought your outfit in Seattle and steamer passage to Skagway, with little more knowledge than that somewhere beyond those mountains men like yourself were staking out gold claims and getting rich.

The snow clears, and a cold and cheerless sun shines on as bleak and unfriendly a landscape as you've seen on this trip. The mountains rise vertically

Thwaites, 1286.   Mushers, Alaska.

Ready for the North. Klondikers aboard ship, 1897. out of the water; there doesn't even seem to be a beach. The chatter of the crowd fades as all look at the mountains and what lies ahead.

If you were very lucky, your steamer tied to a wharf, but for those in the first wave in 1897, there were no wharves. Most gold seekers unloaded their outfits from steamers onto lighters, shallow-draft barges. If the tide was up, the lighters took you right in to shore. If it wasn't, the lighter got as far as the flats and you had to cross 200 or 300 yards of sand and mud to get to shore.

Many had brought animals and staked them out with their piles of boxes and gear while they made the first trips across the flats to shore.

Some weren't familiar with the big tides in the northern fjords of Alaska. They rested, perhaps, after lugging their first load up the beach, and visited with others about what they might expect in the rough-hewn town, visible through the snow, and hiked back to find their outfit underwater, their animals drowned. Few were really prepared for the rigors of that journey, or the true nature of the gold country.

The steamers didn't wait; their owners wanted them back in Vancouver or Seattle as soon as possible, "To get another load of suckers," as one bitter Klondiker put it.

The Gold Rush

Rough as Skagway was in 1897, it was only the beginning. Ahead lay the grueling trek over the passes to the frozen headwaters of the Yukon River.

For most of the hundred thousand or so who came north in 1897 and 1898, their Gold Rush experience had three phases. The first was often the hardest: the passes. The mountain wall that lay between the salt water of upper Lynn Canal and the edge of the Yukon had but two routes over it: Chilkoot Pass and White Pass.

The most powerful image from '97 and '98 is the long line of climbers, each bent with his load, on the steps cut into the ice on Chilkoot Pass. At the top lay the Canadian border and the North West Mounted Police. No one could pass without a year's supplies, about 1,000 lbs.

Wealthy men hired porters, but most just carried it all up themselves, load by backbreaking load, caching it at the top and hoping no one would rob them before they got back. A solid stream of upward-bound men filled the steps. If you wanted to rest, you stepped off to the side, but when you wanted to get back in, you had

LOOKING DOWN THE RAPIDS, BETWEEN LAKES LINDEMAN AND BENNETT   COPYRIGHT 1899

UW Hegg 227

The first of the rapids: Once over the passes, the Klondikers cut trees, built boats, and faced 500 miles of rivers and rapids.

to wait for a gap in the line; it was that crowded. By 1898 cable tramways could carry your gear over the pass for a fee, but the men in the first wave had only their feet.

Down the other side from the summit was Lake Bennett, and after that it was the boats and the rivers. They were 50 miles from salt water, but there were another 500 to the gold country. Arriving in winter, the men camped on the shore, cut down trees, whipsawed them into planks and built boats, and waited for the ice to melt to launch their boats and begin the journey:

> "Some leaked, some didn't steer. They had lots of things wrong with them. But a lot of the boats, made of whipsawed lumber, had beautiful lines and sailed as pretty as anything I ever did see on the Columbia. Yes, sir, that was an expedition, that fleet of boats getting ready to set out from Lake Bennett, come spring of '98."
> —Martha Ferguson McKeown, *The Trail Led North*

The trip became a journey of true epic proportions. Down the canyons and through the rapids they came, some capsizing or breaking up, the survivors trying to hitch a ride with the next boat that had room. The wealthier switched to Yukon steamers as soon as the river got wide enough, but all were heading for Dawson Creek and the last phase of their epic sagas: the diggings.

The best claims were staked before most of the gold seekers arrived. Many who started north gave up before they got to the Yukon. Only half who made it staked a claim. Just a very few struck it rich. Most found some kind of work in Dawson City or in the diggings, made a little money, and moved on.

Yet their adventure transcends time. All experienced the powerful drama of **The North**. Those who returned to the lower 48, even penniless, brought back stories and memories to entertain generations of breathless children and grandchildren.

Arctic Brotherhood Hall, Skagway

The Lucky Few

With no convenient banks, many miners simply brought their gold south with them. One woman, hearing that her husband might be coming home on the steamer, brought their children to meet it, hoping he'd have enough money to buy them groceries (he'd been gone six months and they were out of money). He staggered down the gangplank under the weight of his duffel and its 116 *pounds* of gold.

Alaska gold at Scandinavian American Bank, Seattle, 1897.

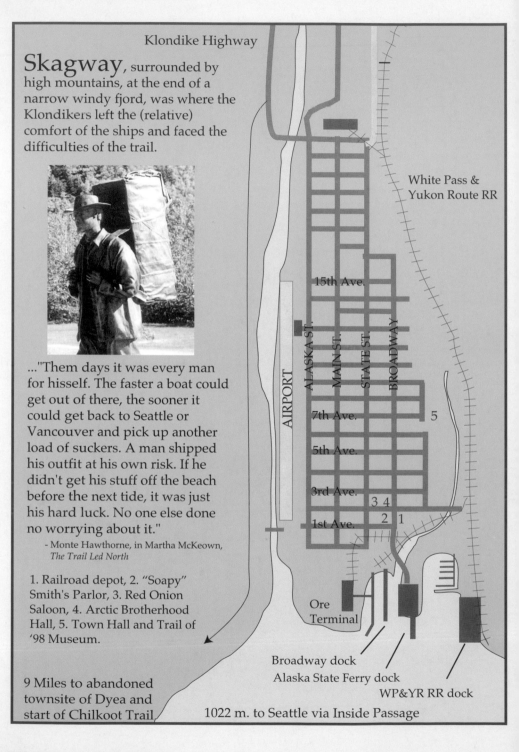

Klondike Highway

Skagway, surrounded by
high mountains, at the end of a
narrow windy fjord, was where the
Klondikers left the (relative)
comfort of the ships and faced the
difficulties of the trail.

White Pass &
Yukon Route RR

15th Ave.

AIRPORT   ALASKA ST.   MAIN ST.   STATE ST.   BROADWAY

...."Them days it was every man
for hisself. The faster a boat could
get out of there, the sooner it
could get back to Seattle or
Vancouver and pick up another
load of suckers. A man shipped
his outfit at his own risk. If he
didn't get his stuff off the beach
before the next tide, it was just
his hard luck. No one else done
no worrying about it."

- Monte Hawthorne, in Martha McKeown,
The Trail Led North

7th Ave.   5

5th Ave.

3rd Ave.   3 4

1st Ave.   2 1

1. Railroad depot, 2. "Soapy"
Smith's Parlor, 3. Red Onion
Saloon, 4. Arctic Brotherhood
Hall, 5. Town Hall and Trail of
'98 Museum.

Ore
Terminal

9 Miles to abandoned
townsite of Dyea and
start of Chilkoot Trail.

Broadway dock
Alaska State Ferry dock
WP&YR RR dock

1022 m. to Seattle via Inside Passage

Skagway

It is the drama of '97 and '98 that fills this town. Skagway blossomed for but a few years, lawless and rough, then almost disappeared.

The gaunt-faced men have passed through to whatever fate The North had in store for them. But the town the boom built at the jumping-off place for the Klondike remains, looking much as it did in 1897 and 1898, when some 80 saloons and many professional women were anxious to serve the lonely men on the trail north.

Today, Skagway offers a unique experience to visitors. Even the vegetation is different from the rest of Southeast

The White Pass & Yukon Route RR train pulls right onto the dock. The train ride, along the route followed by many headed to the Yukon during the Gold Rush, is one of the most popular excursions in Alaska.

This steam-powered rotary snowplow, recently restored to operating condition, kept the passes open. The black cab houses the locomotive engine that was used just to turn the plow! Another steam engine, coupled behind, did the pushing!

Alaska, as the town is under the influence of the harsher temperature extremes of the interior instead of the milder, cloudier maritime climate elsewhere in the region. Some of the native craftwork available here, especially of ivory, is truly excellent

Sam's Tour: "Ever since my dad showed me some old photos of the Gold Rush, I've always wanted to see Chilkoot Pass—not by chopper or plane, but to see it, even maybe hike the whole route. It's a tough hike for my old bones, and I didn't have the time for it this trip—the guidebooks say allow for 3 to 5 days of strenuous going—but I just wanted to get a taste of it. So I rented a bike, checked in with the Park Service for trail conditions, and had a great six mile ride to the trailhead. Then I parked my bike and just started, with a lunch pack, and an extra sweater. What a gorgeous trail—winding along the riverbank, but all I could think about was those who went before—you know, left their families behind, to make it in The North! I only went a couple hours in, ate and hiked out, but I made a vow: someday, I'll get in shape and do the whole thing! And that beer back at Moe's Frontier Bar, back in town, went down pretty smooth, too!"

Skagway entrepreneur Dennis Corrington used to be an ivory trader along the Yukon River. His museum houses some of his excellent collection, along with some unusual items for sale. Don't miss it!

Elsie's Tour: "What a train ride, what views—It was super! I had thought that once the gold rush guys got over the pass, they were there! No way—turns out they still had another

500 miles to go—not only that, but most of them went over in winter and had to chop down trees, and handsaw planks to build boats to go down the rivers, after the ice melted. Those guys were tough!

Downtown Skagway in 1900 didn't look that different from how it looks today.

I loved Skagway—I like the way they've got all those old buildings fixed up. I found this beautiful carved ivory cribbage board, with whaling ships and scenes all over it, almost like stuff you see in museums!"

Note: Only ivory harvested by Native carvers in accordance with federal regulations may be sold legally. Make sure to get a export/transit permit if you buy ivory and plan to transit Canada on your way home. You'll need it to bring the ivory into the United States.

Skagway entrepreneurs wasted no time when the Klondikers came to town—this curio store opened in 1897.

Look for northern lights if it's dark after your ship leaves Skagway.

Your ship usually will leave Skagway around eight P.M., and retrace her route down Lynn Canal to Point Retreat, where she will swing southwest toward Icy Strait and Glacier Bay, or southeast towards Juneau.

Point Retreat, mile 960, was named by Vancouver's Lieutenant Whidbey after being repulsed by armed natives each time his party tried to land for the night: "Where they drew up in battle array, with their spears couched, ready to receive our people on landing."

The flashing white light, off to port, nine miles south of Point Retreat is Naked Island, beyond which is **Funter Bay**, site of an abandoned cannery and small settlement, accessible only by boat or floatplane.

Your ship makes a big swing to the west here, around Point Couverden and into Icy Strait

It was near here that my first Alaska skipper would usually turn the steering wheel of the old salmon tender *Sidney* over to me on our night runs from Icy Strait down to the cannery at Metlakatla, on Annette Island, near Ketchikan.

Packers or tenders serve as mother ships, buying fish and providing fuel and other supplies to fishing boats operating a long way from their home canneries.

It was always a totally magic time. The mate had bad eyes, the cook didn't steer, the insurance man's kid couldn't be trusted, and the skipper liked his sleep. And so, after a long day of buying fish and attending to the mechanical problems of the Tsimshian seiners that fished for us, I'd get a late dinner, then bring my coffee forward into the wheelhouse, and let my eyes get accustomed to the dark. Skipper would do his routine of showing me exactly where we were on the chart, what to look out for, when to wake him, ask me if I was ready, and then retire.

The dark canyon of Chatham Strait opened ahead of me on the radar, and I'd fiddle with the old AM radio until I found a Seattle rock station, fading in and out.

Sometimes there'd be the lights of another vessel, occasionally the wink of a navigational aid. But the land was always dark, and I was stunned by it: all that waterfront, and never a town, hardly even a house.

Icy Strait—when Vancouver's men explored here in July of 1794, they could barely get through Icy Strait because of the enormous amount of ice in the water: "The space between the shores on the northern and southern sides, seemed to be entirely occupied by one

compact sheet of ice as far as the eye could distinguish."

Look for salmon seiners and trollers working these waters, as well as humpback whales. For many years Icy Strait has been the site of a strong run of silver (coho) salmon. Trollers usually fish them with small, pastel-colored trolling spoons. A good day might be 200 fish, worth a thousand bucks or so to the fisherman.

The big inlet to the south at **mile 988** is **Port Frederick**. Around the point at the eastern entrance is a disused cannery and the Tlingit village of **Hoonah**. On the Fourth of July, salmon seiners put in here for a boisterous celebration.

House and airplane float at Hoonah, south of mile 988

Fishing used to be the community's bread and butter, but today logging on tribal lands is the primary revenue source. Much of the timber goes to Japan.

Accessible by floatplane or the smaller ships of the Alaska ferry system, lodging is available in Hoonah for the traveler who is seeking a quieter time than is possible in the larger towns.

The center of town is the L. Kane Store, founded in 1893, just 14 years after John Muir came to Glacier Bay. There is a new cultural center here, with a rich display of Tlingit art.

Look for whale-watching boats and humpback whales to the south near Point Adolphus.

You are 1,000 miles from Seattle. To the north at **mile 1,003** is **Gustavus**, a pleasant, un-southeastern spot: the land is flat and almost perfect for gardening. Farmers in the early part of the century grew vegetables here for the canneries at Excursion Inlet, Hawk Inlet, and other places. The Gustavus Inn offers lodging and family-style dining. Juneau residents take charter flights over for dinner. A road connects Gustavus with the Park Service headquarters for Glacier Bay at Bartlett Cove.

Pt. Adolphus is a regular summer hangout for humpback whales.

Traveler's Guide to Marine Mammals...................

BELUGA WHALE. Size: to 18 feet. Range: Arctic waters to Bristol Bay, Cook Inlet and Turnagain Arm, Alaska. Distinguishing features: Adults are pure white; juveniles are gray. Likes coastal waters, especially rivers. Especially likes codfish, but also crabs and mussels. Frequently seen in groups. History: Nicknamed "sea canary" because of extensive vocalizing.

BOWHEAD WHALE. Size: 45 to 60 feet, weight to 100 tons or more. Range: Arctic waters. Distinguishing features: Very large head, black with white chin. Plankton eater, skims schools with top of head just above surface. History: A staple of Eskimo diet. Once hunted extensively for its baleen, used in corsets.

HUMPBACK WHALE. Size: 30 to 50 feet, weight to 40 tons. Range: Throughout Alaska and British Columbia in summer. Winters in warm waters. Distinguishing features: Black with white throat and belly, long tail flipper with irregular edges. Knobs and bumps on head and flippers. Likes to breach, or jump dramatically. History: Much studied, commonly seen, sings hauntingly.

GRAY WHALE. Size: 30 to 50 feet. Range: coastal Arctic to Mexico. Distinguishing features: Black with white spots and blotches. Only large whale with overhanging upper jaw. Sometimes pokes head vertically out of water; also breaches. History: Calves its young in one of several lagoons in Baja California after annual migration. Whale watchers count them on their journey.

ORCA, OR KILLER WHALE. Size: to 30 feet. Range: global, especially coastal. Distinguishing features: Bold black and white markings, dramatic tall dorsal fin, especially on male. History: Before 1970s thought to be dangerous to man. Captured whales showed remarkable intelligence and docility. Many in aquariums. Travel and live in pods, or groups.

STELLER'S, OR NORTHERN SEA LION. Size: to 13 feet and 2,400 pounds. Range: California to Alaska; often found in large numbers at remote rookeries. Distinguishing features: Large size, visible ears, bad breath, and occasional loud roaring. History: Now protected by law, these large mammals are commonly seen along the Alaska coast. Eats fish, particularly salmon, to the annoyance of man.

HARBOR SEAL. Size: 4 to 6 feet. Range: Throughout most of the northwest coast. Distinguishing features: Grayish with spots; the most common seal in Alaska. Has no visible ears; clumsy on land. History: Fish and shellfish eaters, they frequently steal salmon from fishermen's nets and lines. Protected by law.

DALL PORPOISE: Size: 4 to 7 feet. Range: Throughout most northwest waters. Distinguishing features: Black body·with dramatic white markings, small triangular dorsal fin. Sometimes mistaken for killer whales, but are much smaller with lower dorsal fin. Usually travels in groups. History: Likes to ride the bow waves of fishing and other craft.

Traveler's Guide to Birds ....

BALD EAGLE. Size: wingspan to 6 feet and larger. Range: Oregon to Bering Sea. Distinguishing features: Large soaring bird, adult marked with white head and tail, juveniles dark brown or mottled. Notes: Uncommon in Puget Sound, these very noticeable large birds are common throughout coastal British Columbia and Alaska. While scavenging dead fish, they will also attack live fish and small animals.

BONAPARTE'S GULL. Size: to 14 inches. Range: Peru to Bering Sea. Distinguishing marks: smaller than most gulls, easily recognized by black head and bill and white wing tips. Notes: Nests and breeds in interior, migrates south in late summer, returns in spring.

ARCTIC TERN. Size: to 10 inches. Range: Circumpolar. Winters in Antarctic, summers in coastal Alaska and British Columbia. Distinguishing features: Terns are noted for their smaller size, slender shape, and distinctive long forked tail. Arctic terns have a prominent black cap on their heads. Notes: These remarkable birds migrate some 8,000 to 10,000 miles each spring and fall.

COMMON LOON. Size: to 20 inches. Range: California to Bering Sea. Distinguishing features: Large diving bird with sharp bill and noticeable white and black checkerboard pattern on dark back. Notes: Dives when approached. Feeds on fish. Requires long flapping takeoff run on windless days. Haunting, *whoooo* call.

RAVEN. Size: to 24 inches. Range: Central America to Bering Sea. Distinguishing features: Crow-like, but substantially larger. Jet black, almost glossy purple color; call is a distinctive *klok* sound. Notes: The raven is a central figure in Haida and Tlingit mythology; raven figures appear on totem poles and dance masks.

MARBLED MURRELET. Size: 10 inches Range: California to Alaska. Distinguishing marks: Very short neck, marbled white markings on brown. Winter plumage is dark above, white below. Notes: This species, seen commonly in all seasons in Southeast Alaska, may be the next Spotted Owl. Nesting in old-growth timber, its numbers are declining.

STELLER'S JAY. Size: to 12 inches. Range: Washington to Bering Sea. Distinguishing features: Bright blue and black coloring with distinctive black crest. Very visible and busy; likes to taunt larger birds, such as eagles. Notes: Named for German naturalist Georg Steller, who was with explorer Vitus Bering, whose 1741 expedition discovered Alaska.

SPOTTED SANDPIPER. Size: to 8 inches. Range: California to Arctic. Distinguishing marks: Easy to identify in summer plumage with large spots underneath. Fall and winter plumage is brown above and white below with no spots. Notes: This little bird is seen over most of the Alaskan coast. When surprised, flies away from the shore with short, jerky wingbeats, and returns nearby.

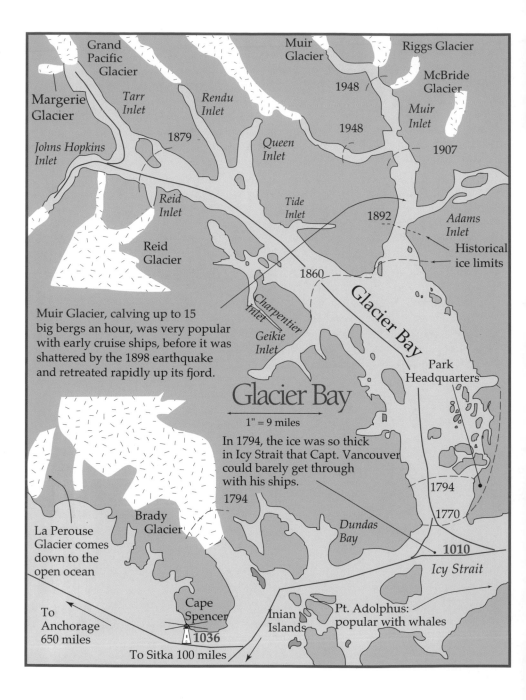

Grand
Pacific
Glacier

Muir
Glacier

Riggs Glacier

McBride
Glacier

Margerie
Glacier

*Tarr
Inlet*

*Rendu
Inlet*

1948

*Muir
Inlet*

*Johns Hopkins
Inlet*

1879

*Queen
Inlet*

1948

1907

*Reid
Inlet*

*Tide
Inlet*

1892

*Adams
Inlet*

Reid
Glacier

1860

Historical
ice limits

Muir Glacier, calving up to 15
big bergs an hour, was very popular
with early cruise ships, before it was
shattered by the 1898 earthquake
and retreated rapidly up its fjord.

*Charpentier
Inlet*

*Geikie
Inlet*

Glacier Bay

Park
Headquarters

Glacier Bay

1" = 9 miles

In 1794, the ice was so thick
in Icy Strait that Capt. Vancouver
could barely get through
with his ships.

1794

1794

Brady
Glacier

1794

*Dundas
Bay*

1770

La Perouse
Glacier comes
down to the
open ocean

1010

Icy Strait

To
Anchorage
650 miles

Cape
Spencer

Inian
Islands

Pt. Adolphus:
popular with whales

1036

To Sitka 100 miles

CHAPTER 6

Into The Ice

Glacier Bay and Icy Strait,
Mile 1000, to Cape Spencer, mile 1035

"Then setting sail, we were driven wildly up the fiord, as if the storm wind were saying, 'Go then, if you will, into my icy chamber; but you shall stay in until I am ready to let you out.' All this time sleety rain was falling on the bay and snow on the mountains; but soon after we landed the sky began to open. The camp was made on a rocky bench beneath the front of the Pacific Glacier, and the canoe was carried beyond the reach of the bergs and berg waves. The bergs were now crowded in a dense pack against the discharging front, as if the storm wind had determined to make the glacier take back her crystal offspring and keep them at home."

—John Muir, *Travels in Alaska*

Around **mile 1010** your ship will swing north and enter Glacier Bay. The great rivers of ice are still almost 50 miles away, but when Vancouver and his men passed this way in July of 1794, Glacier Bay didn't exist! Instead they found only a wide indentation in the shore, filled with a solid wall of ice, and so much floating ice in seven mile-wide Icy Strait that they could barely pick their way through! They named Icy Strait, continued their explorations to the south, and Glacier Bay disappeared into the mists of time for almost 75 years.

The next visitor was a C.S. Wood, traveling by canoe in 1877, just ten years after the United States had purchased Alaska from Russia. What he found was astonishing. Instead of the ice front pushing all the way out into Icy Strait, it had receded almost forty miles, or almost a half mile a year, an event almost unprecedent-

Your ship will stop in southern Glacier Bay to pick up a Park Service naturalist.

ed in geologic history. What caused such a great recession of the vast ice sheets during this period—some earlier version of global warming? No one really yet knows. But events in the late 1890s suggest substantial seismic activity in the Glacier Bay area. As these events were to prove, earthquakes seem to have the ability to shatter the ice in glaciers. Where such glaciers face the water, they will calve off immense amounts of ice after an earthquake, causing them to recede rapidly.

John Muir and Glacier Bay

In the middle of October, 1879, John Muir and his missionary companion, a Mr. Samuel Hall Young, set out from Fort Wrangell by canoe. With a crew of native paddlers, they were bound for the ice mountains of the north that prospectors had told Muir about. As they traveled, the youngest native, Sitka Charley, told Muir he'd hunted seals as a boy in a bay full of ice and thought he could show Muir the way.

Muir was skeptical. Sitka Charley said the bay was without trees, that they'd need to bring their own firewood. The other paddlers, in all their lives throughout the region, had never seen a place without firewood.

They came to a bay cloaked in fog and storm. Sitka Charley became uneasy; the bay was much changed, he said, since he had seen it before. Even Vancouver's chart, a copy of which Muir so much relied upon, failed them, showing only a wide indentation in the shore.

Fortunately, they found a group of natives hunting seals and staying in a dark and crowded hut. One of the men agreed to guide them, and northward they paddled, off the chart and into that astonishing bay that had been birthed from the ice almost within their lifetimes.

The weather got worse, and Muir's paddlers wanted to turn around:

> "They seemed to be losing heart with every howl of the wind, and, fearing that they might fail me now that I was in the midst of so grand a congregation of glaciers, I made haste to reassure them that for ten years I had wandered alone among mountains and storms, and good luck always

John Muir—few people have ever come to the area as prepared to explore and celebrate its beauty as this Scottish-born conservationist. California Historical Society FN26339

followed me, that with me, therefore, they need fear nothing. The storm would soon cease and the sun would shine to show us the way we should go, for God cares for us and guides us as long as we are trustful and brave, therefore all childish fear must be put away."

—John Muir, *Travels in Alaska*

Dark lines are often caused when a glacier scrapes rock and dirt off the mountains on the way down to the salt water.

Look around and imagine yourself in a small canoe with native paddlers, as John Muir was in 1879.

And so on they went, camping in rain, on snowy beaches, pushing farther and farther, only glimpsing the vastness and grandeur of the land.

Finally Muir climbed the flanks of one of the mountains just as the clouds passed, and he gazed, stunned, at the grandeur and the size of the many-armed bay that was revealed below him.

When the party headed back, the lateness of the season was evident. Each morning before they reached Icy Strait, the ice was frozen a little thicker, and the men had to cut a lane for their canoe with an axe and tent poles.

Muir's description of the moment of their departure is a shining icon of Alaskan literature:

"The green waters of the fiord were filled with sun spangles; the fleet of icebergs set forth on their voyages with the upspringing breeze; and on the innumerable mirrors and prisms of these bergs, and on those of the shattered crystal walls of the glaciers, common white light and rainbow light began to burn, while the mountains shone

Your ship must proceed very carefully when the ice is very thick. In thick ice like this, look for seals resting on the ice floes.

in their frosty jewelry, and loomed again in the thin azure in serene terrestrial majesty. We turned and sailed away, joining the outgoing bergs, while 'Gloria in excelsis' still seemed to be sounding over all the white landscape, and our burning hearts were ready for any fate, feeling that, whatever the future might have in store, the treasures we had gained this glorious morning would enrich our lives forever."

—John Muir, *Travels in Alaska*

After Muir's discovery and powerful writings about what he'd seen, the bay soon became one of the premier sights of the Western Hemisphere, and a regular stop for steamers such as the *Ancon*, the *Idaho*, and the *Queen*.

For many of the early steamer excursions, part of the trip was taking the ship's boats to shore and if conditions permitted, taking groups to the top of the glacier itself to climb around amongst the crevasses!

The destination for most was Muir Glacier, the face of which was an ice cliff towering above the decks of the approaching steamers, and calving up to 12 icebergs an hour.

Icebergs don't always fall; sometimes they come from the underwater foot of the glacier, surfacing suddenly and unexpectedly. Watch out for them!

"The Muir presented a perpendicular ice front at least 200 feet in height, from which huge bergs were detached at frequent intervals. The sight and sound of one of these huge masses of ice falling from the cliff, or suddenly appearing from the submarine ice-foot, was something which once witnessed was not to be forgotten. It was grand and impressive beyond description."

—Fremont Morse, *National Geographic*, January, 1908

THE 1899 EARTHQUAKE—At midday on September 10, 1899, as he was waiting for lunch at his salmon saltery in Bartlett Cove, now site of Glacier Bay National Park headquarters, August Buschmann was surprised to see his trunk come sliding across the floor at him. Moments later, the cook's helper came running into the building, frightened. He had been up on the hill at the native cemetery as the ground started to heave around him, and he thought the dead were coming to life.

The earthquake shattered the front of Muir Glacier and others, and within 48 hours Glacier Bay was a mass of floating ice so thick that ships could not reach the saltery at Bartlett Cove for two weeks. Icy Strait filled with ice, making Dundas Bay, 10 miles to the west, inaccessible.

It wasn't until the following July that the steamer *Queen* ventured close enough to Muir Inlet to see what had happened. The bay was still full of ice; only by picking their way along the shore west of Willoughby Island could they make any progress. The closest they could get to Muir Glacier was 10 miles; the rest was solid ice.

Hidden behind a fleet of icebergs, Muir Glacier commenced a rapid retreat up the inlet; today the face is 25 miles north of where Muir found it in 1879.

Steamer Queen *at Muir Glacier, about 1890. This graceful liner was one of the first to regularly bring visitors to Glacier Bay. Passengers could go ashore by small boat and climb ladders up to the top of the glacier. Imagine the Park Service allowing that today!* Photo courtesy of Dave Bohn

In good conditions your ship can get quite close to the face of the ice.

Getting close to Johns Hopkins Glacier.

ROUTES IN GLACIER BAY—the bay is all part of Glacier Bay National Park and Preserve, administered by the U.S. Park Service. In order to allow each visitor to have the richest experience of the park's unusual beauty, cruise ship visits are limited in number. Furthermore, the schedule and routes of the ships that are allowed into the Park are managed to try to allow each major ship to have one of the major glaciers/inlets to itself for a substantial viewing period. Johns Hopkins Inlet and Tarr Inlet are generally considered to offer the best opportunity for cruise ship visitors.

Look for several lone spruce trees near the base of the spit in Reid Inlet. These were planted by gold miners Joe and Muz Ibach, around 1941, in soil they had carried from their homestead on Lemesurier Island, 48 miles away.

Usually large cruise ships travel up the west side of Glacier Bay, often slowing or stopping to allow passengerrs a good view of Reid Inlet, a few miles south of the entrance to Johns Hopkins Inlet. This is the place where Joe and Muz Ibach built a cabin on the spit that blocks much of the mouth of the inlet. Each summer in the 1940s, they would travel from their little homestead on Lemesurier Island, just west of the entrance to Glacier Bay, to this cabin to work a small gold claim. Dave Bohn, in his excellent book, *Glacier Bay: The Land and The Silence*, suggested that rather than the modest returns on their gold claim, that it was the haunting beauty of their cabin site that brought the Ibachs back summer after summer to work in the shadow of the great ice. The active front of the glacier was so close to their cabin site that they could hear the great rumble of calving glaciers as they lay in their bed at night!

Johns Hopkins Glacier has been very active in recent

years, and the outgoing stream of ice is often so thick that ships often do not enter, for fear their propellors would contact ice pieces large enough to damage them. Additionally, seals use the ice flows in this inlet to birth their pups, and during the period when they are actively birthing pups, ship traffic is prohibited here.

Lampugh Glacier pokes its icy snout into the salt water just south of the entrance to Johns Hopkins Inlet.

However, while seal activity is the thickest in the inlet itself, you are apt to see seals, and perhaps even with their pups on ice flows anywhere in Glacier Bay, so be sure to have your binoculars ready whenever you leave your cabin in this area.

HUMPBACK WHALES IN GLACIER BAY—for reasons not fully understood, Glacier Bay seems also to attract a substantial population of these huge mammals, which generally summer here, and then travel, like many other Alaskans, to Hawaii for the winter! Part of the reason for limiting the daily number of visiting vessels in Glacier Bay is to reduce the impact of this sort of activity upon the summer whale population.

BEARS AND MOUNTAIN GOATS— Get your binoculars and look sharp—mountain goats are frequently seen on mountainsides here, appearing like white dots, except that they are slowly moving. Likewise, it is not uncommon to see bears, especially on the beaches in places like Russell Island. So have those binoculars handy at all times!

What's wrong with this picture? Answer: Boat is in danger. Icebergs can topple suddenly as melting changes their center of gravity.

POINT ADOLPHUS

Sometimes the best whale watching is right from the ship: four humpback whales cavorting near Pt. Adolphus, just south of the entrance to Glacier Bay.

If your captain has heard about humpback whales in the vicinity of **Point Adolphus, mile 1000**, he may investigate before continuing. This point is one of those places where the big mammals like to regularly congregate, and there are regular whale watching tours from Gustavus to this particular area.

I was here on a large cruise ship in 1997, and apparently the captain had heard some of the whale watching excursion boats reporting good activity there, and we swung by.

To our very great surprise and pleasure, what from a distance looked like two big humpbacks blowing a few hundred yards off the point turned out to be four.

Regulations require that vessels not approach within a hundred yards, so we stopped our engines a good distance from the cavorting humpbacks.

But then to our excitement and astonishment, the group of four big humpbacks made a beeline right for our ship, stopping perhaps 60 yards away.

I was down on the promenade deck then with hundreds of passengers for a very exciting photo opportunity as the big whales lolled on the surface, lifted their tails, sounded and disappeared for a few minutes before returning to surface almost in the exact same spot beside our ship. Once they surfaced so close that we could not only hear them exhale, but got a strong whiff of their breath smelling of rotted fish!

Look southeast from **mile 1024**—you may be able to glimpse the cove between the Inian Islands, a favorite anchorage for purse seiners and tenders. Even in August, snow clings in the folds of the hills here, and occasional icebergs drift among the anchored fleet at

night. I spent much of my 18th summer in this cove, buying fish from big native-owned fishing boats. These were powered with immense, straight 8 Chrysler Royal gas engines, and one of my jobs was to keep them tuned and running smoothly. In these 50-footers, the fo'c's'le was right in front of the engine, and as I worked, replacing spark plugs and filing points, I could hear the natives talking. Sometimes they spoke their native language, but other times it was English. They spoke of the fishing, but also of the legend of Lituya Bay, over and beyond the ice mountains to the north. I didn't understand all that was said, but they seemed to be speaking of an angry spirit that sometimes lashed out, creating great waves that washed away villages.

How'd you like to have one of these bump into your anchored boat at night? On occasion stray icebergs drift into Inian Cove, a popular anchorage for fishing vessels.

And once or twice that summer, ice drifted into the anchorage at night, a powerful, almost magical experience for me:

"**August 17, 1965, Inian Cove**. Something woke me in the night, and I sat up in my bunk, wondering what it was. And then it came again, a faint but insistent scraping, as if another boat had drifted down on us in the night. I stumbled out on deck and, there, eerily lit by the three-quarter moon, was a big iceberg, moving gently down our port side, pushed by the tide. Its irregularly shaped top was even with my head; I reached out to touch it, to try and retrieve some of the gravel clearly visible within its pale, translucent flank. The gravel had been scraped off a canyon floor, hundreds of miles away, thousands of years before I was born. But the ice was hard, its contours softened by melting. My hand could find no purchase, and after a moment the berg moved away in the tide.

JOE'S JOURNAL

"Outside the point I saw a ghostly armada moving in the seven-knot current of North Inian Pass: eight or nine little bergs, maybe a thousand tons each, showing as big as medium-sized boats above the surface. In the moonlight they seemed to glow as if lit from within. I wanted to wake my shipmates, but then the tide pushed the bergs around the corner and they were gone."

Look for salmon trollers in this vicinity operating out of the settlements of Pelican and Elfin Cove.

Look north at mile 1,029 to Taylor Bay and Brady Glacier. Glaciologist extraordinaire Muir was here the summer after his 1879 Glacier Bay trip, hiking with a dog over the flats and up to Brady Glacier on a cold and rainy August day. In the late afternoon, he had to take a running jump across a very wide crevasse. Fortunately the other side was lower, but even so he barely made it; a few minutes later he realized he and the dog had jumped onto a sort of island, surrounded by wide and deep crevasses. The only ways out were back across the wide crevasse that he had barely managed to jump over, or across a frighteningly precarious ice bridge: curved, drooping, knife-edged, eight feet down in the abyss of a crevasse from the surface of the glacier.

Muir chose the ice bridge, notching steps into the side of the crevasse, and sliding across, straddling the ice, chipping away the sharp-edged top as he went so that the dog could also use it. As he worked, the dog whimpered and cried, refusing to follow. See the picture on P.157.

Only with difficulty did he get across. It began to get dark, and Muir could wait no longer. He moved away, calling to the dog that he could make it if he only tried.

Small craft bound for Sitka and the outside coast usually take a short cut via Lisianski Strait, visible to the south here.

"Finally, in despair, he hushed his cries, slid his little feet slowly down into my footsteps out on the big sliver, walked slowly and cautiously along the sliver as if holding his breath, while the snow was flying and the wind was moaning and threatening to blow him off. When he arrived at the foot of the slope below me, I was kneeling on the brink ready to assist him in case he should be unable to reach the top. He looked up along the row of notched steps I had made, as if fixing them in his mind, then with a nervous spring he whizzed up and passed me out on to the level ice and ran and cried and rolled about fairly hysterical in the sudden revulsion from the depths of despair to triumphant joy. I tried to catch him and pet him and tell him how good and brave he was, but he would not be caught. He ran round and round, swirling like autumn leaves in an eddy, lay down and rolled head over heels."

—John Muir, *Travels in Alaska*

Look for fishing boats coming out of the community of **Elfin Cove**, southeast of **mile 1,029**. This tiny settlement, with its boardwalk and its anchored fish buyers, is the center for the salmon trollers working this area.

Make time in your day to put on warm clothing and walk the upper decks in the evening light. The view is often spectacular

The End of The Inside Passage—the conspicuous lighthouse to the north at **mile 1,036**, is Cape Spencer Light, which marks the end of the Inside Passage. From here on to Prince William Sound, travel is along a rugged and spectacular coast, almost totally untouched by human settlement and unchanged except by the powerful forces of nature.

It is also a coast where small vessels travel with care:

"They shouldn't have been out there—they'd never been outside in that boat... always worked inside waters. So, of course, after dark the wind came up, and then Ed came over the radio, just terrified: 'Bob, get over here, quick... Mary's washed overboard!' It was a bad night to be looking for anyone, blowing maybe 30, with a big sea running, but we swung back and started scouting around with the spotlight, but I figured Mary was gone, washed overboard with no life jacket or anything...

"Then maybe ten minutes later Ed called saying he'd found her. Turns out a big cross sea busted out a galley window and the door, and Mary got knocked under the table, and buried under about 300 pounds of dog food that had split open from some bags they was freighting for somebody. But they never should have been out there..."

It gets lonely out there—for the next 400 miles, there are not too many places to hide when the wind blows!

— Bob Holmstrand, fisherman

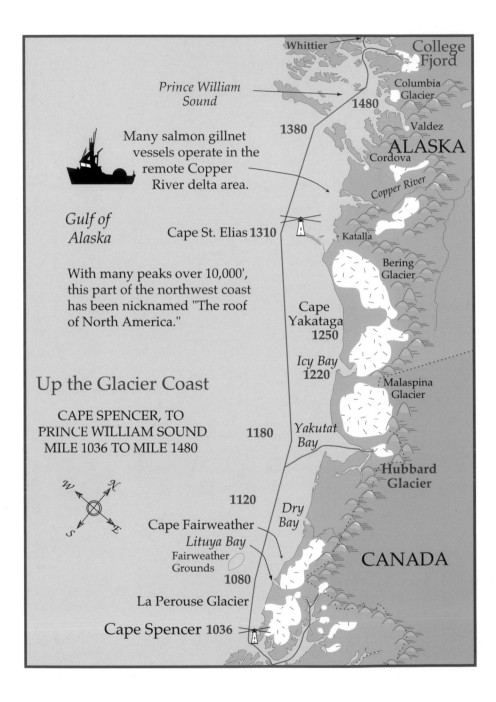

Whittier

College Fjord

Prince William Sound

Columbia Glacier

1480

Valdez

1380

ALASKA

Cordova

Many salmon gillnet vessels operate in the remote Copper River delta area.

Copper River

Gulf of Alaska

Cape St. Elias **1310**

· Katalla

Bering Glacier

With many peaks over 10,000', this part of the northwest coast has been nicknamed "The roof of North America."

Cape Yakataga
1250

Icy Bay
1220

·Malaspina Glacier

Up the Glacier Coast

CAPE SPENCER, TO
PRINCE WILLIAM SOUND
MILE 1036 TO MILE 1480

1180

Yakutat Bay

Hubbard Glacier

1120

Dry Bay

Cape Fairweather

Lituya Bay
Fairweather Grounds

CANADA

1080

La Perouse Glacier

Cape Spencer **1036**

CHAPTER 7

Up the Glacier Coast

Cape Spencer, Mile 1036 to
Cape Hinchinbrook, Mile 1380

"We thought it was an iceberg at first, way out past Spencer - you used to see 'em out there sometimes—but then when we got closer, we could see it was a big crab boat. But ... wasn't she iced over! Just like one big hill of ice, with some rigging and antennas sticking out of the top, and ragged pieces of plywood covering where the pilothouse windows were broken out. Pretty soon we could see the crew was all out on deck, knocking off the ice with baseball bats and shoveling it over the side as fast as they could. We all got up on deck to just stare at 'em—it was a wonder they hadn't capsized with all the weight of the ice. We heard about it later—a big cold northerly had caught 'em south of Kodiak. They busted their windows out trying to get back to the harbor, and finally just had to run before it, for three days, the spray freezing on 'em the whole time and the guys barely keeping up with knocking it off. It gets bad out there..."
— Crab Fisherman Russell Fulton

If the visibility is good, the most spectacular dawn on your trip will be out in the Gulf of Alaska, off this very rugged coast.

Mariners: travel with caution—the next 350 miles is open ocean, with few good harbors.

A few miles past the lighthouse at Cape Spencer, your course will take a long swing to the north, and settle on a new course, paralleling the coast.

Take your binoculars and have a good look around, especially at the shore before you get too far away. This body of water is called the Gulf of Alaska, but it's really part of the North Pacific Ocean.

The Gulf of Alaska has many moods— from life-threatening for the iced-up fishing boat above to serene for the passengers on opposite page.

This is the outside coast: bold, rugged, with few harbors, and backed by the stunning and rugged St. Elias Range. Take the time to go on deck with your binoculars. In North America, only Alaska has a coast like this.

Much of the land you'll see for the first few hours is still part of Glacier Bay National Park. Except for the rare hiker, and occasional fishermen, it is little visited.

If the coast of British Columbia had been like this, the development of coastal Alaska would have been very different. The myriad harbors and sheltered passages of the Inside Passage allowed very small craft to travel to Alaska. Many would never have dared head north if their only route was outside, along a coast like this.

JOE'S JOURNAL

A Journey to West'ard - Part I

(Author's note: These are portions of a journal I kept when I was a 25-year-old crewman on a new 104' crab boat. "West'ard" is the nickname for the part of Alaska west of Cape Spencer.)

"**March 3, 1971**—At dusk, Glacier Bay was to the north. The day faded until just the jagged raw peaks of the Fairweather Range glowed with that last pink light, and the icy wilderness below was all purple-black. In hooded

parkas and gloves we tightened and rechecked the lashings of the crab pots on deck. A thousand miles behind us, we still had that many to go, but from here on the journey would be along the open ocean with sometimes hundreds of miles between good harbors.

"The mood in the pilothouse after supper was subdued. Astern was the sweeping beam of the light at Cape Spencer, the entrance to sheltered, inside waters. Ahead was the Gulf of Alaska. The night was hazy, black, and cloudless. The bow rose and fell with the long Pacific swell, and there was neither star nor horizon to guide us.

"On my watch, I made out the shape of Lituya Bay on the radar screen. I stepped outside into the bitter air, peered intently to the east, trying to get some glimpse of the breakers in the dangerous entrance, of the glaciers, the snow and ice mountains that overhung the bay. But there was only black. Uninhabited, guarded by a treacherous bar, haunted by violent and recurring tidal waves, that invisible bay seemed somehow a taste of all that lay ahead of us."

Look for La Perouse Glacier at mile 1060. With its almost perpendicular 200-300' face, it's an outstanding landmark along this section of coast. It is unique along the North Pacific coast as the only glacier to reach the open ocean. (All other tidewater glaciers are in protected bays.) This is an active glacier: in some years, like 1997, advancing into the ocean, while just a year earlier receding enough to allow foot passage across the front at low tide.

Evening light, on the outside coast north of Cape Spencer. In the background La Perouse Glacier flows down from the mountains to meet the sea.

Spend some time up on deck with your binoculars; this is truly spectacular country.

The Remarkable Survival Suit

It was at Astrolabe Bay, **mile 1052**, that a survival suit—a foam rubber overall style floatation and insulation outfit—first saved the life of an early user. Paul Stratton was traveling south on the 42' seiner *Marmot Cape* in October of 1978, when they ducked into this bay north of Cape Spencer to seek shelter from a gale. The storm got worse and things started happening pretty fast—waves capsized the seiner after her anchor line parted and Stratton washed up on the isolated, wilderness beach in his suit, the only survivor. It was four days before he was rescued, kept alive by the suit.

Remarkable tales such as this one spread quickly through the maritime community, and long before the Coast Guard required these suits to be aboard fishing vessels, most had purchased them. Some with limited space even have them tied to the mast! Many mariners are alive today thanks to these ungainly looking suits.

Halloween? No—this is my crew during a regular safety drill, in their foam survival suits.

Fuel and supplies may sometimes be had from fish buying vessels anchored in Graves Harbor, just north of Cape Spencer.

To the west at mile 1090, is the Fairweather Ground, an area of legendary king salmon fishing. Here the ocean floor humps up to form a ridge, 75 feet deep at the shallowest, pushing nutrient rich water up and creating a feeding ground for the big king salmon. It was discovered by accident in 1954, by a commercial salmon fisherman 'prospecting' or looking for new fishing grounds. See page 103 for more information on salmon trolling.

It is not, however, named for the weather or sea conditions found there, but rather for 15,320-foot Mt. Fairweather, that looms so dramatically 50 miles to the northeast.

This is fishing only for the hardy; when the wind comes, vessels face a difficult choice—travel 4 hours to Lituya Bay, and hope they can get in, or 7 hours to Graves or Dixon Harbor where they know they can get in.

Tragedies in Lituya Bay

Look carefully shoreward near mile 1080 for a bay with a narrow entrance and a high island in its middle. This is Lituya Bay, whose history is pockmarked with tragedy that continues even to the present day.

The Fairweather Ground is is the Grand Prix of commercial salmon trolling—only the most seaworthy vessels need apply.

"Ebb currents, running against a southwest swell, cause bad topping seas or combers in which no small boat can live. Small powered vessels in the bay should stay away from the entrance on the ebb to avoid being swept through."
　　　　　　—*U. S. Coast Pilot,* Vol. 9, 1964 edition

Lituya Bay offers a secure anchorage. But first you have to get in. The problem is simply this: all the tide for this roughly 25-square-mile bay has to pour in and out of a narrow entrance. When the tide is ebbing, the current pours like a river out of the entrance and against the typical westerly swell, creating whirlpools and breaking seas.

The first white man to anchor within the bay was French explorer LaPerouse, in 1786, who had been at sea for 11 months without losing a man to disease or accident. Then in a single hour he lost almost a quarter of his crew when two exploring parties were swept into the tide rip that today still bears his nickname—"La Chaussee"—(The Chopper).

Those who successfully enter the bay (normally safe passage can be accomplished without problems on the

Mariners: Use extreme caution when entering Lituya Bay, especially against an ebbing tide.

Tlingit legends of whole villages being wiped out by an angry god seem to coincide with evidence of regular tidal waves ocurring here.

flooding, or rising tide) find a place of particular beauty, with three tidewater glaciers. Though it is probably the least-visited bay in Glacier Bay National Park, it creates a lasting impression with those willing to accept the challenge of getting there. Many who visit call it the most scenic bay in Alaska.

However, the loss of the French seamen wasn't the first tragedy in that stunning bay whose history gives mariners a good reason to seek shelter elsewhere. Native legend has it that angry gods have inexplicably wiped out whole villages in the past. White men tended to discount the old Indian stories. Until August 9, 1958.

The Giant Tidal Wave of 1958

The evening of August 9, 1958 was gorgeous in Lituya Bay—several salmon trollers had come in to anchor for the night as was their custom, and turned in early. Around 10:20 p.m. Howard Ulrich, on his troller

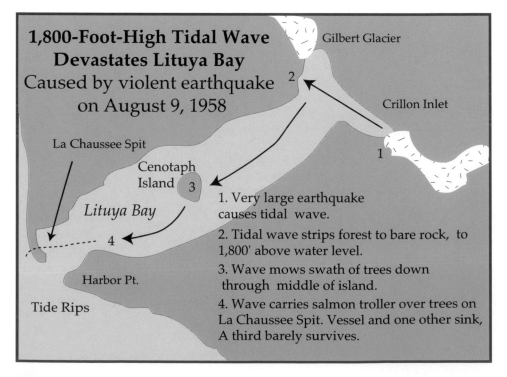

1,800-Foot-High Tidal Wave Devastates Lituya Bay
Caused by violent earthquake on August 9, 1958

Gilbert Glacier

Crillon Inlet

La Chaussee Spit

Cenotaph Island

Lituya Bay

Harbor Pt.

Tide Rips

1. Very large earthquake causes tidal wave.

2. Tidal wave strips forest to bare rock, to 1,800' above water level.

3. Wave mows swath of trees down through middle of island.

4. Wave carries salmon troller over trees on La Chaussee Spit. Vessel and one other sink, A third barely survives.

Edrie, was awakened by the sudden pitching and rolling of his boat. Still half asleep, he jumped up into the little pilothouse to see what was going on. What he saw became etched into his mind forever:

> "These great snow-capped giants [the mountains at the head of the bay] shook and twisted and heaved. They seemed to be suffering unbearable internal tortures. Have you ever see a 15,000- foot mountain twist and shake and dance?
>
> At last, as if to rid themselves of their torment, the mountains spewed heavy clouds of snow and rocks into the air and threw huge avalanches down their groaning sides.
>
> During all this I was literally petrified, rooted to the deck. It was not fright but a kind of stunned amazement. I do not believe I thought of it as something that was going to affect me.
>
> This frozen immobility must have lasted for two minutes or longer. Then it came to a dramatic end. It so happened that I was looking over the shoulder of Cenotaph Island toward the head of the bay, when a mighty seismic disturbance exploded and there was a deafening crash.
>
> I saw a gigantic wall of water, 1,800' high, erupt against the west mountain. I saw it lash against the island, which rises to a height of 320 feet above sea level, and cut a 50-foot-wide swath through the trees of its center. Then I saw it backlash against the eastern shore, sweeping away the timber to a height of more than 500 feet.
>
> Finally, I saw a 50-foot wave come out of this churning turmoil and move along the eastern shore directly toward me."
>
> — Courtesy of *Alaska Magazine*

After 1958, few vessels would ever anchor in Lituya Bay without wondering: Can it happen again?

This was an earthquake so severe that it knocked the needle completely off the seismograph at the University of Washington in Seattle.

Ulrich put a life jacket on his six-year-old son, started the engine, ran all his anchor chain out (there wasn't time to pull it in) and headed into that wave as his only chance. Fortunately the chain snapped and the giant wave carried the *Edrie* on a wild ride over what had been

According to an eyewitness, Lituya Glacier was lifted at least several hundred feet up out of the water for a brief period during the earthquake.

dry land and forest just minutes before. Ulrich got off a quick radio call: "Mayday!, Mayday! This is the *Edrie* in Lituya Bay. All hell has broken loose in here. I think we've had it. Good-by."

Dancing and weaving for survival among heaving seas, icebergs and thousands of floating trees, the *Edrie* finally escaped the wave and managed to stay afloat.

The two other vessels in Lituya Bay that night weren't so lucky. The *Badger* was carried by the wave over the trees and the land on the north spit, finally to sink outside the bay, her crew safe in a tiny skiff. The third, the *Sunmore* was last seen running full speed toward the bay's entrance before the wave engulfed her, never to be seen again.

Bill Swanson, who with his wife Vivian survived the sinking of their troller *Badger*, saw a sight that gave geologists a clue to the almost unbelievably powerful forces at work that night in the mountains behind Lituya Bay:

"...The mountains were shaking something awful, with slides of rock and snow, but what I noticed mostly was the glacier, the north glacier, the one they call Lituya Glacier.

I know you can't ordinarily see that glacier from where I was anchored. People shake their heads when I tell them I saw it that night. I can't help it if they don't believe me. I know the glacier is hidden by the point when you're in

Anchorage Cove, but I know what I saw that night, too.

"The glacier had risen in the air and moved forward so it was in sight. It must have risen several hundred feet. I don't mean it was just hanging in the air. It seems to be solid, but it was jumping and shaking like crazy. Big chunks of ice were falling off the face of it down into the water. That was six miles away and they still looked like big chunks. They came off the glacier like a big load of rocks spilling out of a dump truck. That went on for a little while—it's hard to tell just how long—and then suddenly the glacier dropped back out of sight and there was a big wall of water coming over the point. The wave started for us after that, and I was too busy to tell what else was happening up there."

> — Bill Swanson, in "Where Hell Breaks Loose",
> in *The Alaska Sportsman*®, October 1958

Trollers out on the open ocean reported whales jumping out of the water, and their boats seeming to hit bottom in deep water.

The Hermit of Cenotaph Island

Sometime around 1917, a prospector named Jim Huscroft settled on isolated Cenotaph Island in Lituya Bay to raise foxes. His simple cabin was known as 'Hotel Huscroft' to the members of mountaineering expeditions that started their trek to the high country in the bay. Once a year Jim would catch a boat ride to Juneau, to sell furs, perhaps a little gold, and stock up on supplies. The Juneau Elks Club would save the year's papers for him, and once safely home at Lituya Bay, he would read them one day at a time, just a year late. At times, in the winter, Jim probably was the only human being in the entire 125 miles between Cape Spencer and Yakutat Bay.

When the freighter *Patterson* stranded in December, 1938, Jim was instrumental in showing the rescue parties the trail from Lituya Bay to the remote beach where the shipwrecked survivors were waiting for help.

Bradford Washburn

Jim Huscroft, Cenotaph Island, 1933

This is perhaps the most rugged part of the North American coast that is visited by cruise ships. Make sure you take time to experience its grandeur. Evening or early morning with its dramatic light is often the best time to view the coast.

Out on the Fairweather Ground, Ingvald Ask on the *Scenic* was still trolling when suddenly his boat lurched and shuddered as if it were hitting a rock, and whales began jumping out of the sea around him.

Near Cape Spencer, fishermen said dust and smoke covered the mountains, and one was reminded of a passage in the Bible: "And every mountain and island were moved out of their places."

Eighty miles away, in Lynn Canal, the Alaska-Seattle undersea cable broke in four places.

Today, no one who is familiar with the history of Lituya Bay anchors there without wondering about when such an earthquake and subsequent tidal wave might happen again.

The Inaccessible Coast

Before the advent of helicopters, mariners unfortunate enough to strand along this coast usually had a particularly difficult time. When the little freighter *Patterson* beached herself near **mile 1090** in December of 1938, would-be Coast Guard rescuers stood helplessly outside the surfline on and off for ten days. As Christmas approached the story of the 18 survivors stranded on a remote Alaska beach made headlines all over the country.

But as pioneer Alaska aviator Shell Simmons circled the survivors, dropping supplies, he noticed that when a big sea was running, generally the seventh wave would

run up the beach and slop over into a nearby creek, adding just enough water to allow him to land...quickly. He circled, watching and waiting, and finally timed his landing perfectly and was able take out the two injured seamen. But it was too risky to repeat and finally the other 16 survivors walked far enough toward Lituya Bay to be met by a rescue party.

Hunting for Glass Balls? For generations Japanese fishermen used handblown glass balls of various sizes as buoys for their gillnets. Today the buoys are plastic, but many of the old glass balls eventually drifted ashore along the Northwest coast. The easy-to-find ones have been in stores, homes, and restaurants for decades. Today a glass ball is a rare find along most beaches.

There are parts of the shore along here that have few, if any, visitors. Places like these remote Alaskan beaches are where glass balls are still likely to be found, particularly in the grass and debris above the high tide line.

Did You Know? Tlingit legend has it that several canoes capsized in the entrance to Lituya Bay just before Russian explorer Vitus Bering passed in July of 1714 and that the cargo—sea otter pelts wrapped in waterproof halibut skins—was found, and sold in Kamchatka, sparking the fur rush which led to the Russian fur era.

Just north of **Cape Fairweather**, a low, bare headland at **mile 1096**, vessels may seek shelter from moderate southeasterly or southwesterly winds. In heavy gales, vessels are advised to give the coast from Cape Fairweather to Ocean Cape, **mile 1162**, a wide berth as seas have been observed breaking several miles from shore.

Dry Bay, at mile 1120 is the shallow mouth of the Alsek River. Although a fair run of salmon enters this river, the entrance is shallow. Over the years several

Glass balls, from Japanese fishing nets, often end up on northwest coast beaches. They come in several sizes and shapes, occasionally with netting still attached. Your best chance of still finding them is on remote beaches like those on the Alaska coast. Note how the left middle ball has a pattern etched onto it by the wind blowing the sand against the netting that was originally on the glass. The tubular glass on the bottom is a gillnet float, quite a rare find!

Caution: The entrance to Dry Bay changes frequently and should only be attempted in calm seas, at high tide, and with local knowledge, if possible.

Roughly 1200 people a year float through the vast wilderness east of Dry Bay and down the Alsek River in kayaks. All but a handful take the Tatshensheni - Alsek Route. A few hardy souls always try the infamous Turnback Canyon route.

entrepreneurs have tried canning fish here, but in the end were always defeated by the rough seas and shifting sand bars at the bay's entrance. After a particularly tragic mishap in 1944, when six Coast Guardsmen were lost as their surfboat capsized in the breakers trying to reach two stranded fishing boats, vessels tended to stay away from Dry Bay. Today, a small salmon processing plant is located on the northern shore of Dry Bay, but owing to the difficulty of entering the river, the fish are transported by plane to Yakutat.

The land to the east, from the coast up over the Fairweather Range, and into the Yukon Territories of Canada, almost to the Alaska Highway, is for the most part a vast wilderness. It does present, however, an opportunity for kayakers or rafters willing to travel for long distances far from any help or source of supplies.

For the truly brave hearted, the **Dezadeash-Kaskawulsh-Alsek route** includes the infamous **Turnback Canyon**. It was named after the 1898 gold prospectors who tried the Alsek as a route to the interior, had one look at the ten-mile chute of churning 34 degree water and turned around.

This unforgiving canyon has become to kayakers what K2 or Everest is to climbers. A word of caution - sometimes high water and current conditions make this canyon truly impassable and kayakers are urged to have a contingency plan for a helicopter to shuttle them around the canyon.

The other route, via the rough **Tatshensheni River** involves less white water, but is no less of a wilderness experience:

"..you almost have to do it to really sense what it's like back in there. We started off right from the Haines highway, and as soon as that bridge disap-

peared, it was like, except for our little group of four guys, humans had ceased to exist. It took us a week, and never did we see a plane, or a bit of trash, another kayaker... nothing. The amazing thing was that the river goes right through the middle of this range of mountains that go all the way up to 15,000'.

"Of course we just trashed the kayaks—they were just beaters to begin with, and we just left them on the beach when the plane came to pick us up. But the thing that I'll always remember was at the very end, when we had all our stuff on the shore at Dry Bay, waiting for the plane to come in and pick us up. It was a clear day, the river looked like it just came from a solid mountain wall, with no possible way through, and I just felt, 'Wow... we came through there...' "

—A kayaker

The sun deck of a big liner is often deserted after dark. Find a place out of the wind and let your eyes get accustomed to the dark. You'll get a unique perspective on this vast land.

This area is also a good place to look for Northern Lights. While the Aurora Borealis is most commonly seen in the winter, when, with the sky very black, it can be bright indeed, don't discount the possibility of seeing it on your trip.

What to look for: Northern Lights seen in the summer will be much more subtle. What I reccomend is this: each night before you turn in, put on warm clothing and go up to an upper deck in the forward part of the ship, away from any deck lights, and give your eyes a chance to get accustomed to the dark. If you're travel-

Near Dangerous River, mile 1140. The shore is wild and remote, little-visited by man.

Early travelers reported that the Tlingits were able to travel from Dry Bay to Yakutat in their large, 40' - 50' canoes, without ever going out into the open Gulf. They followed the shallow lagoons and streams behind the beaches.

ing around the time of the summer equinox - June 21 - it might not be dark enough even at midnight. But in any case, give your eyes time to adjust - at least ten minutes, and look around.

What you are looking for would be very subtle, often pale pastel beams that could appear to be moving.

"**From Alsek River to Yakutat Bay,** the mountains are 5 to 15 miles from the coast, and between is a low wooded plain cut by numerous streams. The principal rivers between Alsek River and Yakutat Bay have shifting sand bars at their entrances and lagoons or tidal basins inside; they can be used only by small boats and launches at high water and with a smooth sea."
— *U. S. Coast Pilot*, Vol. 9, 1964 edition

The Land—The 'low wooded plain' mentioned above is hardly a plain in the sense most travelers might think. A more apt description might be 'an almost impenetrable thicket of Devil's Club (a particularly sharp-thorned bush), alder and other plant life'. Many mountaineering parties have begun their ascents of the peaks here by being transported to these shallow rivers by float plane. It is not uncommon for these experienced climbers to find that the most difficult part of their whole trip was just getting through the woods to a place where they could begin their climb! Climbers, sportsfishermen, and others usually reach this part of

Brenda Carney

the coast by charter plane from Yakutat.

Lights at night? There are no navigational lights or settlements in the 110 miles of coast between the lighted buoy at Graves Harbor, **mile 1045**, and the Yakutat airstrip beacon (a green and white flashing light) at **mile 1155**. However, the rivers that meander behind the barrier beaches in this area are rich with salmon and trout, and fishermen come sometimes from all over the world to camp and fish this lonely region. Some choose to pay for a guide, who may even have a small cabin available for lodging. But many simply arrange for an floatplane to drop them off and come back for them later. For either style of traveling, a stay on this coast often leaves a lasting impression:

400 bucks a night for this shack? Some guides maintain remote cabins for their fly-in fishing clients. Some of these are on the spartan side...

"I just never had any idea of how much lonely country was out there until that trip. We were lucky—the weather was good—five days and no rain. Mostly we'd just fish, up and down all the streams. We were camped a little ways behind the beach, to get out of the wind, but after supper, we'd always go and sit behind some logs, and just look out. Behind us you could see the snow on the mountains, bright in the moonlight, but ahead and to both sides was just nothing, never a ship at sea, not another light anywhere, just nothing. Sometimes I'd get up early, bundle up, and go out and just walk the beach in the early morning light, with the surf in my ears and a lot of times fresh bear tracks..I tell you it was a very powerful experience. And we caught a lot of fish too!"

— A fisherman

Caution: Give this stretch of coast an offing of several miles, especially at night. There are no lights along the shore, and breaking seas have been reported as much as two miles out.

Today's outdoorsmen, with radios and pre-arranged return trips with bush pilots, have it a lot better than some of the earlier residents, who were sometimes beset by unexpected bad weather:

A Trapper's Journal

"Oct 4, 1917: Getting sick packing, now looking for camping place. Cold in the lungs with a high fever."

"Dec 7, 1917: River froze except for a few riffles. Too much snow and too rough for sleighing. Snow getting deeper now."

"Dec 19, 1917: Can't travel. Don't believe there will be ice a man can run a sled over this winter. Very little grub, snow too deep and soft for hunting goats. Stomach balking at straight meat, especially lynx."

"Jan 8, 1918: River open as far as can be seen. Health very poor... Wolverines been here eating my skins, robes, and moccasins, old meat, and also my goatskin door. They tried to run me last night, came through a stovepipe hole showing fight."

"April 3, 1918: Cooking my last grub, no salt, no tea."

"April 22, 1918: My eyes are useless for hunting. The rest of my body is also useless. I believe my time has come. My belongings, everything I got I give to Jos. Pellerine of Dry Bay; if not alive, to Paul Swartzkoph, Alsek River."

— Courtesy of *Alaska Magazine*
and *The Alaska Sportsman*®

Trapper's food cache and skins. A trapper would often build a number of simple cabins along his trap line for shelter in case of bad weather. Food caches were built high off the ground to keep food away from bears and other predators.

About four months after this last entry, two prospectors found a body, apparently a suicide, in a rough and remote cabin near the Alsek River with the above journal nearby.

Three bare, light colored bluffs distinguish Ocean Cape, the entrance to Yakutat Bay, at mile 1162. This bay is the only really good anchorage for large vessels, in the 350 miles between Cape Spencer and Prince William Sound. Nevertheless, in very heavy weather, breakers or very high swells have been observed all the way across this 15 mile-wide entrance.

Yakutat, some 5 miles inside the bay from Ocean Cape, is the northernmost village of the Tlingit Indians, many of whom fish for salmon nearby. The same earthquake that shattered Muir Glacier in 1899 also hit this village pretty hard. It lifted part of the shore some 50 feet and created several tidal waves and waterspouts that left furrows in the sand 5 feet wide and 20 feet deep, according to some natives.

Russell Fjord, at the head of Yakutat Bay, contains Hubbard Glacier and Nunatak Glacier which both discharge ice into the bay.

The 1898 Harriman Alaska expedition found this Tlingit seal hunters camp near Yakutat. Notice seal skins stretched on frames to dry.

Glacier Dams Russell Fjord

In April of 1986, Curt Gloyer, a pilot for Gulf Air Taxi, in Yakutat, returning from dropping off a climbing party noticed that Hubbard Glacier had surged all the way across the channel and essentially dammed Russell Fjord. He circled lower to make sure, amazed at the unusual sight.

This was an event without precedent in recent geologic history, and as soon as word got out, people and groups from all over the world converged on Yakutat to try and rescue the marine mammals trapped by the ice dam—primarily seals, sea lions, and porpoises. As the weather got warmer and the streams filled with snow melt, the water behind the glacier/dam began rising

Hundreds of marine mammals were trapped by the sudden and rapid surge of Hubbard Glacier.

At times, when glaciers are very active, there is so much ice in the water that your ship must proceed very slowly.

rapidly, eventually reaching almost 90 feet higher than the level of Disenchantment Bay on the other side.

Finally, in the middle of an October night, the water pressure became too great and burst through the glacier wall. By the time the first pilots got out the next morning, the big lake in Russell Fjord was pouring out a crack in the ice like a huge waterfall!

The Roof of North America—East and north of Hubbard Glacier is an area that has been nicknamed 'The Roof of North America'—an immense rock, ice, and snow world with many of the continent's highest peaks. Ten thousand-footers are common here, and there are at least four over 15,000'. Much of this area is the Wrangell St. Elias National Park and Wilderness. This mountain wall catches the eastward flowing moisture-laden air, which falls as heavy snow. The immense

Surging Glaciers

Usually glaciers move slowly, say 3 to 10 feet a day. On occasion, however, they can surge forward at much higher speeds: 150 feet a day or even faster! They can also retreat (breaking off icebergs or simply melting back). John Muir's native paddlers, in 1879, almost didn't recognize Glacier Bay, as the ice had retreated so much since they had been there last.

Variegated Glacier, in Russell Fjord, has been an ideal site for studying these sudden onrushes, as it surged regularly every 20 years.(give or take a few!) When the glacier finally lurched forward in 1982-3, scientists were ready.

The surprising conclusion of these geologists was that normally, water is flowing in channels under the ice. When pushed by the weight of the snow and icepack in the mountains above it, the glacier speeds up, it fractures more readily and these water channels become clogged. This raises the water level to the point where it partially floats the glacier! The result—a fast glacier. Variegated Glacier hit 164 feet a day in June 1983! Of course this speed wouldn't crush your tent while you were trying to get out of your sleeping bag, but still, at over an inch a minute, it is actually noticeable motion - a good trick for something weighing millions of tons!

Naturally, as such a glacier surges forward, all that ice has to crack and flow to accommodate the twists and turns of its canyon or fjord. The result is a continuous rumbling and cracking that is truly awesome.

weight of the snow pack creates the largest glaciers on the entire Pacific coast. Hubbard Glacier is part of a vast ice mass that extends along a few miles behind the coast in an unbroken line (except for two places) almost to Anchorage, nearly 400 miles away. Today the glaciers have all receded substantially back from the shore, but a century ago, the ice reached the ocean in many places.

When this glacier advanced to the right, it blocked off the entrance to Russell Fjord creating a major problem for the trapped fish and mammals.

Are those DC-3s? If you think you see 50-year-old twin engined DC-3s circling to land at Yakutat airport, you're right. They haven't come for an air show—they're part of a fleet of so-called fish freighters that come to Alaska every year to move salmon out of remote areas to where they can be shipped out or processed. In Bristol Bay, 650 miles west, big four-engined DC-6s and -7s land and take off from sand bars to move fish. The DC-3s at Yakutat are probably transporting fish from the Dry Bay area.

Look for Malaspina Glacier, visible west of Yakutat Bay, and rising almost to 15,000' above sea level in places. Today the glacier has receded back from the shore, but just 100 years ago it was a very different story, with much of the coast along here a solid wall of ice extending out into the open ocean.

Malaspina Glacier is a conspicuous landmark for mariners traveling this coast.

If it's clear, look for 18,008-foot Mt. Saint Elias, which will appear behind Malaspina Glacier as you pass Yakutat Bay. Sometimes visible further north and east, in the Yukon Territories, is Mt. Logan, at 19,850' almost a mile higher than Puget Sound's impressive Mount Rainier, and just 400 feet shy of Alaska's Mt. McKinley.

Even if it's dark, get your binoculars and look for these spectacular peaks. Many nights starlight or moonlight gives good visibility.

JOE'S JOURNAL

Our steel crabber seemed invincible tied to the dock in Seattle, but the further north we got, the smaller she felt to us. When we finally left Yaku-tat again after the storm we had a keen sense of heading out into a very hostile world.

A Journey to West'ard - Part II

"March 4, 1971 - Tonight, 20 miles north of Yakutat, a wind came up. After five minutes it was blowing seventy. The temperature was fifteen degrees. The first spray over the bow froze instantly on the wheelhouse windows; we turned around with hardly a discussion. Our vessel was the best that the finest Northwest shipyard could produce, built for winter in the North Pacific, but turn around we did.

"In the outer part of Yakutat Bay, a sobering sight had us all up in the wheelhouse. The 140-foot trawler *Deep Sea*, pioneer of the whole king crab fishery, lay at anchor with a big covered barge in tow. The whole front of the structure on the barge was crumpled in, the top and sides mangled for a third of the way back and in places the aluminum sheeting was ripped like paper. Our skipper got the story over the radio—the barge was a floating shrimp cannery, headed for Kodiak, four hundred miles to the west. They had gotten within 10 miles of the shelter of Cape Saint Elias when the wind came up. Two hours later, the seas had punched in the front of the barge, forcing it to turn and run more than a hundred miles back to Yakutat.

"We tied with frozen lines to a silent cannery wharf, and I walked up to the village with a shipmate in the blowing, drifting snow. In the whole settlement we saw only two lighted windows, and nowhere a footprint or car track. We trudged back to the boat through the knee-deep snow with the trees only dark shapes on our left, and the cove on our right lit up by the brillant crab lights. Our boat, with the bark of her auxillary engine filling the night, seemed almost like a visitor from another planet.

"In the night, a blizzard swept in from the Canadian Yukon to the east. At the head of the harbor, in the lee of the great mountains, we lay sheltered from its force, but morning showed a grey and eerie world. Outside the windows of the pilothouse, a steady plume of snow settled down on us, drifting down from the wharf above. By noon, what little free deck we had was drifted rail to rail, almost waist deep with snow."

Did you know?—'Snoose' (Copenhagen or Skoal brand smokeless tobacco) is extremely popular among the Northwest's many Norwegian-descent fishermen. One notable spring, as the halibut fleet was getting ready to leave, there was not a can to be had anywhere around Seattle and the entire fleet waited at the dock until the snoose arrived.

Waiting out a blow in the shelter of a cannery at Yakutat. We walked the streets of the nearby settlement, but found only two dimly lit windows to show that anyone was even there.

Shipwrecked

"Ah, I shouldn't have let Dad steer at night...that's how it all started—he was almost seventy then and his eyes were starting to go. We were headed up to fish Prince William, and I just laid down for a bit, and then the next thing I knew we were in the breakers—he'd just gotten in too close to the beach. The boat started to break up and that was way before survival suits, so we just ended up on the beach in our woolies, [long woolen underwear]...

"It all happened so quick there really wasn't any time for a radio call. The snow was right down to the water's edge in places—it was late April—so I figured our only chance was to try and make it back to Cape Yakataga. I knew there was at least a lodge or something there...

"It was really tough going—seemed like every mile there was a stream that we either had to wade across, sometimes up to our chests, and all snowmelt—just icy cold.

Many small salmon gillnet vessels—in the 30-35 foot range —travel up the coast every year to Prince William Sound.

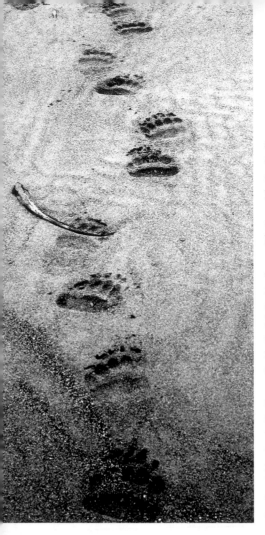

Bear tracks on beach, near Cape Yakataga. This was from a big one, probably a brown bear.
Brenda Carney

"We slept just huddled together, and then on the afternoon of the second day, Dad told me to leave him—that he couldn't go on any longer... The worst part of it was that we'd lost our snoose [powdered or so called 'smokeless' tobacco] and our chew both with the boat.

"If we hadn't stumbled across an old trapper's cabin, and found some old moldy pipe tobacco that we could chew on, I don't think we would have made it. But we spent the night in there, and each of us got a good chew in our mouths the next morning so life seemed a little more bearable...

"Turns out BP had some sort of drilling operation at the Cape back then, and the first building we came to was the mess hall. It was noon, and we walked in the door, all scratched up, just in bloody ripped woolies and our rubber boots. Everyone turned as we came in the door, and for a long moment, you could have heard a pin drop in there..."

—Dick Kietel, fisherman

Mt. St. Elias marks the spot where the Alaska border changes from an irregular zigzag along the top of the coastal range to veer sharply north to follow the 141 degree west longitude line, arrowing across rivers, lonely mountains and tundra to Demarcation Point on the Beaufort Sea, some 650 miles north.

Icy Bay, to the north at Mile 1220, has the usual shallow entrance, though in recent years it has been the scene of considerable logging activity. One hundred years ago, the bay wasn't even there—it was filled with a glacier that extended several miles out into the ocean!

These are active glaciers—there is often much ice in the bay, and sometimes icebergs will drift out of the bay and form a regular line of stranded bergs along the outside shore, all the way northwest to Cape Yakataga.

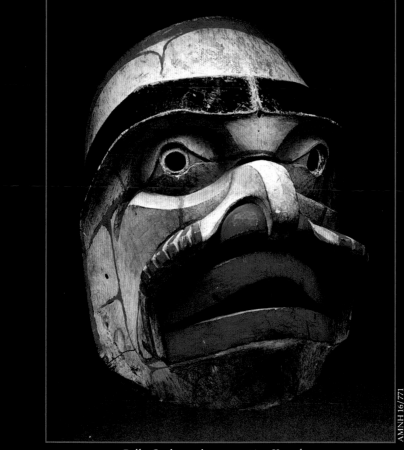

*Bella Coola mask representing Komokoa,
the chief of the undersea world.*

Northwest Native Art

"My wife's uncle told me this more than once. He told me that everything has a **yuk**, a spirit. He told me that he had seen them. He said that even a piece of wood that was split in half was half of a person. It was their life. Everything has a person."

—Paul John, Tooksook Bay, Alaska, quoted in
Agayuliyararput: The Living Tradition of Yup'ik Masks
by Ann Fienup-Riordan

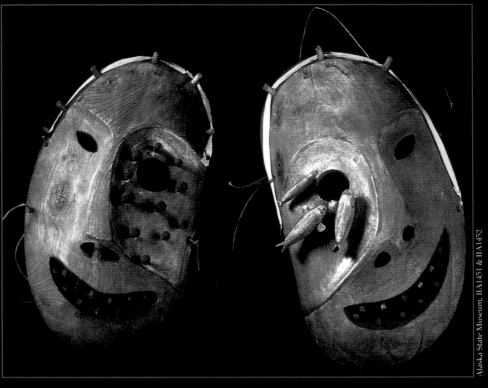

Alaska State Museum, IIA1451 & IIA1452

Masks were often made as pairs with asymmetrical features. These were collected near St. Michael on the Yukon River around 1900.

Yup'ik is the name for the Native American tribes living in the Yukon - Kuskokwim delta area of Southwestern Alaska. They are members of the larger family of Inuit or Eskimo cultures that extends from Alaska, all the way across the top of North America to Labrador and Greenland.

Freeze-up marked the end of the fishing and berry gathering seasons and a time for celebrating. Traditionally masks were created for eleborate dance ceremonies, and most were destroyed afterwards in ritual cleansing ceremonies. Some survived to be traded for various goods, slowly making their way into the hands of collectors and museums,

Christian missionaries generally discouraged masked dancing, but beginning in the mid 20th century, there has been a revival in masks and masked dancing.

One of the best Alaska mask collections is in the Sheldon Jackson Museum in Sitka.

Some masks were so large as to be almost sculptures. This represents two birds flying side-by-side. Pairs of human hands are common features of masks coming from the central Yup'ik area. Collected by Ellis Allen at Goodnews Bay in 1912

Blue killer-whale mask holding small beluga whale or porpoise in mouth. This mask was carved for the 1946 Hooper Bay dances. Initiated by the arrival of filmakers for the Disney film, Alaskan Eskimo, the native community was genuinely excited by the opportunity to make new masks and begin dancing again.

Human / Fox Ircit mask. Many masks represent the Yup'ik view of the dual nature of reality, with half human, half animal faces. Nunivak Islanders believed Ircit were extraordinary persons who were able to appear as humans, or as various animals including wolves and killer whales. Many of the contemporary masks found in galleries today have this round style.

Tlingit dance headdress, wood, inlaid with abalone shell. It represents a fish and a man's face. Used during ceremonies at the feast after the fishing season. Collected at Angoon around 1890

The tribes of Southeast Alaska and the British Columbia coast —Bella Coola, Haida, Kwakiutl, Tsimshian, Tlingits and others— are blessed with a much more temperate climate than their Yup'ik brothers.

Due to the availability of huge cedar trees they were able to create their well-known totem poles. Masks were also an important part of their art and mythology. As with the Yup'iks, masks generally reflected the view that all creatures have spirits who must be honored.

Thunderbird mask, open and closed. The Kwakiutls, of lower coastal British Columbia, produced some particularly remarkable art. Some masks, like this one, were designed with moveable parts. Dancers would, by skillfully moving their heads, present themselves alternately as birds or humans. Collected by George Hunt in Hopetown, B.C., in 1901

Kwakiutl mask of Born-To-Be-Head-Of-The-World. Collected by George Hunt at Hopetown, B.C., in 1901. This mask opened to reveal another human face, with hands painted on the inside of the opening sections.

AMNH 16/1507

*Bella Coola wooden sun mask, collected by George Hunt and Franz Boas in 1897.
Ironically, while waiting for the steamer that was to take them farther north, Boas
ran into a competing collector from the Field Museum of Chicago. He was very
annoyed to have competition!*

Detail, Kwakiutl Totem, Brockton Point, Stanley Park,
Vancouver, British Columbia.

Totems

One fair July day in 1981, when I was a young fish buyer
waiting for our boats to come in, my wife and I rowed ashore
to the long-abandoned site of a Tsimshian village near the
southern border of Alaska. Mary Lou searched the fine white
sand for glass trading beads, and I poked through the nearly
impenetrable undergrowth for the remains of the village.

The beach yielded a dozen exquisite glass beads, some little larger than the grains of sand that hid them, yet all of
bright color, hardly faded with the passing of centuries. In the
forest was a single totem base, decayed from decades of rain
and wind.

A century earlier, there would have been high-prowed
canoes drawn up below the simple cedar plank-and-beam
houses. In front would be art: carved cedar in its many forms,
the most dramatic of which were the totems.

Totems were a highly visible sign of the success and
wealth of the native cultures that evolved along the coast,
whether Haida, Kwakiutl, Tlingit, or Tsimshian. Sheltered by a
benevolent forest, blessed with a food-filled sea, the tribes
could afford the luxury of permanent village sites and orna-
mental art. Their art celebrated legends, events, or simply the

wealth and crest of the family for whom it was carved. The poles had no religious significance, but were records of the past in a society where there was no written language.

At first, the coming of the whites was the catalyst for a burst of creative energy among northwest tribes. Steel tools, and the cash from the fur trade and native employment, led to an affluence celebrated in larger potlatches, with more carved masks and totems.

By the 1860s, the situation had changed radically. Epidemics had ravaged the coast, and missionaries and government worked to reform a way of life they viewed as pagan and against the spirit of modern commerce.

At the beginning of the 20th century, travelers remarked on the curious combination of the presence of sophisticated carved art and its apparent abandonment. The reason was simple: so many natives had died that villages were abandoned.

The result was that much native art disappeared—either rotted into the forest, was purchased by individuals, or, fortunately for us, was collected by museums. But in many villages, where the people struggled with poverty and alcoholism, the tradition of art, as it was practiced in the 19th century, essentially disappeared.

Fortunately the 1960s and '70s brought a rekindling of the flame of carved art among northwest coastal tribes. Today, intricate newly-carved totems fetch high prices and are in demand—from Disney World to corporate offices.

Detail, Bishop totem, Sitka NHP.

Detail, top of Haida style mortuary pole, Stanley Park. The Haidas of the Queen Charlotte Islands were the only tribe to built this unusual style of totem.

Alaska Cruise Handbook **225**

Haida village of Skidegate in the Queen Charlotte Islands, British Columbia, circa 1881.

Totems have become cultural icons for the northwest coast. We shouldn't forget what they were carved to celebrate: the centuries-old success of a native culture that suffered badly with the coming of the whites.

Eskimo and musk-ox herd group, of carved ivory on a humpback whale vertebra. Musk-oxen tend to line up like this when confronted by a situation with which they are unfamiliar. Very fine carvings such as this are still being produced by native carvers and are available throughout much of Alaska. Author's collection.

Northwest Artists Gallery

Marvin Oliver

Box of Daylight 1992

This carved and painted door represents Raven releasing the sun. According to legend, Raven stole the box containing the sun, the moon and the stars, and placed them in the sky.

Marvin Oliver is an internationally recognized contemporary Native American artist. He is best known for combining a variety of materials: bronze, copper, steel, glass, wood and paper. Marvin merges the spirit of past traditions with those of the present, creating a unique and innovative style. His works can be found in private and public collections worldwide, and are on display in Ketchikan, Alaska at The Alaska Eagle Arts Gallery at #5 Creek Street and 407 Dock Street.

Northwest Artists Gallery ....

Rie Muñoz

Whaling Camp, 1983

"A beluga whale has just been spotted and pandemonium breaks out. The villagers rush to the boats, taking oil, gas, floats, rifles, and outboard motors. This is another scene from the whaling camp at Sigik."

Juneau artist Rie Muñoz's cheerful watercolors are perhaps the most widely distributed Alaskan images from any contemporary artist. For some 40 years, she has been traveling the state, to the most rural and remote areas, to gather ideas for her remarkable pieces. Whaling Camp, like much of her work, celebrates village or native life.

Available from fine art galleries or Rie Muñoz Ltd., 2101 N. Jordan Ave., Juneau, Alaska, 99801, 907-789-7441.

Nancy Stonington

Detail from *Cloudscapes*

In the fjord country of Prince William Sound, the low-lying clouds lift for a moment, revealing the rugged, high, and glaciated mountains that ring the sound.

Each year artist Nancy Stonington divides her time between Alaska and Idaho, with stops up and down the northwest coast in between. Her particularly realistic watercolors of the northwest scene have become a regular presence in this region's homes and galleries.

Nancy's work is seen in galleries throughout Alaska and also from nancystonington.com.

Northwest Artists Gallery...............................

John M. Horton, C.S.M.A., F.C.A Detail from *Close Quarters*

The historic tug *Ivanhoe* tows a log raft into Vancouver Harbor, circa 1910. As she comes up on the Moodyville Mill, she passes a big three-masted sailing ship, deck-loaded with freshly cut lumber and being pushed downstream with the tide by another tug.

Canadian artist John M. Horton is well-known for the accurate detail of his historic marine paintings. Presently he lives and paints in Steveston, British Columbia, where as a volunteer he is also active in marine search and rescue.

Available from Gulf of Georgia Galleries, #5-3500 Moncton Street, Steveston, British Columbia, Canada, V7E 3A2. 604-271-3883.

Further information on John Horton and where to view and purchase his art is available at johnhorton.ca.

A Fisherman's Tale

"We were headed out to west'ard for crab. It started to blow up by Yakataga, so we decided to run back and duck into Icy Bay until it got better. Of course it was snowing, so you couldn't see that much, even with the radar, but we felt our way in, dropped the anchor and we just all sacked out, for we knew that once crabbing started, sleep could be a scarce commodity.

"This awful racket woke me up in the middle of the night, and I jumped out and went out on deck. 'Course in them rigs we always keep the generators running and the deck lights on all night, so I stepped out on deck, just as another couple hundred pounds of ice came crashing down from this big berg that was scraping down our side! Damn! This thing must have been sixty feet high—it just towered over us! Spookiest thing I ever seen—it dropped off another corner of itself, and disappeared off into the snow. And them other guys never even heard it!"

— a friend

The Ruby Sands of Cape Yakataga

The tiny mining and hunting settlement at Cape Yakataga, **mile 1250**, is the only permanent settlement on the coast in the entire 150 or so miles between Cordova and Icy Bay. With patient effort, the 'ruby sands' (because of the high garnet content) around the Cape still yield a bit of gold.

The Cape House Lodge—more like a big log cabin - offers simple accomodations for the occasional hunter or traveler. Sometimes in winter there was only a watchman at the old lodge, which had the only phone for many many miles:

Cape Yakataga is the best landing place along this shore, but it is only possible with smooth seas—a somewhat unusual occurrence.

"A bush pilot told me about the phone, and flew me in there. I mean it's remote, there's just a few buildings and that's it. Anyway, there were a bunch of old magazines by the phone, you know, hunting and fishing magazines and such—the watchman who lived there subscribed to them, I guess.

Watching the wild outer coast slide by is a great way to pass the time in an upper deck hot tub.

Anyway, I hadn't seen a magazine in a month or so, so I started reading, and then I notice the address the old guy had given himself: '122 Bearshit Drive, Cape Yakataga!' "
—Terry Johnson, fisherman

"**Cape St. Elias, the south end of Kayak Island, is an important and unmistakable landmark**. It is a precipitous, sharp, rocky ridge, about one mile long and 1,665 feet high, with a low, wooded neck between it and the high parts of the island farther north. About 0.2 mile off the cape is the remarkable Pinnacle Rock, 494 feet high."
—*U.S. Coast Pilot 9*, 1964 ed.

JOE'S JOURNAL

Northbound vessels will often be off this dramatic cape around dawn, so if you're an early riser be sure to get a good look to the east as soon as you get up.

A Journey to West'ard - Part III

In that winter of 1971, this was such an isolated and remote part of the Alaskan coast, that even radio communication to the outside world in case of an emergency would have been difficult.

"**March 5, 1971**—Underway at four A.M. The storm had blown out to sea in the night. The dawn, when it came, was truly awesome—first a faint yellow line, then a dozen peaks tinged with pink. But the sun when it rose, was red and angry, lighting up a couple hundred thousand square miles of bleak ice and rock with its eerie long-shadowed light before it disappeared into a strange, thin, hazy cloud cover.

"All day we steamed northwest, a few miles off the beach. The wind was offshore and light, our ride easy, but

there was something about the day and place that made us all somber. The land to the north and east was a strip of beach, rising to icefields and mountains as far as the eye could see, range after range of cold, white peaks. The coast was broken here and there by little bays, all ice-choked and shallow, offering only limited shelter to small vessels.

"Night came early and inky black, but without a breath of wind. It seemed as if we were traveling through a featureless void. We ate early, and all gathered in the darkened pilothouse, anxious to make Cape Hinchinbrook, to put this long and exposed passage behind us."

"**March 6, 1971**: Sometime after midnight I awoke suddenly. The engine was only rumbling along at an idle, but it was something else that had woken me—the boat's motion—she took a roll, slow and loggy, seeming to hesitate at the end. I stumbled up into the pilothouse, instantly saw the problem: The wind had come up suddenly at Cape St. Elias and we'd iced up badly. Outside the window was a terrible sight—the two-inch pipe rails around

A solitary crewman is witness to a dramatic dawn off Cape St. Elias. If you look carefully, you can just see Pinnacle Rock, almost 500 feet high, just to the right of the cape.

Catching king crabs could be exciting. But just getting up to the fishing grounds could be very challenging.

the foredeck were swollen into foot-thick bloated sausages, and in a few places they had already grown together into a solid wall of ice. The anchor winch was an unrecognizable white mound. I took a quick look out the back windows, and just as quickly looked away. What had been a neat stack of big crab pots, was now a lumpy hill of white ice, broken here and there by the black steel edges of the pots.

"It was easy to see how vessels died—after just a couple of hours, we'd accumulated enough ice to make the boat dangerously top-heavy—and we were only carrying 75 pots in two layers on deck. Some vessels traveled north with several hundred pots stacked three high.

"Without a word, the engineer and I suited up with oilskins over insulated coveralls, grabbed the baseball bats and edged cautiously out onto the foredeck, clipping short safety lines around the rails, knocking the ice off as we went. It popped off easily, but it was awkward work—the boat rolling, the footing treacherous, the bitter wind turning the spray to slush on our oilskins. Once a sea larger than the others loomed suddenly out of the night, came right up over the bow—solid black water. It tugged at our knees for a moment and was gone.

"But it was a terrible feeling—the bow sinking, the water swirling around us, clutching at our legs. There was a white and strained face in the window, my hands fastened to the rail, but then the bow rose sluggishly and the water cleared.

"When we'd cleared off the tons of ice from the bow, we worked aft, knocking the ice off the rails as we went. An hour's work, just to clear the bow and boat deck area, but our little ship seemed to ride a little higher, roll a little quicker.

"The back deck was another story, for even the nylon meshes of the pots had swollen with the ice, finally grown into an almost seamless mound of solid ice. Much of what we chipped fell on deck, had to be tediously shoveled over the side. And all the while the wind picked the water off the sea, froze it to every surface that we uncovered. It

was blowing perhaps 25. No one spoke of it, but we all knew that it would only take another 20 knots of wind to make ice faster than we could chip it off, and it would only be a matter of time before we became too top heavy and simply rolled over. It had happened to other vessels in just those same conditions. We knew we had to find shelter and soon, to get as many pots below deck, into our holds, to reduce the area where ice could accumulate.

"It's the Copper River wind, boy," the skipper's brother told me in the galley when we were done and warming up. "It just sucks down off the flats and ice after a little sou'west breeze. All that ocean air just gets frozen up there, and all of a sudden decides to roll back to the sea. And I told that guy down in Seattle to put the pots into the hold when we loaded them. 'Oh, no,' he said. 'We won't have to do that...' Those guys down there don't even know what ice is except when they see it in their drinks...they think these new super boats can take anything."

"Even at less than a quarter throttle, we iced up again badly before we found a few acres of shelter behind a tiny dot of an island off the abandoned copper boom town of Katalla. We pulled the big steel hatch covers off, loaded as many of the heavily iced pots into the holds as would fit, laid the rest flat on the deck, lowered the boom and lashed it to the stern. The icy wind still clawed at us, but there was no sea. When we were finally done I looked around. We were probably the only humans within 50 miles and the vista—frozen islands, shore and mountains, now hidden, now revealed by moon and racing clouds was unspeakably bleak."

This was a coast waiting to trap the unwary, and we traveled with the utmost caution. When this steamer went ashore in 1914, her crew waited weeks to get rescued.

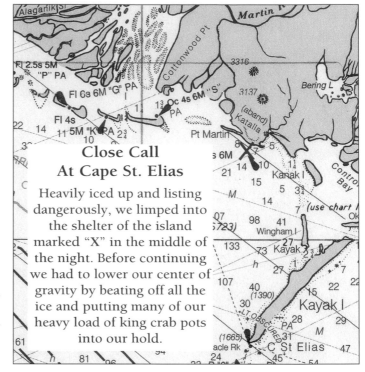

Close Call At Cape St. Elias

Heavily iced up and listing dangerously, we limped into the shelter of the island marked "X" in the middle of the night. Before continuing we had to lower our center of gravity by beating off all the ice and putting many of our heavy load of king crab pots into our hold.

After icing up badly at the cape, we found a tiny bit of shelter near the abandoned settlement of Katalla to lick our wounds and chip ice.

The Perils of an Exposed Townsite

Today, Katalla, 25 miles north of Cape St. Elias, is little more than another ghost town. But around 1907 high hopes were raised when Eastern capitalists J. Pierpont Morgan, the Guggenheim Brothers and others formed The Alaska Syndicate to develop the copper and coal resources along the Copper River to the northeast. The then tiny settlement of Katalla was picked as the place—"Where the rails meet the sails"– and between 5,000 and 10,000 construction workers poured into town.

Without a breakwater, steamers would stop at Katalla only when the sea was calm, and load passengers and freight into small boats which either land on the beach, or proceed into the shallow river.

Katalla's harbor, or lack of it was notorious among steamer captains. But when the "Googies" brought the famous railroad engineer M.K. Rogers to construct a 2,000-foot-long breakwater, who could have doubted that a protected harbor bringing prosperity to all was just around the corner? Indeed two different railroad companies, each with its own plan for a breakwater and harbor, were literally racing down the river valleys from the copper country.

Alaska State Library

However, what looked good on paper was no match for the seas that a hundred-mile-per-hour November gale drove in from the west on top of some of the highest tides of the year. When the three-day storm finally blew off to the east, it had taken Katalla's prospects with it. All that was left of the 2000-foot breakwater were a few bent pilings and rock scattered along the beach. That was the end of Katalla's short lived boom as the railroad men quickly rerouted their track toward Cordova with its more protected harbor.

Busy days in Katalla —looking out toward the site of the new breakwater. The big fall storms of 1907 shattered the breakwater and dashed Katalla's hopes.

The shore to the north, between Cape St. Elias, **Mile 1310**, and Cape Hinchinbrook, **Mile 1380**, is low and marshy in places, and is dominated by the deltas of several rivers, and a string of barrier islands, also low and grass-covered.

The Copper River emerges from the mountains between Miles and Childs Glaciers. The river deltas and the myriad sand bars are the scene of considerable activity in the late spring and summer with shallow draft salmon gillnetters seeking the well-known Copper River Red Salmon. Marketed as **Copper River Reds**, they are some of the first fresh Alaska sockeye on the market and traditionally command a high price. Much of the fishing is in and among the sand bars on the flats, in and out of the breakers, a challenging fishery. Tenders (fish buying vessels) typically anchor in sheltered coves nearby.

While hunting guides may have cabins in Katalla for seasonal use, no supplies or fuel are available here.

The nearest town and the home port for these vessels, is **Cordova**, northeast of **mile 1380**. There is a native settlement, Alaganik, 10 miles up Alaganik Slough, the main channel of the Copper River.

A shallow channel for vessels with local knowledge exists over the shifting sand bars east of Hinchinbrook Island.

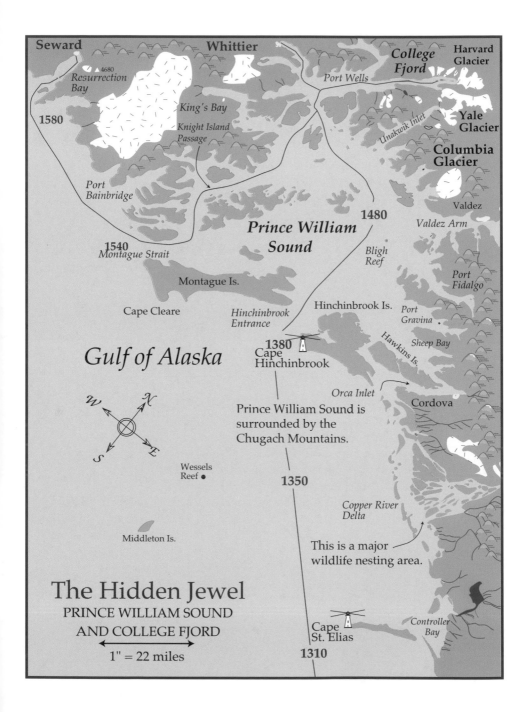

Seward

Whittier

College Fjord

Harvard Glacier

4680
Resurrection Bay

Port Wells

Yale Glacier

1580

King's Bay

Unakwik Inlet

Knight Island Passage

Columbia Glacier

Port Bainbridge

Valdez

Prince William Sound

1480

Valdez Arm

1540
Montague Strait

Bligh Reef

Port Fidalgo

Montague Is.

Cape Cleare

Hinchinbrook Entrance

Hinchinbrook Is.

Port Gravina

Gulf of Alaska

1380
Cape Hinchinbrook

Hawkins Is.

Sheep Bay

W   N

Orca Inlet

Cordova

S   E

Prince William Sound is surrounded by the Chugach Mountains.

Wessels Reef •

1350

Copper River Delta

Middleton Is.

This is a major wildlife nesting area.

The Hidden Jewel
PRINCE WILLIAM SOUND
AND COLLEGE FJORD

Cape St. Elias

Controller Bay

1" = 22 miles

1310

CHAPTER 8

The Hidden Jewel

College Fjord and Prince William Sound

"Prince William Sound is an extensive body of water with an area of about 2,500 square miles. It is very irregular in outline, with great arms spreading out in all directions. The entrance, from Cape Hinchinbrook to Cape Puget, is 58 miles across, but is almost closed off by islands. The largest is Montague Island which extends well out into the ocean.

Many of the islands and peninsulas in the sound are low and tree covered, but behind these rise eternal barriers of ice and snow."

— *U.S. Coast Pilot 9*, 1964 edition

C ape **Hinchinbrook, mile 1380**, is the entrance to a many-armed Prince William Sound, an area about the size of some small states. Except for three towns, Cordova, Valdez, and Whittier, and a few settlements, the area is mostly uninhabited, a dramatic island archipelago wilderness with many active glaciers.

It was here that the square-rigged ships full of Chinese workers and Italian and Norwegian fishermen came to build canneries and harvest salmon in the earliest days of the salmon fishery in Prince William Sound beginning in the 1890's.

Not OSHA approved—working conditions in those days were rough. Injuries were common, but often the

The terrain in Prince William Sound is similar to that in Southeast Alaska.

Mohai 16233

Asian laborers frequently traveled from the San Francisco area each summer aboard sailing ships to work in fish processing plants. Many canneries had separate bunkhouses and even cooking areas for Asian workers, and cultural artifacts like old opium containers may still be found at old cannery sites.

same crews of workers and fishermen would return year after year. Sometimes the ships would bring up building supplies as well. They would put into a bay with a promising fish run, but without a cannery and then the crew would build the cannery in time for the season. It was a remarkable enterprise, one that continues strong to the present day.

When the ships arrived, little processing settlements, inhabited in the winter by only a watchman, would come alive for the summer months with the rattle of steam-operated canning equipment and the chatter of many languages. In September, when the salmon runs were over, the cans and workers would be loaded aboard ship and sail hoisted for the run south to San Francisco or Puget Sound.

This relatively easy life was well-suited for these older ships, who by the 1920s had been largely displaced by steam powered vessels on most world trade routes. It wasn't until the late 1940s that the *Star of Shetland* or one of her sisterships hoisted aboard her last case of canned salmon, raised her sails, perhaps off Cordova in Prince William Sound, or Karluk Spit, on Kodiak Island, or Ugashik in Bristol Bay, and disappeared into history.

UW 8326

Early Explorers—Captain James Cook briefly explored this area in 1778. Setting out from England in the spring of 1768, he made three voyages to become one of the most famous explorers in history. Much of his work was spent in filling in the vast blank space on the map that was the Pacific Ocean. Exploring this section of the coast was to be his last hurrah. Returning to Hawaii, he was killed in a scuffle with natives in February of 1779.

But when Cook's men beached and caulked his ship in Prince William Sound, they traded a few fishhooks and trinkets for sea otter pelts, which were made into clothes to protect themselves against the cold. A year later, returning to England via China, the crew was amazed at what the worn-out clothes fetched—$10,000! —and nearly mutinied, wanting to get back to Alaska and get more furs.

But it wasn't until 1794 that George Vancouver, one of Cook's lieutenant's, returned with his own exploring expedition, and more thoroughly explored and charted this region.

The principal occupation of area residents is commercial fishing, much of which is centered in Cordova, in Orca Inlet, the easternmost arm of Prince William Sound. Access to Cordova is only by ferry.

Headed north—the Alaska salmon trade was the last livelihood for many old square riggers. Based in San Francisco, they made seasonal round trips to Alaska until the 1940s. For the Bristol Bay-bound fleet, a steam tug waited at tide-swept Unimak Pass in case they needed a little help.

The classic sea otter position—floating on its back. Once hunted almost to extinction, the sea otter has made a remarkable comeback in Alaska. Today the population is estimated at around 100,000 otters.

Brenda Carney

When the Harriman Alaska Expedition stopped at nearby **Orca** in June of 1899, they found a bustling cannery, staffed with Oriental workers, brought up on the nearby anchored full-rigged ship sailing from San Francisco.

The Sound teems with **sea life** such as sea lions, seal, and frequently, humpback whales. Sea otters in particular have made a remarkable comeback. After being hunted almost to extinction, their population has risen to over 100,000 statewide.

Before regular ferry or mailboat service, remote settlements, and fox farms were often served by trading vessels with irregular schedules.

Like Southeast Alaska, the Sound's islands were an excellent site for raising foxes for the fur trade. So-called blue foxes were most in demand, and to get started a person need only buy a pair of adult foxes, set them out on a small island, make sure there were no predators, provide plenty of food, and let nature take its course. Generally, fox farmers either raised the animals in cages, or let them grow wild, and trapped them once a year. Sometimes trading vessels made regular runs through the islands, trading furs for supplies. Usually located far from the nearest town, these fox farmers relied on the visits of these trading vessels.

A Fur Trader's Tale

"When the Depression came, I knew a lot of them fox farmers were desperate for supplies. Of course no one had any money, but I was able to talk the Seattle merchants out of a boatload of trading goods on credit.

"So off we went, through Prince William and through the islands out to west'ard...everyone was glad to see me come, so I was just trading supplies—flour, bullets, nails, etc.—for fox furs.

Problems with Sea Lions

Twenty years ago, a fisherman encountering a sea lion eating salmon out of his fishing net might be tempted to get his rifle. Today, however, sea lions, like all marine mammals in the United States, are protected by law, with severe penalites for violators.

This has given rise to problems, particularly with California sea lions, like the one above. No longer having the experience of being harassed by man, some have become quite bold, even aggressively charging unwary fishermen.

Although large (up to a ton), these mammals can be suprisingly agile. The individual above jumped three feet up of out the water to land on this barge's narrow side deck.

However, population levels of another species, the Stellar sea lion, is dropping substantially, especially in the western Alaska - Bering Sea area. This reduction has alarmed biologists. If the decline warrants, the Stellar sea lion could possibly be classified as an endangered species. Such a designation would probably severely impact commercial fishermen by forcing them to reduce catches of pollock, a species Stellar sea lions are thought to feed on.

"So pretty soon I'm low on supplies, and I just know furs weren't worth much, so we were pretty much in a pickle. But then when we got to Dutch [Dutch Harbor in the Aleutian Islands] there were telegrams waiting for me from all the major fur buyers in Seattle.

"Turns out Eleanor Roosevelt wore some fur-trimmed coat at some blamed play or dinner and just that turned the whole fur market around, and I was able to unload them all, pay off what I owed and even make a little money."

— Fisherman Mike Jacobsen

Port Etches, on the west side of Hinchinbrook Island, is a secure anchorage but subject to williwaws. (See left.)

Williwaws—"The williwaw is an especially dangerous wind due to the suddenness of its occurrence as well as to its violence and extreme gustiness. It occurs when the air dams up in great quantity on the windward side of a mountain and then spills over suddenly as an overwhelming surge."

—*U.S. Coast Pilot 9*, 1964 edition

Red salmon, also known as sockeye, are the most valuable species caught by Prince William Sound fishermen.

These winds are dependent on local topography—some harbors are known as "blow holes" specifically because the shape of the surrounding mountains is conducive to williwaws.

Herring Pounds—Spring visitors to Prince William Sound may see fishing vessels clustered around rectangular raft-like structures. These are herring pounds, essentially pens in which a particular type of kelp is suspended. Once the kelp is hung in the pens, a seiner tries to locate a school of "ripe" (i.e. ready to spawn) herring. These are then surrounded by a net, and fish and net are towed to the pen, into which the herring are released. If all goes well, the fish spawn and the eggs fasten onto the kelp fronds, producing "roe on kelp," a popular Japanese delicacy.

The very best kelp, however, is less abundant here than in Southeast Alaska, and during the short herring season, Alaska Airlines' 737s are sometimes pressed into service as "Kelp Freighters," ferrying loads of kelp to Prince Willim Sound!

A decade or so earlier, divers used to harvest kelp on roe in Southeast Alaska. But competition was fierce and biologists worried about the resource, so wild harvest is today illegal.

But it is salmon that has been the bread and butter for most fishermen here. During the summer season, tenders or fish-buying vessels spread out to the farthest reaches of the many fjords of the region, to buy fish from both purse seiners and gill-netters. These tenders acted like mother ships, often supplying groceries, water, and fuel for their boats.

Many fishermen lived in remote communities like Cordova where fishing was the only game in town.

A Fisherman's Tale:

"The best part of seining (salmon purse seining) Prince William is that there's basically only two ways for the fish to get in—Hinchinbrook Entrance and Montague Strait. If they're not in one place, then they're in the other.

"The most money I ever made in my life was 1988—we were getting a buck a pound for pinks, and a buddy called me on the radio over to Danger Island. 'Better get over here,' he said, 'It's big.'

"First set we totally loaded the boat, 60,000 pounds. We got a tender in there quick, unloaded, and set again, *another 60,000 pounds. We deck-loaded her...*"

—Henry "Ike" Issacson

In the hierarchy of salmon fishermen in Alaska, (there are many salmon fishing districts in Alaska, each with its different style of vessel and gear) the "Prince William Sound Boys" in the 1980s were doing well. Salmon prices were high, and there were plenty of fish to be had. Life was good.

This comfortable world was shattered on March 23, 1989, when a long nightmare began—the oil spill.

Happiness is a hot apple pie from the fish buyer when you deliver an extra big load. For Prince William Sound fishermen in the 1980s, prices were high, salmon were plentiful and life was good. That's your author and mapmaker in the middle.

John VanAmerogan

Pushed off course by drifting ice from Columbia Glacier, the Exxon Valdez *piles up on Bligh Reef, March 23, 1989.*

Ice, Oil, and the *Exxon Valdez*

"It was Sunday morning. I was just laying in bed, playing with the kids, trying to read the paper. The TV was on, some news thing about a tanker, but I wasn't paying any attention... Then Nancy, my wife, said, 'Hey Ron, have a look at this—isn't that where you fish?'

"God! So I looked out and there's this tanker, with oil it seemed like for miles around it. And it was right at Bligh Reef, right where I put my herring pound!

"Yeah, we got some money, but the herring never came back."

— Ron Hames, fisherman

"The only guys that win are the lawyers."

— many fishermen

Look for Bligh Reef, mile 1475. Generally your ship will stop briefly in this vicinity for a smaller vessel to deliver the pilot alongside. This is where the *Exxon Valdez* oil spill occurred.

The evening of March 23 was calm, with a little fog, when the big ship departed the Valdez tanker terminal

John VanAmerogan

Oiled sea otter at washing station. These small, graceful critters suffered most from the oil spill. Many died from hypothermia, when their coats became oiled, losing its insulating property.

around 9 p.m. Two hours later the ship slowed near Rocky Point, about 15 miles out of town, to drop the pilot.

The *Exxon Valdez* was a huge (987 feet long by 166 feet wide) modern single-skinned tanker carrying 211,000 tons of North Slope crude oil from Valdez to California refineries.

As was frequently the case, a substantial amount of ice—small icebergs and drift ice—was moving with the current across the shipping lane near Bligh Reef, just to the east of the channel, some seven miles farther south.

Captain Joseph Hazelwood elected to dodge the ice by crossing from the southbound traffic lane to the northbound lane (tanker traffic in this area is restricted to special traffic lanes), and then out of the channel entirely. Such a maneuver was neither dangerous nor uncommon, but required careful execution.

Look for Columbia Glacier to the north, just after your ship turns west toward College Fjord.

In a move he was to regret deeply later, Captain Hazelwood stepped into his stateroom to take care of some paperwork during this maneuver, leaving Third Mate Gregory Cousins in charge.

The problem with very large vessels like this one is that that they have such terrific mass and inertia. Even after the rudder is turned, the huge momentum of 211,000 tons of steel and oil tends to keep the ship traveling in the original direction.

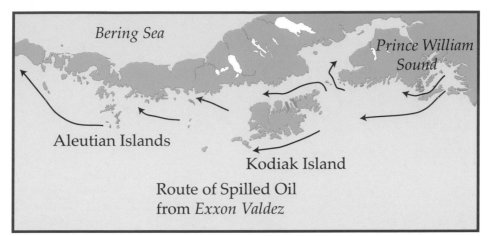

Bering Sea

Prince William Sound

Aleutian Islands

Kodiak Island

Route of Spilled Oil
from *Exxon Valdez*

The currents of the Gulf of Alaska carried the oil through many of the region's salmon fisheries.

Everything from old ferries to out-of-work cannery bunkhouse barges were pressed into service to house oil spill workers. To Exxon's credit, they spared no expense to try and get the oil spill cleaned up.

In this case the ship wasn't turned quickly enough and shortly after midnight, the *Exxon Valdez* slid up on Bligh Reef, instantly rupturing several of her crude oil tanks.

About three hours later, the first small Coast Guard cutter arrived on scene and its officers were stunned by what they found—the huge tanker aground on a well marked reef, with crude oil literally blowing out of the hull, bubbling almost two feet out of the water. It was their worst nightmare.

Within 24 hours some 10 million gallons of crude oil had spread into a slick that covered about 18 square miles.

Fortunately, the three days following the grounding were unusually calm—perfect weather for skimming and recovering oil from the surface of the water.

Unfortunately, much of the oil spill response equipment was temporarily unavailable. The reaction of fisherwoman Riki Ott after arriving on the scene the day after the spill said it all:

"I was stunned. There was no (oil spill) boom, no containment. Just a tanker on the rocks with two fishing boats coming up to it. Where was everybody?"

By the time a modicum of oil spill recovery equipment arrived on scene, the opportunity had been lost—the oil had thickened into a hard-to-skim "mousse," and the wind and tide had started it on its journey to blacken many thousands of miles of shoreline, and wreck economic havoc on many of the state's salmon fishermen.

The spill was an unmitigated disaster for Prince

William Sound and particluarly those fishermen who depended on the area's salmon and the herring stocks.

Of course the spill created a mini boom for thousands of scientists, technicians, reporters, and clean-up workers. Fishermen chartered their vessels at top dollar to work on the clean-up, and marine suppliers gladly wrote up orders for tons of buoys, line, boots, foul weather gear, etc.

The surprising recovery—in Prince William Sound, nature has shown itself to be remarkably resilient. Many affected sea life populations have returned to previous levels and the area appears to be as pristine as it always was. For salmon and herring fishermen however, the picture is not as rosy. Neither herring nor salmon have returned to pre-oilspill levels.

The Columbia Glacier, 40 miles west of Valdez, is a big one, even by Alaska standards—some 450 square miles—and with its towering (over 200 feet high in places) six-mile-long face is as dramatic a sight as any in Alaska. It was ice from this glacier that the *Exxon Valdez* made its ill-fated turn to avoid.

Actually, this glacier is discharging so much ice that it is retreating rapidly up the bay, and it's expected to retreat as much as 20 miles in the next half century or so. So if you want to see it, do it now!

All over Alaska, boats were beached or tied up hoping that the oil spill would pass.

There are a few isolated native villages in Prince William Sound.

Alaska Cruise Handbook **249**

The face of the Columbia Glacier, accessed via excursion boat from Valdez.

Mariners should use particular caution in Prince William Sound due to substantial bottom changes caused by uplifting in the 1964 earthquake.

Did you know? Probably the fastest-moving glacier in history was the **Black Rapids Glacier**, north of Valdez. In 1927 it was big news when it began surging, hitting <u>almost ten feet an hour</u> at one point, headed for the road link to the outside world, the Richardson Highway. Reporters were disappointed when it stopped just short of the road and began a slow retreat.

Valdez—More Than the Tanker Terminal. This town of some 4,000 residents, backed by high mountains, has been called Alaska's Little Switzerland. Don't, however, look for traces of its gold rush past. The entire town was essentially built after the 1964 earthquake and tidal wave destroyed what is now known as Old Valdez, four miles east. One of only two roads into the Prince William Sound area, the Richardson Highway, follows the pipeline out of Valdez north toward Fairbanks, some 230 miles north.

Valdez' main feature, of course is the terminal for the Alaska pipeline. It takes roughly one supertanker a day to keep up with the flow through the insulated four-foot diameter pipe that stretches 800 miles from Prudhoe Bay on the frozen Beaufort Sea.

At times, when the ice flow from Columbia Glacier is particularly heavy, substantial amounts of ice move into the entrance to Valdez Arm.

If you are on a northbound ship, the early morning light here can be truly spectacular. First light comes real early in the summer, so as soon as you wake up, have a look out your window or if you have an inside cabin, dress warmly and step outside with your camera. Above is a picture I took around 5 a.m. in late May. I took a whole roll here and most were gorgeous.

Early morning off Cape Hinchinbrook, looking toward the Wrangell - St. Elias mountains.

Prince William Sound is also going to be the best place on your cruise to look for sea otters. They especially like to hang out on ice flows, which you will be passing through in the College Fjord area. What is very distinctive about these creatures is that they very often swim on their backs. They will also dive down to pick up crab, sea urchins, etc. off the bottom, return to the surface, place whatever they have brought up on their stomachs, and paddle along, eating slowly.

The Fur Trader's Language

Words in the Chinook jargon, a language developed by Northwest Indians and fur traders to communicate with one another, from John Muir, *Travels in Alaska:*

Boston: *English, white men.*

Chuck: *Water, stream.*

Delait: *Very, or very good.*

Friday: *Shoreward.*

Hi yu: *Much, a lot.*

Hootchenoo: *A native liquor.*

Hyas: *Big, very.*

Klosh: *Good.*

Kumtux: *Know, understand.*

Mika: *You, your* (singular).

Poogh: *Shoot, shooting.*

Sagh-a-ya: *How do you do?*

Skookum: *Strong.*

Skookum-house: *Jail.*

Tillicum: *Friend.*

Iola: *Lead* (verb).

Tucktay:*Seaward.*

UW - NA2098

The Harriman Expedition's chartered steamer George W. Elder receives visitors.

Much of the Alaska coast was not surveyed when the Elder *made this trip; many times they had to sound carefully with the lead line.*

The 1899 Harriman Alaska Expedition

After suffering a nervous breakdown, railroad magnate (Union, Southern, and Northern Pacific) Edward H. Harriman was ordered by his doctors to have a "long vacation at sea." Prohibited from taking railroad men, he instead assembled one of the most remarkable literary, scientific, and artistic expeditions ever to come to Alaska. Chartering the steamer *George W. Elder*, Harriman arranged for a well-stocked library and some of the leading naturalists, artists, and scientists of the day including naturalist **John Muir**, photographer **Edward Curtis**, and many others.

Perhaps their biggest contribution was their extensive observations in Glacier Bay in June of 1899, just three months before a huge earthquake shattered many of the glaciers.

Entering Prince William Sound, they again found what some have called the two Alaskas—the spectacular beauty of the land in stark contrast to the grubbiness and even squalor of those who lived there, or like gold

UW NA2113

miners or cannery workers, exploited the resources.

Several days later, as their ship approached what is now known as College Fjord, they made a startling discovery—while the chart showed Barry Arm ending at Barry Glacier, in fact, the glacier had receded enough for the ship to squeeze through, into the uncharted and unknown waters beyond. It was a genuine thrill for the group to discover and map this new territory that came to be named Harriman Fjord. A group including John Muir (naturally) spent two days camped in the new fjord while the ship returned to Orca for propeller repairs, after striking a rock.

Next was another unique opportunity—to name a fjord and its glaciers. As many of his party were "Easterners," they surveyed many of the glaciers here, and named them for New England colleges like Dartmouth, Harvard, Wellesley and Vassar.

After leaving Prince William Sound, the *George W. Elder* proceeded "to the west'ard," touching at many places that are still extremely remote almost 100 years later, including King Island, Alaska, and Plover Bay, Siberia, on the Bering Strait.

Plover Bay, Siberia. Note the whalebone structure over the fire for hanging pots. After leaving College Fjord, the expedition worked its way west and north up the coast to Siberia and Bering Strait.

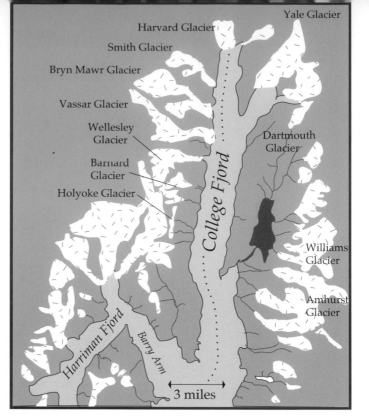

Ice cavern, Wellesley Glacier, measuring more than a hundred feet high.

College Fjord

The hidden jewel of Prince William Sound is remote College Fjord. Within an eight-mile stretch at the upper end of this fjord five major tidewaters reach the salt water. While Glacier Bay has emerged from the ice so recently that substantial trees have not gained foothold close to the ice, College Fjord is a place where the forests and glaciers have coexisted for centuries.

The result is a perspective on the great rivers of ice not seen in Glacier Bay. To see a glacier towering above the 100-foot-tall trees of a spruce forest, like **Wellesley Glacier** is really impressive.

Study the hillsides here. The upper slopes of these big glacial fjords, stripped of trees an covered with many berry bushes, are excellent bear watching territory. What you are looking for are brown or black dots that appear to be moving - these will be bears foraging for berries. Look also for white dots, often found in small groups - these will be mountain goats. Sometimes you will see goats in places that an experienced rock climber would probably have trouble in.

Have your binoculars on deck with you - this is the place to look for sea otters on the ice flows as well as bears on the hillsides or down on the beach.

Bears are also found down on the beach, especially if the tide is low. They are pretty good clammers, despite a crude technique. It goes like this: they look for the tell-tale water spurts of clams, dig them up with a big paw, smash them open with their other paw, and press the whole mass, shells and all, up to their mouth.

So where are the really big icebergs? By the time most of this ice gets to the salt water, it has been fractured so much by those twisting mountain valleys, that most of the ice that breaks off is fairly small, say the size of a small apartment building at the most.

But remember that roughly 7/8 of an iceberg is below the surface of the water, so that something that looks small on top, like the size of a garage, still poses a significant danger to ships. (Small icebergs and so-called "bergy bits" are notoriously difficult to see on radar.)

Calving bergs: before Alaska cruising got so popular, few big ships penetrated right up close to the glaciers here and in other places. The captains of those ships that did discovered that if the glacier wasn't actively calving when they were there, they could often dislodge some ice with a blow of the ship's steam whistle. Today such practises are prohibited, so it's just a waiting game. Often major calving is proceeded by small bits breaking off. I was here aboard a big cruise ship in 1997, and the captain spied an apartment-sized ice spire that seemed to be tipping toward the fjord. We circled slowly for more than an hour, watching and waiting, and were finally rewarded with a splash that must have been 280

If the conditions are right, your ship might get very close to the face of glaciers here.

Make sure you try to make an effort to listen when your ship gets close to the ice. The grinding and rumbling of millions of tons of ice pushing forward is not to be forgotten.

In several places, such as Wellesley Glacier here, a spruce forest grows alongside the ice, giving a clear sense of the glaciers' size.

feet high and a huge boom that echoed up and down the fiord. See the photo on page 79.

Directly astern as you swing to the east to leave College Fjord is **Passage Canal**, at the head of which is **Whittier**, a small fishing community. Before the new road was finished in 2000, the only access was via the Alaska Railroad and several tunnels through the mountains. Cars and buses drove onto flatcars for the scenic trip. See pages 260-261.

If your ship continues west, you will swing past Perry Island and into **Knight Island Passage**. The land is forested and wild. Around you passages lead back to bay after lonely bay: Copper Bay, Herring Bay, Mummy Bay.

A Cash Buyer's Tale

Look for "CASH" signs on some of the fish-buying vessels.

"The main trouble with cash buying is you end up carrying so much cash around. It's not so bad in a small boat, when you know all the gang pretty well. But in '68, we were cash buying with a floater with thirty guys onboard, and we didn't have a safe. Well, usually we had at least sixty or eighty thousand bucks in the cash box, so each night when I hit the sack, I'd hide it in a different spot. You can imagine how many places there are to hide a cash box on a 120' floater! Then one morning, I forgot where I'd put it. *I couldn't find the cash box!* I was wild! I spent the whole day hunting for that sucker before I turned it up. I got a safe after that!"

— Bob Holmstrand, fish buyer

Once many of these bays and islands were home to fox farms, herring plants, prospectors cabins and the like. But today, except for the settlements around **Sawmill Bay**, to the west at **Mile 1520** this part of the Sound is for the most part uninhabited.

Prince William Sound is also the site of one of the largest "ocean ranching" operations in the world, at **Sawmill Bay**, near Whittier. Conceived after a series of poor runs in the 1970s as a way to stabilize the fishery, the project succeeded spectacularly—until the *Exxon Valdez* hit Bligh Reef. Pink salmon returns to the Sound declined dramatically after the oil spill.

If your cruise ends at **Seward**, you'll probably be spending part of your evening packing after you leave College Fjord.

However, the area between Prince William Sound and Seward is also some of the most dramatic of the whole trip. So try to find some time to go up to a lounge or viewing area where you have a view forward, and just take in some of this magnificent scenery. I have nicknamed the coast west of Prince William Sound, "The Ironbound Coast." and if you can take a few minutes in the late evening to study it, you will probably agree.

Seward where some cruises may begin or end, is some 1,500 miles from Vancouver, and lies at the head of long and deep Resurrection Bay, past Fox Island.

Today Fox Island has a small guest facililty on it used by a tour boat operator. But it was here that noted

In these remote reaches of Prince William Sound, fish were sometimes processed on a "floater"—floating cannery or freezer-ship, such as the Moku. Life aboard these ships sometimes has its own unique problems. (See story on opposite page.)

Even if this is your last evening—don't spend it all packing—the landscape here can be particularly dramatic in the evening light.

artist and author Rockwell Kent spent the winter of 1918-1919 with his nine-year-old son.

Kent was a true Renaissance man and adventurer. In addition to being a talented artist, he had a penchant for living close to the edge. His adventures, some of which he was lucky to survive, are in a powerful account, along with some of his excellent woodcuts and drawings, published as *Wilderness, Journal of A Quiet Adventure in Alaska* in a new edition published by the University Press of New England in 1996.

Fishing—sport and commercial—and tourism, are the engines that run the economy here. Look just south of the small boat harbor to the big parking lot for campers and motor homes. Every Alaskan is entitled to a subsistence catch of salmon. Originally intended for natives and other rural residents who traditionally depended on fish, today many city dwellers take advantage of its provisions to load up on salmon either frozen or put up in jars for the winter. If you look around the beach and parking lot, you're apt to see regular little home canning operations, set up on tables outside motor homes.

There are several sea lion rookeries in the Resurrection Bay area.

The Alaska SeaLife Center is part rehabilitation center for species damaged in the spill, and part aquarium/visitor's center. It's located close to where your ship docks and is definately worth a visit if you have time before your bus leaves for anchorage.

One of Seward's biggest attractions for visitors is the

Kenai Fjords National Park, a dramatic series of narrow bays and glaciated fjords to the west of town. The land in most of the fjords has only recently emerged from the ice—actually the Harding Icefield, which once covered much of the entire Kenai Peninsula.

Fat and sassy: a harbor seal at the Alaska Sealife Center in Seward. You can see what a gorgeous coat these mammals have. Only Alaska natives can legally harvest them to use their skins for clothing.

As most of the park is rugged, roadless country, most folks visit it by boat. Several vessels operate out of Seward on daily excursions to the park.

Eight miles west of town by road is **Exit Glacier**. It's about a 15 minute walk from the parking lot to the face of the glacier, but the reward is getting right up to the ice itself. Be careful though - this is an active glacier, and chunks large enough to injure or kill folks fall off regularly.

Coach to Anchorage - though the Alaska Railroad operates from Seward, most passengers take a bus. It's about 125 miles, takes around four hours, and will usually include at least one scenic rest stop.

You'll be traveling along the Seward Highway that runs over the old dog sled trail and over a series of low divides among the Kenai Mountain Range. To the west and the east are several substantial ice fields with dozens of large and small glaciers. Back in dog sled days, this was a treacherous winter route indeed, as the low passes formed a highway for the powerful weather systems that march back and forth between the Arctic Highs to the north and the North Pacific Lows out in the Gulf of Alaska.

Whittier: The Road's End

The surprise Japanese occupation of the western Aleutian Islands in World War II put Alaska in a frenzy as ships full of men, equipment and supplies crowded into the ice-free port of Seward. Concerned that so many ships crowded into a single port would be a tempting target for aircraft, planners chose tiny Whittier (and usually covered by thick clouds) as an alternative. Punching a railroad tunnel through the mountains was completed in 1943.

Next was "the city in a building." That ugly abandoned six story building that stands out like some bombed-out relic was for many years the home of almost all of Whittier's residents. In a place like this with heavy deep snow on the ground for most of the long winter, it was convenient to have all the homes and town services, stores, movie theatre, etc. all under a single roof. Why worry about plowing the streets if there's no place to go?

Another big concrete building—14 stories this time —and Whittier was a busy place, with its population rising to 1,200 at the end of the Korean War. But then in 1960 came the dreaded word: "Deactivation." The military pulled out and the population plummetted to around 70.

The Good Friday Earthquake of 1964 almost finished Whittier off—13 of the 70 residents were killed, the big oil tank farm burned up, and the small boat harbor and the big docks all disappeared into the sea.

Rebuilding was slow, but when the small boat harbor was rebuilt much larger in the 1970s, Anchorage residents suddenly had a reason to come: boating in Prince William Sound. (The extreme tides at Anchorage discourage all but the most determined boaters.) Access was still a problem— you could drive your car onto a flatbed railcar and get pulled through the tunnel with the rest of the train, but it was hardly convenient.

Finally, in 2000, a widened tunnel was opened that accomodated both cars (one way at a time) and trains. This better access was a boost for Whittier residents, and a number of businesses have sprung up to serve the increased numbers of visitors.

If you want to keep your boat in Whittier's expanded small boat harbor, be prepared for a long wait—at present around ten years to get a slip. However, for the 350 folks lucky enough to have one, the boating in Prince William Sound, with its abundant sheltered anchorages and dramatic glaciers, is nothing less than spectacular.

Whittier is also one of the wettest places in the entire United States— averaging 176 inches a year. So in the winter the snow gets deeper and deeper and deeper...

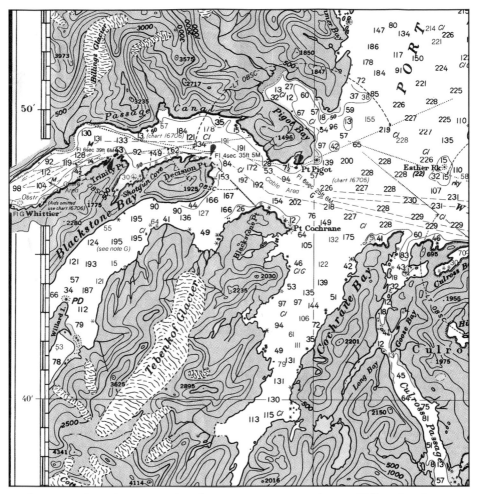

The new road to Whittier opened up the intricate waterways of Prince William Sound to Anchorage area boaters and sportsfishermen. Whittier is on the lower left corner of Passage Canel on the left side of the chart.

Kayaking Prince William Sound

The secret is out: Prince William Sound is one of the best places to kayak in Alaska. With many islands, protected harbors and good camp sites, a number of outfitters offer trips here. Often a larger vessel will drop off kayakers at a remote location with supplies for a number of days, with a rendezvous set for a later place and date.

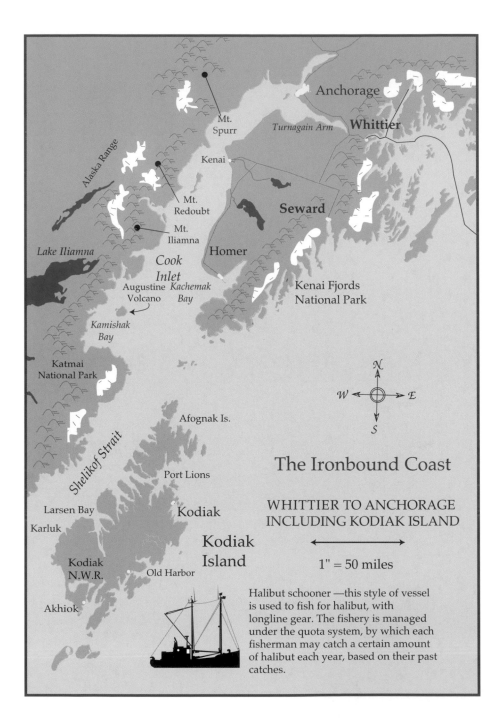

Anchorage

Whittier

Turnagain Arm

Mt.
Spurr

Kenai

Seward

Mt.
Redoubt

Mt.
Iliamna

Homer

Lake Iliamna

Alaska Range

*Cook
Inlet*

Augustine *Kachemak*
Volcano *Bay*

Kenai Fjords
National Park

*Kamishak
Bay*

Katmai
National Park

Shelikof Strait

Afognak Is.

N
W E
S

Port Lions

The Ironbound Coast

Larsen Bay

Karluk

Kodiak

WHITTIER TO ANCHORAGE
INCLUDING KODIAK ISLAND

Kodiak
Island

1" = 50 miles

Kodiak
N.W.R.

Old Harbor

Akhiok

Halibut schooner —this style of vessel
is used to fish for halibut, with
longline gear. The fishery is managed
under the quota system, by which each
fisherman may catch a certain amount
of halibut each year, based on their past
catches.

CHAPTER 9

The Ironbound Coast

Whittier to Anchorage Including Kodiak Island

"It was good money alright - two seasons in a row I made over eighty grand on deck. But don't ever think we didn't earn it. Our skipper, for example, he kept a little toothpick on a string in the wheelhouse and when coffee and pills wouldn't keep him up no longer, he'd stick that toothpick into his mouth. That way, see, when he nodded off that toothpick'd jab him in the cheek and wake him up. The cook'd make cakes and leave them on the table right by the porthole that gives out onto the deck, so we could reach in and get a piece. Twenty hours straight on deck, thirty hours sometimes. Sure it was big money, but I know you'd take two years off your life for every one you were up there."

—A king crab fisherman

Watch out around salmon streams— bears in this part of Alaska are apt to be large brown bears.

I f you explore the coast west of Whittier and Prince William Sound, you'll be traveling a route taken mostly by fishermen and workboats. This is a rugged, remote, and isolated coast; the next settlement west of Seward is Port Graham, almost 100 miles away.

Much of the coast here is part of the **Kenai Fjords National Park.** The park headquarters is in Seward, but there are few facilities in the park itself except for several remote cabins, available to fly-in visitors.

On our trip north to the Aleutian Islands in March of 1971, we left Seward genuinely humbled by the power of the North, and apprehensive about what lay ahead:

The best small craft anchorage along this stretch of coast is Taz Basin, a remarkable cliff-walled harbor, 35 miles SW of Seward. Among local mariners it is known as "Hole-In-the-Wall."

Seattle Historical Society 17588

Where it all began— large King Crab with Bertha and Clarence Anderson, circa 1950. Anderson was captain of the pioneering crab boat Deep Sea. *The very sweet meat of these large crustaceans created a boom fishery that remains legendary in the Northwest to this day. Many fortunes were made by the fishermen who managed to contend successfully with the very difficult weather and sea conditions of the North Pacific and Bering Sea. The remarkable part about king crab is that when abundance is high they travel in herds. Sometimes fishermen encounter such volumes of crab that they wonder how many are being killed each time a heavy pot hits the floor of the ocean.*

JOE'S JOURNAL

"**Resurrection Bay, March 17, 1971**— Had to break ice again to get out of the harbor. When I got all the tie up lines put away I joined the rest of the crew up in the pilot-house. Only the palest yellow-pink hue in the east showed the dawn was coming, even though it was past 8 a.m. The temperature hovered at 5 degrees; a thick cloud of fog-like frozen water vapor covered the ocean's surface. When the sun's burning disc finally made it above the horizon, its long shadowed light illuminated a cold and smoking ocean and an icy forbidding shore of sharp snowy peaks dropping steep and sheer into the sea. The most lonely and difficult part of the trip still lay ahead: Shelikof Strait. Here the vast and frozen Alaska mainland to our north created a cold air mass through which we traveled with utmost caution. Any wind would begin the dangerous icing conditions that had so nearly overwhelmed us earlier."

Kodiak Island

One of the largest islands in the United States, its early residents were the Koniag Indians, whom the Russians found to be particularly strong, cunning, and aggressive.

Kodiak today is the home of a particularly hardy group of Alaskans, most of whom depend on fishing and live in or near the main town, also named Kodiak.

This town has had its share of natural disasters. On June 6, 1912, residents observed a curious-looking fan-shaped cloud, getting closer, higher and darker, with flashes of lightning inside the cloud. This was the tipoff that something very unusual was occurring as lightning was a rare event. The sky got even darker and then small earthquakes could be felt, and finally ash began falling from Mt. Katmai, some 100 miles away.

Visibility dropped to almost nothing—people groped their way toward the foghorn of the Coast Guard Cutter *Manning*, and some 500 sought refuge aboard as the cutter steamed away from the shore and anchored in total blackness.

Flunking the bear test at Katmai National Park. After we were briefed on bear etiquette (Don't run; they'll think you're food!), a momma bear and two cubs appeared out of the woods, maybe 20 feet in front of my 14-year-old son and me. I began walking backwards, rapidly, but when I turned to check on my son, he was a hundred yards down the trail, kicking up dust and sprinting as fast as he could!

Did you know? At the time of the California gold rush, some entrepreneurs set up an ice company on Woody Island, on the east as you enter the harbor, and hired natives to cut and store some 10,000 tons of ice each winter in buildings with sawdust insulation. Before the Woody Island venture most of the ice used in California came around Cape Horn from Boston. The Alaskan ice cutters had horses to haul the ice and the first road ever in Alaska was built here to exercise the horses during the summer.

The business went well until mechanical refrigeration developed, but the makers of that machine paid the Alaskans not to ship ice for a while!

Most of the Kodiak fishing fleet ended up in the streets of town after the 1964 earthquake and tidal wave.

Salmon fishing is a critical component of the Kodiak economy

Two days later, it seemed safe enough to return. The town was buried in almost two feet of ash and many roofs had collapsed. Ash piles may still be seen today in many parts of the Alaska peninsula.

Then in March of 1964, as the town was getting ready for the salmon season, it was shattered, like Seward and Anchorage, by the Good Friday Earthquake. After five minutes of terrifying shocks, the radio station broadcast warnings of possible tidal waves. Many people moved to higher ground, and watched in horror as a huge tsunami roared into the harbor, snapped mooring lines, threw boats up into the streets and knocked houses off their foundations. Over 200 vessels were lost or destroyed, and canneries and cold storage plants simply disappeared. Fortunately, there were few fatalities.

After the earthquake devastated the town and essentially swept all the crab and fish plants into the bay, processors had to do something quickly. The easiest solution was to bring up ships and beach them with processing facilities built inside. The *Star of Kodiak*, an old World War II liberty ship, right by the docks, had a new life in Kodiak as a cannery.

Most of Kodiak Island is unsettled and wild, with seasonal fishing settlements located in several of the larger bays. With less than a hundred miles of roads, many residents get around by boat or floatplane.

Did you know? Tidal wave is a misnomer. The proper name is tsunami, and they are essentially shock waves emanating from an undersea earthquake. In deep water they are tiny - perhaps a foot high - and travel at high speeds - up to 500 MPH. It is when they reach shallow waters that they become giant waves of sometimes 100 feet high or more.

Katmai National Park

When 6,715' Mt. Katmai erupted in 1912, several feet of ash buried Kodiak and the blast was heard hundreds of miles away.

Cape Douglas

Shelikof Strait

Shuyak Is.

Mt Katmai

Raspberry Is.

Afognak Is.

Marmot Is.

Marmot Bay

Ferry.

While we anchored here in March, 1971, the wind picked up pebbles and small rocks from the beach and drove them against our hull.

Port Lions

Kodiak

Puale Bay—

known to mariners as the windiest bay in Alaska

Uyak

Karluk

Larsen Bay

Chiniak Bay

Cape Chiniak

Kodiak Island

Old Harbor

Ugak Bay

Cape Ikolik

Olga Bay

Dangerous Cape

Sitkalidak Is.

Kodiak Area: Islands of Adventure

Akhiok

Alitak Bay

1 inch = 45 miles

King Crabber

Trinity Islands

The harvest of the sea - these are king crab, caught in a single pot, after an overnight "soak" in the incredible boom days of the 1970s. The bag is an experiment; most crab pots are just frameworks of steel rods wrapped with nylon netting.

UW NA 1995

The traditional bidarka, used by natives both in Kodiak and the Aleutian Islands. Note rain gear made of seal intestines sewn together, and shelf for coiled line.

Russian Kodiak - this town was a major base for the early Russian merchants and settlers who were primarily interested in sea otter pelts. This was not a gentle period in Kodiak history - if the hunters of a particular village resisted hunting sea otters, the village might be destroyed by the Russians.

Of course, like other native groups up and down the coast, the Alutiiq people of Kodiak Island had no immunities to the diseases brought by the Russians and other traders. This combination of disease and murderous tactics to induce sea otter hunting took a heavy toll on the native population.

Kodiak became the first capital of Russian America (the capital was later shifted to Sitka). Today the biggest reminder of the Russian period is the Russian Orthodox religion, a major influence throughout much of western Alaska. Look for the blue onion domes of the Holy Resurrection Orthodox Church, just a block from the docks. It is one of many active Russian Orthodox parishes in the state.

A Native Cultural Renaissance - in 1995, the eight Kodiak Island area native groups formed the Alutiiq Heritage Foundation as part of an effort to celebrate and preserve their native traditions.

The Foundation created the Alutiiq Museum and Archaeological Repository, located on Mission Road, just two blocks from the docks. Featuring an excellent display gallery as well as a gift shop, it is well worth visiting. If your schedule allows, you may also wish to see the Kodiak Alutiiq Dancers perform. Dancing, once discouraged by missionaries, is now part of this cultural renaissance, as these tribes celebrate their past.

If you haven't been flightseeing yet, consider doing it here. As well as having an excellent chance at seeing some bears, you'll get a unique perspective on this spectacular area.

Downtown Kodiak has most attractions within easy walking distance. In addition to those listed above, the Baranof Museum—just across the street from the visitor information center—has a good display on Kodiak's Russian and early American history.

How far did the the tidal wave carry boats? Three blocks from the harbor on Mill Bay Road, is a plaque marking where the 86' power scow *Selief* ended up after the water receded. Patched up and refloated, she is still working and fishing up and down the coast.

Want to see sea lions up close? You'll probaby find a few hanging out near around the shore, just outside the harbor. Don't expect cute - these brutes are big, smelly and sometimes aggressive. Keep your distance!

Sometimes "bleak" and "austere" don't seem to be strong enough words to describe the Aleutian Islands. Extremely windy, with few settlements, strong tidal currents and few good anchorages, these lonely islands are the hunting grounds of capable fishing vessels like this one.

The King Crab Fishery

In the 1970s Alaskan fishermen found a truly remarkable concentration of these spidery crabs. When fishing was good, the big pots would come up with up to 2,000 pounds of crab after less than 24 hours in the water. Boats would get a 200,000-pound load in 48 hours! It was legendary money, but legendary work as well—when you were on the crab, 18 - 20 hours on deck a day were routine.

The heaviest concentration of crab was found in the Alaska Peninsula - Bering Sea - Aleutian Islands area. In the winter, this area has some of the stormiest weather in the world, and many able vessels and crews were lost to violent winds, big seas, and low temperatures.

Of the many disasters in the king crab fishery, none was more tragic and puzzling than the loss of the 123 foot sisterships *Americus* and *Altair*, in good weather on Valentine's Day, 1983. Both vessels, loaded with some 230 king crab pots, left Dutch Harbor, in the Aleutian Islands, and were never heard from again. Only the capsized hull of the *Americus*, which sank shortly thereafter, gave a clue to their fate.

It took months of detective-like work to find the cause. After offloading some 28,000 gallons of fuel, and loading the heavy crab pots, the vessels, unknown to anyone aboard, had such a high center of gravity that

The sea claims another. While riding out a severe Bering Sea Storm in 1978, several crab pots broke loose on deck aboard the brand new 150' Key West. It was too rough to try to secure the heavy pots, and one broke off a 12" air vent pipe, allowing water to flood into the vessel. Fortunately, another crab boat was able to rescue all aboard. Crab fisherman Walter Kuhr and friends are pictured at right. For many, this was nothing less than another "gold rush." Many crewmen worked their way up from deck work to owning large crab vessels, in just a few years.

they were rolled upside down by mild seas.

Today all crab vessels operating in these waters carry a certificate specifying exactly how many pots they may carry and in what conditions. (In summer, with no danger of icing, they may carry substantially more pots than in winter.)

After almost two decades of spectacular growth both in catch and fleet size, the crab population crashed in the early 1980's. For a while the joke in Alaska banks was that when you started a new account, you got a crab boat free as a premium.

Fortunately, it was in this period that foreign fishing effort in the rich waters of the Bering Sea was being reduced, creating much needed opportunities for the crab fleet to convert to trawling—towing funnel-shaped nets for cod, pollock and other species.

Today the crab fishery continues, but at a much lower harvest level than in the boom days of the '70s and early '80s.

Is this a boat? The Expansion *iced up at Seward. Icing up was a constant problem for vessels traveling the western Alaska coast in winter.*

Tales of "Cap" Thomsen and The Aleutian Mailboat

In the 1950s, the only outside contact for 19 isolated native villages on the Alaska Peninsula and Aleutian Islands was the 114-foot mailboat *Expansion,* which made regular round trips from Seward. Niels "Cap" Thomsen was one of those entrepreneurs that Alaska seems to attract. (We met "Cap" a few chapters earlier, running a freight boat into Ketchikan.)

About the first thing "Cap" noticed on his stops was how some native villages seemed to have a lot of single young men, and another village, maybe a hundred miles away, single women, but neither group of singles was aware of the others:

"So I bought a Polaroid camera and took pictures of the unmarried natives. I'd write their names and towns on them: 'Nona Polapalook from Gambrel Bay,' etc. I put the pictures up on two bulletin boards, one for single women and another for single men. Pretty soon after that the word was out, and any time we'd round a point to come into a harbor where a native village was, the singles would be jumping into their boats and rowing out as fast as they could to meet us even before we got the anchor down! They'd come aboard and head right for the singles bulletin boards. Also back in those days, to be legally married, the natives had to go to Cold Bay, a long way away. So I got a Justice of the Peace license, so I could marry them right aboard the boat!"

— "Cap" Niels Peter Thomsen

"Cap" Thomsen's boat also served as a general store, many times taking furs in trade for rifles, flour, etc. He also was a traveling branch of the Bank of Kodiak for the native villagers, some of whom had taken to burying the money they made fishing in jars in their back yards until they needed it.

An early cruise ship? "FOR ROMANTIC ADVENTURE, Sail to The Aleutian Islands, 'Land of the Smoky Sea,' See majestic steaming volcanoes, Witness the drama of life

"Cap" Thomsen aboard the iced-up Expansion *after a difficult trip up Shelikof Strait to Seward in wintertime.*

at sea, See roaring sea lions, precious sea otter." So went the pitch on Thomsen's brochure, seeking travelers wanting an off the beaten path experience. He might have added, 'Help the Captain work on his crab processor,' for on each trip, Thomsen managed to lay over in remote Dutch Harbor, for three or four days—long enough for the passengers to see the local sights, as well as a little scraping and painting on Thomsen's floating crab processor, the *Bethel I.* These were the days when the king crab fishery was just starting. Most of the activity was in the Kodiak area, but wherever "Cap" anchored the *Expansion*, he set a crab pot over and noted how many of the big spiny fellows he caught. A few years later, when his crab processor was ready to go, he recruited some boats from Kodiak by telling them that he knew most of the good crab fishing spots in the Aleutian Islands. Thomsen was able to ride the king crab boom to the peak, eventually selling his little company for some five million dollars, and heading to the Caribbean to build a resort!

Thomsen also wrote a remarkable book, *The Voyage of The Forest Dream,* about some of his early sailing days as a lad of 18, aboard a big square rigger loaded with lumber on a trip across the Pacific.

North of Kodiak is the 25 mile-wide entrance to Shelikof Strait, the passage between Kodiak Island and the mainland. This area has long had a particularly bad reputation among mariners, because of the violent and cold winds that blow out of some of the passes on the Alaska Peninsula during winter gales.

Caution: Tide rips in the Barren Islands area can be hazardous to small craft.

"Anchorages in Puale Bay are indifferent to poor...Williwaws are frequent. Even in westerly weather the winds funnel through the low passes to the west of the bay with greater velocity than that encountered in Shelikof Strait."

—U. S. Coast Pilot 9, Pacific and Arctic Coasts, 1964 edition

A day after leaving Seward in our crab boat, we felt the fury of Shelikof Strait:

A Journey to West'ard - Part V

"**March 17, 1971, Shelikof Strait**—By day we saw no other boats; by night, no lights. Inhospitable ice mountains rose from every shore. I yearned to see another boat, a town, but there was nothing.

"In the evening, in the below zero degree dusk, we anchored up right next to the beach in Uyak Bay, on the southwest side of Kodiak Island.

"An hour later, the wind came on, slamming into us. When the big gusts hit, all conversation in the galley would cease, and we'd listen to the shriek, audible even through the insulated steel hull, seeking any weakness.

"At 3 a.m. an unusually violent gust of wind followed by rattling pops and cracks had us all in the pilothouse.

"'Rocks and pebbles picked off the beach by the wind, and we're almost a quarter of a mile away,' said our skipper, George Fulton. 'One winter I saw a boat whose whole bow looked as if it were sandblasted—the paint gone right down to the bare metal, just from anchoring too close to the beach.' His brother, Russell, stepped into the circle of light over by the chart table, tapped a thick finger on a narrow bay across the straits from where we lay.

"'See this spot? Puale Bay—it's the windiest bay on the whole coast. Sure, you look at it, and think it's a great anchorage; you think you're safe if you manage to get in there, especially if it's your first time. But see these lakes up here, frozen maybe twenty feet thick, and this river valley? Well, you get the right conditions and it's worse than the Copper River flats. Thirty, forty, fifty below up there, and all that air gets real heavy and dense, and just starts running like water down that river valley, speeding up, picking up saltwater over the bay, makes kind of an ice mist, and you'll ice up unbelievably fast, even when you're anchored up, even close to the beach.'"

Most of Alaska's coastal communities have a memorial to those lost at sea. This one is in Homer, and overlooks Cook Inlet, a particularly tide - wracked patch of water.

He was righter than he knew; two years later, the shrimper *Jan and Olaf*, icing up badly, was abandoned in these waters. The crew was never found, but the boat, a frighteningly thick mass of ice, drifted ashore in a sheltered cove without major damage.

Cook Inlet is the wide body of water west of the Kenai Peninsula that stretches from Anchorage to the Gulf of Alaska. Like the notorious Bay of Fundy on the east coast of Canada, this bay narrows towards its head, producing very large tides and the strong currents required to move those huge volumes of water.

Homer

Four-mile-long Homer Spit sticks south into Kachemak Bay. The harbor and many visitor-related businesses are located along the spit.

Once a remote coal mining settlement, today Homer is a town of 5,000 set in a truly exquisite location. Looking south across Kachemak Bay to the snow covered mountains on the Kenai Peninsula, it is becoming a well-known arts community as well. Commercial fishing is the lifeblood here and in the surrounding small communities. Like Seward, Homer is at the very end of a road from Anchorage

The Spit—Homer's most unique feature is a four-mile sand spit sticking out into Kachemak Bay. At the end of the spit is the harbor as well as marine support facilities, a few eateries and gift shops.

The headquarters of the Alaska Maritime National Wildlife Refuge is in town. Its 3.5 million acres are spread across much of the coast of Alaska to the west. The visitors center has exhibits and displays of the wildlife found in the refuge.

Sportfishing, as you may have guessed, is excellent here. One of the local hot spots is the lagoon just north of the boat harbor—hatchery-raised fish are moved to cages in the lagoon, causing them to imprint the lagoon's location and return there as adults to try to spawn. Sometimes, toward the end of a run, "snagging," or dragging a bare hook through the water, is allowed to harvest all the rest of the fish. Kids especially like this—this way the fish are really easy to catch!

Halibut Cove, on the opposite shore of Kachemak Bay from Homer, is a roadless fishing settlement with a strong arts flavor. Not having a road creates a community that is very different from any of the places visited by most cruise ships. One's schedule tends to revolve around the weather and the tides.

On the road to Homer, a cabin overlooks the vastness of Kachemak Bay.

Seldovia, 20 miles west of Halibut Cove, is another commercial fishing oriented community, accessible only by charter plane or boat.

Cook Inlet is named for its discoverer, British Captain James Cook, who passed through in May of 1778 looking for the Northwest Passage. Cook continued his exploration west and north, through the Bering Strait into the Chukchi Sea, where he was blocked by the permanent ice pack. He eventually made his way to Hawaii, where he was needlessly killed in a squabble with natives. Two of Cook's officers, William Bligh and George Vancouver were to become famous in their own right, Vancouver as the Northwest Coast explorer extraordinaire, and Bligh as the captain of the *Bounty,* during the famous mutiny.

Tidal currents in Cook Inlet are especially strong, due to its funnel-like shape. In a large tide, the current in places may reach up to 8 knots. (9.8 MPH!) Also as the glacial sheet retreated centuries ago, it dropped many boulders which form hazards to mariners traveling in shallow waters. Fortunately the tide is usually so strong that these can be seen by wakes created by the current:

Homer is off the beaten track for cruise ships.

Backroads travel in winter here requires a bit more caution than in most places.

"Heavy swirls with overfalls should be avoided, and any disturbance which has a recognizable wake in the water should be avoided as indicating a dangerous rock or shoal."

—*U.S. Coast Pilot 9, Pacific and Arctic Coasts.* 1964

The current posed quite a challenge when a substantial body of oil and gas was discovered underneath the lower inlet. Drilling platforms not only had to contend with the strong current, but the ice that sometimes moved with it in winter. Platforms were developed resting on a single pillar, which reduced the chances of ice damage.

As an added precaution, powerful tugs were stationed at the rigs in the winter to push the bigger ice flows away before they could cause damage.

There is a road, along the shore on the east side of Cook Inlet which connects Homer and other communities to Anchorage. It is the first road that connects to the continental highway system, since the road stopped, about 80 miles north of Vancouver.

The town at **mile 1760CI**, is **Ninilchik**, first settled by Russians and now a fishing settlement. If you see what looks like hordes of people on the beaches in this vicinity, they might be clamming. The first good low tides of the spring (the range of the tide varies in a 28-day cycle, according to the relation of the moon and the earth) are popular with those seeking razor and other clams.

Fishing with tractors—there are many salmon fishermen operating set nets along this part of the eastern shore of the inlet. These are usually set along a beach or mud flat at low tide. As the tide comes in, it floats the

net, and any passing fish are caught. Several fishermen with several sites to tend, use tractors to pull the nets in and out.

The town to the east at **mile 1795CI** is **Kenai**, well-known for its salmon fishing and recreational activities.

The western shore of Cook Inlet is for the most part unpopulated, except for a few very small seasonal fishing settlements, and an ARCO oil facility at Drift River, opposite Kenai. The area is popular as a destination for fly-in fishing and camping.

Look carefully at the water here. As you get nearer the head of the inlet, the water becomes in places more like liquid mud which can be very damaging to salt water pumps and other machinery.

The wide bay to the east at **mile 1850CI** is Turnagain Arm. It is mostly shallow and widely covered with mud flats. At times the incoming tide rushes over these flats as a moving wall of water. In places, the surface of the exposed tide flats contains a quicksand-like mud, and in rare instances people have been trapped, and drowned by the incoming tide.

If Seward is an ice-free port, Anchorage most definately is not. There is regular freight service to this port, but at times, these vessels cannot get into the docks without the help of an icebreaker.

Russian Orthodox church in Ninilchik. The influence of this religion is widespread throughout the Kenai Peninsula and Western Alaska.

Belugas, cream colored whales, typically 12-18 feet long, are frequently seen here in summer.

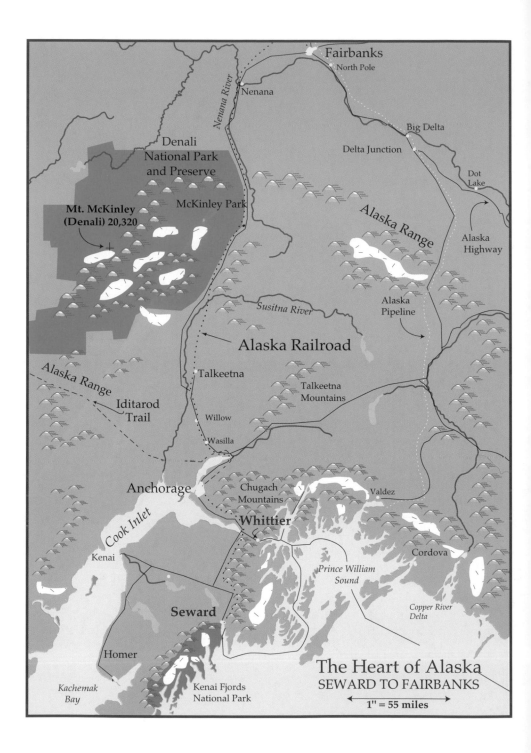

Fairbanks
North Pole
Nenana
Nenana River
Big Delta
Delta Junction
Denali
National Park
and Preserve
McKinley Park
Dot Lake
**Mt. McKinley
(Denali) 20,320**
Alaska Range
Alaska Highway
Alaska
Pipeline
Susitna River
Alaska Railroad
Alaska Range
Iditarod
Trail
Talkeetna
Talkeetna
Mountains
Willow
Wasilla
Anchorage
Chugach
Mountains
Valdez
Cordova
Whittier
Cook Inlet
Kenai
*Prince William
Sound*
Seward
*Copper River
Delta*
Homer
*Kachemak
Bay*
Kenai Fjords
National Park

The Heart of Alaska
SEWARD TO FAIRBANKS
1" = 55 miles

CHAPTER 10

The Heart of Alaska
Whittier to Fairbanks

"So off we went, the four dogs and I, to explore high mountains new to us.

"As the days went by, I wondered what the dogs got out of it. I had a supply of dried salmon on the sled, and they eagerly looked forward to their meal each evening. They loved to be in harness; as a matter of fact, as they were being hooked up in the morning, they were so happy that it was hard to handle them. The minute we were ready, off they would go in a great burst of speed."

— Olas J. Murie, *Journeys to the Far North*

The Iditarod—Today the famous dog sled race begins each year in Anchorage. But it's important to remember that the diptheria vaccine to combat the outbreak in Nome actually arrived in Seward by ship in January of 1925. From here it traveled by train to Nenana to begin the 674-mile dog sled relay through blizzard conditions to Nome.

Another big event in those days was the arrival of the dog teams that brought the heavy loads of gold from the interior to meet the southbound steamers:

"The town was stirred by the arrival of the Iditarod gold shipment...The populace stood packed about, but fully one half their interest was centered on the perfectly matched dog teams that had pulled the treasure from the banks of the Kuskokwim, four hundred miles to the northwest... Their harness was perfect from the silver bells that jangled so sweetly, to the red pom-poms that bobbed gaily on each furry back."

— Terris Moore, *Mt. McKinley, The Pioneer Climbs*

For generations, the rivers of interior Alaska were the only highways. Paddlewheelers took freight and passengers to the most remote locations. But once the rivers froze up for the winter, travel was either by dog, horse-drawn sled, or by foot. The arrival of the first paddlewheeler in the spring with the first new food supplies and mail, was always a big event.

Ice floes in Cook Inlet. Some of th e peaks in the background are active volcanoes. Cook Inlet is also a good place to look for beluga whales which often chase salmon here.

In fall or spring, look for migrating birds along this route.

Road: Whittier to Anchorage—typically around two to three hours. Almost all two-lane road, winding through a tunnel, past Portage Glacier, Turnagain Arm and many salmon streams. There is usually at least one rest stop, at a particularly scenic spot of the driver's choice.

Until 2000, to drive to Whitter, you had to put your car onto a railroad flatbed car: fun if you had the time, but not particularly convenient. Then the rail tunnel was widened to accommodate a one-mway road as well. However, in the spring of 2004, things were still a little rough—the unlined tunnel (most highway tunnels have a concrete lining) posted "Watch For Falling Rock" signs, and traffic was often delayed by tunnel closures and by the necessity of waiting for traffic in the opposite direction. And as one recent driver said: "How do you watch for falling rocks in a dark single-lane tunnel?"

Nevertheless, Whittier access is now much easier, and many Anchorage residents are enjoying Prince William Sound, perhaps for the first time.

Early travelers headed over these mountain from Whitter and Seward, had to fight the winter storms. The low passes form a highway for the powerful weather systems that march back and forth between the Arctic highs to the north, and the North Pacific lows out in the Gulf of Alaska. The power of these storms became part of the lore of The North as soon as early Alaska novels became popular reading:

"It was early in the afternoon when the Indian stopped and began testing the air; Balt also seemed suddenly to scent a change in the atmospheric conditions.

"What's wrong now?" Emerson asked, gruffly.

"Feels like wind," answered the big man with a shake of his head. The native began chattering excitedly, and as they stood there, a chill draught fanned their cheeks. Glancing upward at the hillsides, they saw that the air was now thickened as if by smoke, and, dropping their eyes, they saw the fluff between their feet stir lazily. Little wisps of snow vapor began to dance upon the ridges, whisking out of sight as suddenly as they had appeared. They became conscious of a sudden fall in the temperature, and they knew that the cold of interstellar space dwelt in that ghostly breath which smote them. Before they were well aware of the ominous significance of these signs the storm was upon them, sweeping through the chute wherein they stood with rapidly increasing violence. The terrible, unseen hand of the Frozen North had unleashed its brood of furies, and the air rang with their hideous cries. It was Dante's third circle of hell let loose - Cerberus baying through his wide, threefold throat, and the voices of tormented souls shrilling through the infernal shades... There was no question of facing the wind, for it was more cruel than the fierce breath of an open furnace, searing the naked flesh like a flame."

— Rex Beach, *The Silver Horde*

Coach stops along the road to Anchorage may include viewing salmon in streams many miles from the salt water.

Brenda Carney

Big fishing on the Kenai Peninsula. Most out of state anglers freeze or smoke their fish and have them shipped home.

The road exits the tunnel near Portage Lake and Glacier. An excellent visitor's center and its proximity to Anchorage make it one of the most visited glaciers in the state. A tour boat operates here to take visitors up to the face of the fast receding glacier.

A few miles further you'll come to Turnagain Arm, a shallow arm of the sea named by Captain Cook, for turning them around yet again in the search for the elusive Northwest Passage. Here you'll turn right to follow the shore to Anchorage.

> "**Turnagain Arm** is noted for the violent winds which blow out of it whenever the wind is easterly, and is locally referred to as the Cannon, which expresses the opinion held of it."
>
> —*U.S. Coast Pilot 9*, 1964 edition

Quicksand and Bore Tides in Turnagain Arm. Aside from the violent winds, this shallow, funnel shaped arm has a bad reputation for the combination of forces waiting for the careless traveler—deep, unstable sands and quickly rising tides. Imagine, you're out on the flats at low tide, hunting or beachcombing. An unexpectedly soft patch of sand suddenly swallows your

On the Kenai Highway - convenience stop, Alaska style.

leg up to the knee. You struggle, but can't free it. Then you hear an odd sound, like a faraway roaring, and realize it's the tide, coming up the arm, a low wall of water.

It turns out that the particular glacial silt here has a large number of triangle-shaped grains. When the right amount of liquid is present, they float loosely in suspension, but when disturbed, by a leg, for example, seem to lock together. Struggling only locks the grains tighter.

In a few particularly tragic episodes, rescue personnel arrived in time to try, without success, to extricate the victim, who quickly drowned as the tide rose.

The tides in this area are among the biggest in the world—in the larger tides up to 35 feet of water must move into this arm in the six hours between low and high. The size of the tides is governed by the relative position of moon, earth, and sun. But what happens in Turnagain Arm on these larger tides, is even more dramatic. The water actually enters as almost a wall, moving at up to 10 mph. The reason is the funnel-like shape, which concentrates the water flow, similar to the way it does in the Bay of Fundy.

*Close to Anchorage,
Portage Glacier is a
popular attraction.*

*Small craft opera-
tors and travelers on
beaches and mud
flats should exercise
particular care here
due to powerful tides
and areas of quick-
sand.*

Look for beluga whales chasing salmon here.
Belugas, white, or cream-colored, (young may be gray)
are a toothed whale, typically 15' - 18' in length. They
seldom travel much farther south than Cook Inlet on
the Pacific Coast, and especially seem to like the shallow rivers in western and northern Alaska. It is not at
all uncommon to find these whales almost nudging the
riverbank in just four or five feet of water, miles upriver.
They are popular with aquariums as they are particularly vocal, and early sailors nicknamed them sea canaries,
after hearing their many sounds through the hulls of
their ships.

The volcanoes across Cook Inlet—you'll glimpse
three of the region's active volcanoes as you travel
along. Minor eruptions are a regular part of contemporary Alaskan life.

Most recently, in 1992, the tallest at 11,070', **Mt.
Spurr**, erupted, disrupting air travel, and covering a
wide, but mostly uninhabited area, with fine ash. When
the wind changed direction and brought the ash to
Anchorage, the local remedy for keeping car engines
running was a homemade filter of ladies' panty hose
wrapped around the air cleaner. The ring of fire continues out along the Alaska peninsula, where **Mt.
Aniakchak** continues to vent steam through its year-
round snow cover and others like **Mt. Pavlof** and **Mt.**

Shishalden occasionally cough up steam and hot ash.

Sometimes fishermen working after dark on the Bering Sea would be startled by the fireworks of one of the many volcanoes throwing up a few tons of ash and cinders in a show that filled the sky.

While most recent Alaska eruptions are of the "throat clearing" variety—fireworks and a bit of ash, the 1912 Mt. Katmai blast was more along the lines of a nuclear bomb. The explosion was heard in Juneau, 750 miles away and sulphuric fumes drifted all the way to Vancouver, B.C.

In Kodiak, the ash fall was so heavy that houses collapsed, and much of the town's population took shelter in a Coast Guard cutter. For two days there was no sun and only constant lightning pierced the black clouds.

It was to be almost three years before anyone ventured into the area of the volcano. When the first visitors arrived in the Katmai area, they found a desolate moonscape with so many smoking fumaroles that they named the area **The Valley of 10,000 Smokes.** Today just a few of the fumaroles are still active and the area is known more for its bears.

Little visited, seldom climbed, lonely Aniakchak volcano rises from the tundra west of Ugashik Village, on the Alaska Peninsula. Note steam vent on left slope. Also if you look sharply, there is a bald eagle over the left-hand building.

The Bears at Katmai

Waiting for that perfect fish. The bears don't catch the jumping fish with their paws, but actually grab it out of the air with their mouths!

At the peak of the run, some 200-300 fish a minute are leaping these falls, so the bears have a pretty good chance.

The Valley of 10,000 Smokes is pretty quiet these days (most of the old fumaroles have stopped smoking), but this "size-of-Rhode-Island" national park is well known for another feature: the bears.

If you are near this part of Alaska (Katmai is about 250 miles west of Anchorage) in late June or July, and want to see bears, up close and personal, this is the spot.

For the bears, the attraction is the salmon. The park encompasses several major salmon-producing lakes, and in spawning season, the streams that feed them are full of literally hundreds of thousands of fish.

The visitor center is at Brooks Lodge, built in the 1930s as a sportsfishing camp. Today it is a classic Alaska lodge, with individual log cabins overlooking the lake and the mountains.

I flew in there in July of 1997, with my son, and some friends, after just finishing our commercial salmon fishing season in Bristol Bay, 80 miles to the west.

The only way in is by floatplane; it pulls up to the beach, and you walk up to a small log cabin that is both the park headquarters and gift shop. Our group crowded in to watch the "Bear Etiquettte Video" a short presentation on how to avoid those unpleasant one-on-ones with bears.

As we were watching there was a clatter outside, and we looked out to see a brown bear about the size of a Volkswagon, rattling the bolted-down, bear-proof trash cans.

As we walked the paths to the viewing platforms, we were accompanied by a walkie-talkie-equipped park ranger, who was monitoring bear movements. Several times on the way to the viewing stand at the falls on the Brooks River, we had to move off the trail to let bears pass. (They have right of way!)

Then we got to where we could see the falls through the trees, and my feet stopped walking. There, in plain sight were at least six very large brown bears, intent on the business of catching the fish that were leaping up the four-foot falls, oblivious to us humans.

Several viewing stands afford an excellent opportunity to watch and photograph the bears. This is not for the squeamish as sometimes the bears are literally rubbing on the posts that support the elevated platforms.

We climbed the ramp to the viewing platform, our guide latching the gate behind us. In front, arrayed across the falls, and in the stream below were the bears, wading, chasing fish in the pools, snatching them out of the air as they leaped the falls.

In a tree, just twenty yards from the platform, were two 100-lb. bear cubs. When they got bored and began climbing down, their mother would amble quickly over from the stream and indicate to them in no uncertain terms that they were to remain where they were.

When a bear got a fish, it would walk into the shallows, hold the fish down with one paw, and neatly strip off a fillet with the other, flip the fish and do it again—an impressive performance.

The park ranger said there hadn't been a bear incident in 12 years, but we forgot to ask what the park's definition of an incident was—did you have to get stitches, or would a few scrapes and bruises do it?

Orca whale mural on J.C. Penny building, Anchorage

Anchorage - Downtown Alaska

The old saying, "You can see Alaska from here," basically describes the relationship of Anchorage and the rest of the state. While some 40% of the entire state's population resides in the greater Anchorage area, it's a good bet a lot of them blast out of town each weekend, judging from the number of planes, campers, snowmobiles, 4-wheelers, kayaks, etc., in the back yards all around town. Don't be surprised to see a moose meandering around town, though wandering bears are also regularly seen.

The eight-mile-long, paved Tony Knowles Coastal Trail, starting at the end of 2nd Avenue, is a great walk, and an opportunity to watch shore birds.

Though Anchorage overlooks **Cook Inlet** and **Knik Arm**, it's hardly a waterfront town in the mold of Ketchikan or Juneau. There's no place for boats to tie up downtown—the rivers draining into the inlet bring a big silt load and there are extensive tide flats making it difficult to even get to the water in most places. Most marine activity is centered in Ship Creek, north of town.

The newest and shiniest high-rise office buildings usually belong to Big Oil in this town. The revenue from this industry basically redefined Alaska economics, and gave its citizens the unique distinction of getting the only state dividend checks in the country. Farsighted leadership in the early days of the oil boom established a large and so far untouched "Permanent Fund" which yields enough income for checks typically in the $1,000 (U.S.)range annually for each of Alaska's citizens.

Cheating on the Permanent Fund. There's a lot of

P.O. Box addresses in a state as rural as Alaska. There are also a lot of people who like to get that check, regardless if they qualify as a resident or not (Alaska's residency definition is pretty strict). Fish and Wildlife Protection officers (game wardens) who enforce the state's many fishing and hunting regulations, and other law officers, are usually alert to ID's with post office box addresses:

Downtown Resolution Park with a statue of Captain Cook offers a view of the inlet and a fitting tribute to this remarkable and courageous explorer.

"We were way back up the Koyukuk, fishing, and this fish cop appears out of nowhere in his boat and asks to see our licenses and our photo ID, I mean, that's lonely country up there—we hadn't seen anyone for days...

"So anyway, when he asks for my photo ID, I gave him my Alaska driver's license. He checks it out, then says, 'Hey, pal, this here says you live in King Salmon. Well, I've lived in King Salmon for the last 10 years. How come I've never seen you?' I finally had to admit I spend most of the year in Idaho.

"Damn. I had to go to court, and got fined a thousand bucks for falsifying a residency and another hundred bucks for not having a fishing license...and way up the Koyukuk."

— A sportsfisherman

Belugas and orca whales are occasionally seen right in front of town.

Take a few minutes and walk to the **Captain Cook Memorial**, overlooking the water at the end of 3rd Ave. You can get a clear sense of the very different shoreline below, but also it's an opportunity to reflect on the many unusual deeds of this English sailor, who charted much of the vast reaches of the Pacific Ocean.

UW 14501

When the earth shook: Some sections of town were so shattered that survivors could only be reached by helicopter.

Good Friday, 1964—Most folks were just settling down to supper when the most powerful earthquake to hit North America this century struck. Anchorage was mostly built on unstable clay, which is particularly susceptible to movement in an earthquake. So move it did—splitting apart, dropping whole blocks and tumbling expensive waterfront homes down steep bluffs. Within minutes, much of the downtown core was a ruin of fallen storefronts, crumpled streets, and shattered businesses.

Property damage was extremely heavy, but fortunately only nine people died.

Shopping—if your cruise is over and you haven't done all of your shopping, it's all here in downtown. Take an evening to explore these shops and especially the galleries of native arts and crafts. There are pieces here that would be hard to find anywhere outside Alaska.

Galleries and other notable places—**Alaska Center for the Performing Arts**, 6th & F; **Wolf Song of Alaska**, inside J.C. Penny Mall, 6th & E; **Reeve Aviation Picture Museum**, 343 W. 6th; and **Anchorage Museum of History & Art**, 121 W. 7th.

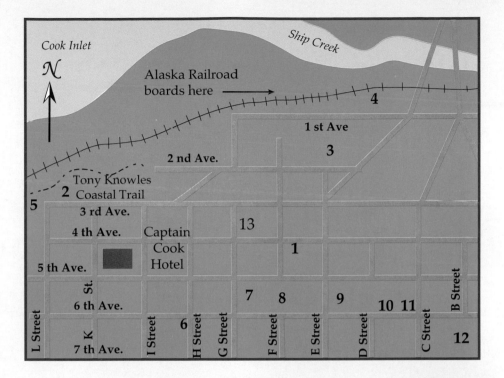

Downtown Anchorage

1. Log Cabin and Visitor Information Center
2. Tony Knowles Coastal Trail - ten mile trail that follows the shore with great views.
3. Alaska Statehood Monument
4. Alaska Railroad Depot
5. Resolution Park with Captain Cook Monument
6. Oomingmak Musk-ox Producers Co-Op— unique garments from strange creatures.
7. Alaska Center for the Performing Arts
8. Town Square Municipal Park
9. Reeve Aviation Picture Museum
10. Alaska State Trooper Museum
11. Wolf Song of Alaska - large wolf exhibit.
12. Anchorage Museum of History and Art— excellent collection; gift shop and cafe.
13. Alaska Public Lands Information Center

Be sure to save some time for the shops and galleries here.

UW 17956

Surveyor returns to camp, Turnagain Arm, circa 1920. Building the Alaska Railroad was hard, cold, and dangerous work.

"**Anchorage, September 14, 1997, 7:45** A.M.: Our train sits waiting on a siding, near the water. The other passengers board quickly, their breath white in the chill morning air, but I stand aside, let the bus leave, to take in the surroundings. The days get shorter quickly in the fall this far north and the sun is still behind the Chugach Mountains to the east, yet just illuminating the volcanoes along the snowy wall of the Alaska Range, across Cook Inlet. The shiny sides of the coaches are yellow and pink, reflecting the sky, while all around is almost dark. Here and there along the waiting train, steamy air vents from beneath the coaches, cloaking all in a mysterious otherworld feeling. The last whistle finally blows, and I have to board. Yet I linger until the very last, unwilling to leave the drama of this moment."

The Alaska Railroad

This route is one of the most scenic in North America.

The engines and cars all came by barge, from "outside;" there's no connection to any Canadian railroad, no way to get to the rest of the United States by rail—there's just too much rugged territory in between. Begun in 1915, it was finished after much difficulty in 1923.

Until just 20 years ago, when the George Parks Highway north to Fairbanks was completed, the train was the only transportation there was for the folks along much of the Anchorage - Fairbanks corridor.

Whistle stops were an everyday part of train life as the "local" trains dropped homesteaders off with their bags and boxes of groceries and supplies, often at trail heads where horses or four-wheel-drive vehicles waited to take them down some lonely dirt track to a remote home. Since the road was completed, the railway is strictly freight for seven months out of the year.

But every spring the passenger specials begin, with the domed cars that make it one of the most scenic rail rides in North America. Each day there is a northbound and a southbound passenger run. These trains generally have three different kinds of domed cars. The Alaska Railroad domed cars are essentially the Vistadome cars still seen on some routes through the United States west today—only part of the car has a dome, and passengers either pay extra or rotate through the domed section. Several cruise lines have had special railcars constructed for their passengers. These dome cars are usually a modification of dome cars used by railroads in the US western states. The domed section is usually made longer along with other improvements. Recently a few totally brand new cars have appeared, having been built from the ground up specifically to cruise line specifications. These would include gift shops and other passenger amenities.

However you travel, these dome cars provide a wonderful opportunity to experience this dramatic country.

Just north of Anchorage, the train passes just east of the runways of **Elmendorf Air Force Base**, essentially a self-contained town with its own schools, shops, etc.

In the stillness of a September morning, dome cars wait for their northbound travelers. A number of cruise lines have their own custom built train cars that are travel this route along with Alaska Railroad cars.

You might get a close-up view of F-15 fighters as you pass the Air Force base. Although showing their age, they can still climb vertically, and accelerate at the same time with their afterburners lit.

Shortly after passing Elmendorf, you will be transiting an area of marsh and lakes around the delta of the Knik River. This whole area is part of the Northern Flyway, the route that hundreds of thousands, perhaps even millions, of birds and waterfowl travel each spring and fall in their annual migrations.

Some of these birds, like the Arctic Tern (see drawing on right) make truly remarkable migrations. Sometimes called the migration champion of the world, each year they summer along the shores of the North Pacific and Bering Sea, where they breed and hatch their young. Then in late August, they and their young start flying south - and keep going. down the British Columbia coast to Washington and California, along the Central and South American coasts, to wait in the Cape Horn area to wait for good weather conditions for the last leg - across hundreds of miles of the stormy Drake Passage to the Antarctic Peninsula. When the southern hemisphere fall begins, they head north, 8,000 miles or so, back to Alaska, Greenland, and northern Canada.

The red-necked Phalarope is common on lakes and marshes here.

The number of birds involved in these annual migrations is stunning. When I was a crewman on a king crab boat in the spring of 1971, we would often anchor in the bays on the north side of the Alaske Peninsula. At the head of the bays, valleys ran back to low mountain passes that connected to the North Pacific side of the peninsula. On some mornings we would look out in awe as a dark cloud of birds would be flowing down from the passes, out low onto the water,

directly for us, dividing at our bow, rejoining behind our stern, hundreds of thousands of birds, driven by the mysterious power of their annual migration to the vast complex of lakes and marshes around the mouth of the Yukon River.

I've had fishermen tell me about coming upon waiting flocks on the Alsek River flats in the fall. Thousands of ducks and terns, just laying in the rippled sloughs, waiting for weather. Then when a morning came still, or with a breeze out of the north, they'd be off the water at very first light, some wheeling east, to follow the Alsek and the Tahshensheni through that icy wall of the Fairweather Range, and then south through the interior valleys. But others headed southeast, down the outside coast, following the shore towards Cape Spencer. And I remembered our own struggles to get south in our little boats. Traveling when we could, sometimes just harbor to harbor, two days of waiting for one of traveling, a long month of it from Skagway to Seattle. In some ways, I suppose we weren't that different from these birds, waiting, waiting, for weather.

Truly remarkable travelers, the Arctic Tern (black cap, red bill and feet, with a long, forked tail) summers in Alaska then takes off each fall for a 10,000 mile journey to winter in the Antarctic. You might see them in the Knik marshes.

The Matanuska Valley Experiment

During the Great Depression, 202 families were chosen from the distressed northern Midwest, and brought by the federal government to found an agricultural colony and begin a new life in the rich bottomland of the Matanuska River valley, northeast of **mile 150**.

It didn't work out as the planners had hoped. The first summer was unusually wet; many children grew sick; the soil quality was uneven. The sizes of the plots

weren't really big enough from which to make a living. Some families gave it up, but the remainder stayed, fighting the challenges of high latitude farming. Today the valley farmland is a natural target for developers creating more suburbs for Anchorage commuters; but the long hours of summer daylight still produce some spectacularly large vegetables, most notably the legendary 90-pound cabbages.

They grow them big up North – cabbages at Fairbanks.

UW UW13591

Racing sled dog team, circa 1920. Does it sometimes seem there are two Alaskas— Southeast and the vast interior? It does so to many Alaskans who want to have the capital moved closer to the Anchorage Fairbanks corridor.

"Fer Cris'sake, all it would take is for one of those Alaska Airlines jets to cream into Mt. Juneau and it'd take the the whole legislature with it..."
— Heard around Alaska

Now that you've taken the cruise, seen Southeast Alaska and steamed up the wild and lonely coast to Seward, doesn't it seem a bit like there are two Alaskas? The drizzly, grey one down there with Ketchikan and Juneau, and the wide open one up here with Anchorage, Fairbanks and the whole really, really, big rest of the state? And doesn't it seem just a little odd that the capital, Juneau, is way down there, and well, really isolated from the whole rest of the state?

Don't think that this same thought hasn't occurred to many Alaskans. In the 1970s when the state was flush with oil revenues—just the oil lease sale, in 1969, eight years before a drop of oil flowed down the pipeline, brought in 900 million dollars— "Move The Capital" was a bumper sticker seen all over the state.

The only problem was where to move it. In true Alaska fashion, Anchorage and Fairbanks were such rivals that neither would accept the other as capital. So why not pick some centrally located spot in between, and make that the capital? Brillant! So, in 1976, Alaskans voted to build a new capital near Willow, mile 185.7. So where is it, you say? Cooler heads prevailed a few years later, when the first cost estimates came out, and the capital remained in Juneau.

Now and again, through the trees, you'll glimpse a road, the George Parks Highway, just to the west, or left of the train. Between this highway and the Bering Sea coast, 500 miles to the west, there are no roads. (Well, O.K., there are a few exceptions—the 20 miles of

bumpy pavement between Naknek and King Salmon, on Bristol Bay, a few miles around Dillingham and a few more around Nome. But, basically it's pretty lonely out there.)

This is an airport? Sometimes vast seems an inadequate word to describe the interior of Alaska.

The forest here is known as taiga, very different from that of Prince William Sound and Southeast Alaska. Gone are the tall hemlocks and cedars, replaced by low white and black spruce, poplar, birch, aspen and larch. Where the trees seem particularly stunted is a sign of either wet muskeg or frozen permafrost close to the surface.

Sometimes the train slows near mile 224, to let travelers get a good view of the Alaska range across the Susitna River: Denali at 20,320', and her lower sisters, Mt. Hunter, 14,573', and Mt. Foraker, 17,400'.

The Susitna is normally placid, but about 65 miles northeast of here the river turns violent in a five-mile rapids named Devil's Canyon. It was here in August of 1955, that one of the more remarkable feats of Alaska flying took place.

Get ready for a glimpse of Denali and the Alaska range near mile 224.

Talkeetna pilot Don Sheldon saw the wreckage of a U.S. Army survey boat in the canyon on a charter flight to a nearby lake, and upon returning, spotted survivors huddling on the rocky shore with almost no way out, unless he could somehow land in the river canyon. The rapids in the river created 6-foot waves—certain death to land on, but after a couple of passes through, Sheldon found a little strip of calmer water, just above the survivors, where he thought it might just be possible to land. Sheldon made his approach, swallowed hard, and set his little Aeronica down. Once he was in the water, he had to let the river carry him backwards, into the rapids, for him to get to where the survivors were:

Land a floatplane here? In a true feat of bush flying, Talkeetna pilot Don Sheldon landed in the rapids in a river canyon to save a surverying party whose boat had been destroyed by the rocks and churning white water.

"As the plane backed into the first of the combers, I felt it lurch heavily fore and aft. It was like a damned roller coaster. The water was rolling up higher than my wingtips, beating at the struts, and I could barely see because of the spray and water on the windows. All of a sudden the engine began to sputter and choke, and I knew it was getting wet down pretty good..."

—Don Sheldon, in *Wager With the Wind*, by James Greiner

Somehow the engine kept going, and Sheldon managed to maneuver close enough to shore for one of the men to clamber aboard. Getting out was almost as hard—backing the plane down the rapids, until he came to another stretch just barely long enough to effect a take-off. Sheldon had to repeat this remarkable performance three more times to get all the surviviors out.

Look for the little airstrip, through the trees to the east at Talkeetna. This village is the staging area for almost all expeditions to the top of Denali, and for most it begins with a flight to Kahiltna Glacier at 7,000', where base camp is established and the climbing begins.

Denali

Early explorers sometimes got a glimpse of a very high mountain to the north of Cook Inlet, a peak the natives of the region called Denali, which meant "The High One." An early prospector named it Mt. McKinley, but most Alaskans today refer to it as simply Denali.

At 20,320, it is the tallest peak in North America. If this mountain were in California, or perhaps Peru, it would be a world class climb, but it wouldn't have the particular challenges that come with its high latitude.

The Alaska Range is a wall between Yukon - Arctic highs and North Pacific lows. The result is a highly volatile microclimate, and a mountain that can basically create its own weather very rapidly. Most climbing fatalities here are caused by rapid weather changes, combining wind, cold, and snow.

Denali on the right and Mt. Foraker on the left. In the foreground is the Susitna River.

I was lucky to have gotten a clear view of the mountain, for as most residents of this region can tell you, Denali often hides itself in clouds.

"On the northern side of the range there was not one cloud; the icy mountains blended into the rolling foothills, which in turn melted away into the dim blue of the timbered lowlands, that rolled away to the north, growing bluer and bluer until they were lost at the edge of the world. On the humid south side, a sea of clouds was rolling against the main range like surf on a rocky shore."
—Belmore Browne, *Conquest of Mt. McKinley*

Voices from Denali

Alfred Lindley and Harry Liek, after their successful ascent of Denali, May 1932. On their way down the mountain they encountered tragedy—two members of a scientific expedition had fallen to their death in the treacherous crevasses.

"...The storm now became so severe that I was actually afraid to get new dry mittens out of my rucksack, for I knew my hands would be frozen in the process... The last period of our climb is like the memory of an evil dream. La Voy was completely lost in the ice mist, and Professor Parker's frosted form was an indistinct blur above me... The breath was driven from my body and I held to my axe with stooped shoulders to stand against the gale; I couldn't go ahead. As I brushed the frost from my glasses and squinted upward through the stinging snow, I saw a sight that will haunt me to my dying day. The slope above me was no longer steep! That was all I could see. What it meant I will never know for certain—all I can say is that we were close to the top."

— Belmore Browne, *The Conquest of Mt. McKinley*

"I was snowshoeing along about fifty feet back of the sled, with Harry (Liek) right behind me when, without warning, the snow fell away under my snowshoes. I plunged into sudden darkness.

I had time to let out a feeble shout. Then for a couple of long, long seconds I plummeted downward. I remember thinking, 'This is it, fellow!' Then my pack scraped against the slide of the crevasse, my head banged hard against the ice wall and I came to a jarring stop.

When my head cleared and I could look around in the blue darkness, I saw I was on a plug of snow wedged between the ice walls. On either side, this wedge of snow fell away into sheer blackness.

About forty feet above me I could see a ray of sunlight, slanting through the hole I had made in the surface crust. The crevasse was about twelve feet wide up there, it narrowed to two feet down where I was. Below was icy death."

— Grant Pearson, *My Life of High Adventure*

Climber Emilio Gunther towing a sled with extra supplies.

"But in half an hour, we stood on the narrow edge of the spur top, facing failure. Here, where the black ridge leading to the tops of the pink cliffs should have flattened, all was absolutely sheer, and a hanging glacier, bearded and dripping with bergschrunds, filled the angle in between...I heard Fred say, 'It ain't that we can't find a way that's possible, taking chances. There ain't *no* way.'

"We were checkmated with steepness, at 11,300 feet with eight days of mountain food on our hands. But remember this: also with scarce two weeks provisions below with which to reach the coast and winter coming. The foolishness of the situation, and the fascination, lies in the fact that except in this fair weather, unknown in Alaska at this season, we might have perished either night in those two exposed camps."

— Robert Dunn, *Shameless Diary of an Explorer*

Climber Belmore Browne made three attempts on Denali, but was defeated each time.

"We tried to take some snaps, but had to give it up. For four minutes only did I leave my mittens off, and in that time, I froze five tips of my fingers to such a degree that after they had first been white, some weeks later, they turned black, and at last fell off, with the nails and all.."

Erling Strom, *How We Climbed Mt. McKinley*

"... My mind was racing. I had to grab the rock near Dave with my left hand; it was bare, no mitten or sock. It would be frozen. I had to. Suddenly my bare hand shot out to grab the rock. Slicing cold.

I saw Dave's face, the end of his nose raw, frostbitten. His mouth, distorted into an agonized mixture of compassion and anger, swore at me to get a glove on. I looked at my hand. It was white, frozen absolutely white."

— Art Davidson, *Minus 148 Degrees, The Winter Ascent of Mt. McKinley*

On Denali, 1932. When we look at all the high tech equipment today's climbers consider essential, our respect for the feats of the pioneer climbers grows.

Many climbing parties have had the bitter experience of getting close to the top, only to be turned back, sometimes just a few hundred yards short of the summit by wind and cold. Experienced Denali climbers know that they can only get near the top and hope that the mountain gods will allow them to tread on the top of the continent.

The Pioneer Climbers—for the first climbers, in the early 1900s, just getting to where they could start their climb was an immense task in itself. The 1912 Browne - Parker expedition left Seward on February 1, with dog teams, and took almost five months to reach within a few hundred feet of the summit, only to be turned around by weather on two different days. When they finally gave it up, and turned to leave that desolate spot, their last memory was of the continual roar of wind from the summit somewhere in the clouds above them.

An Imposter's Claim—One of the oddest episodes in Denali's history was the 1906 claim by Dr. Frederick Cook, a very experienced Arctic explorer, that he and a companion had made it to the top of the mountain, the first to do so, bringing down photographs for proof. Climbers familiar with the mountain doubted Cook's claims, but it wasn't until 1910 that a group, specifically climbing to dispute Cook, found the supposed summit photographed by Cook: 10,000 feet lower and 20 miles away from the actual summit.

First to the Top—In 1910, a group of hardy Alaskan prospectors, tired of the the controversy stirred by Cook's claims, decided to prove that Alaskans could do the job. This was the so-called "Sourdough Expedition." They reached the top of the North Peak, (actually the South peak was slightly higher but they didn't realize it at the time) put up a 14' pole and flag, and then went back down, and got back to prospecting!

Of course, many folks doubted their claim (until another expedition, years later, saw the pole) and the credit for being the first to climb McKinley went to Alaskans Hudson Stuck, Harry Karstens, and their party in 1913. They were fortunate in having a window of clear and relatively calm, though bitterly cold, weather at the top:

> "There was no pride of conquest, no trace of that exultation of victory some enjoy over the first ascent of a lofty peak, no gloating over good fortune that had hoisted us a few hundred feet higher than others who had struggled and been discomfited. Rather...that a privileged communion with the high places of the earth had been granted... secret and solitary since the world began. All the way down, unconscious of weariness in the descent, my thoughts were occupied with the glorious scene my eyes gazed upon, and should gaze upon never again."
> — Hudson Stuck, in *Mt. McKinley: The Pioneer Climbs,* Terris Moore

Leaves, Mt. McKinley National Park, 1997

Denali today—The mountain has become a very popular climb, sought each summer by expeditions from all over the world.

However today's climbers face a much easier prospect than the early climbers. Instead of starting on the ground near Talkeetna, and struggling for several days before they even got to the top of the first glaicer, they hop a plane from the Talkeetna airstrip and get dropped off at the base camp at Kahiltna Glacier at

7,000 feet. In a typical summer literally hundreds of climbers try to find a break in the weather and make it to the top so, this base camp is a busy place, with a ranger station, aircraft, and climbing parties coming and going. How very, very different from the rigors faced by the mountain's true pioneers!

For the Talkeetna folks more interested in a subsistence lifestyle

Don't surprise bears, don't run from a bear (but walking backwards rapidly is OK!), and being careful with food are rules in bear country.

than catering to the needs of the climbers and summer visitors there are some gold claims back in the hills. The combination of semi-wilderness living and gold mining for those cash needs allows them to have a satisfying version of the Alaska dream many came to the state seeking.

But as Alaska grows, and the pressure on state and federal parks mounts, even these remote folks aren't immune from its impacts. Presently state agencies are considering this area for an entrance to Denali State Park, setting up the classic battle of old timers vs. developers.

Trumpeter Swans—the bus driver's tale:

"...I live on a lake, back off the road a bit, just two other cabins on the whole lake. There's always been a pair of trumpeter swans there, each summer as long as I can remember. They mate for life, and they're sort of solitary, so usually you'll just get one pair on a lake.

"But for the last couple of days there's just been one swan out there, honking like crazy. So finally this morning, I went out to where they nest, and found wolf tracks and a bunch of feathers..."

Rules for Bear Country

Brown, or grizzly (or just 'griz'), as well as black bear are common throughout this part of Alaska. While for the most part bears are content to mind their own business, visitors should remember a few rules. First, let bears know you're around by talking, singing, wearing bells, etc. when you hike though the woods or wherever visbility is reduced. If a bear knows you're coming, he'll probably want to get out of your way. If however, you surprise one on narrow trail, it could get ugly, for you.

Don't get between a mother and her cubs, or a bear and its food. Sometimes people have been mauled when they inadvertently got between a mother and cub, without knowing it, in thick bushes.

Don't run—it could trigger an automatic, "chase food" reaction. Bears may look big and lumbering, but when they want to do so, they can accelerate faster than a man ever could.

Be careful where you put your food. Problems have sometimes arisen from campers carelessly leaving food out or stored near or in their tent or vehicle. Put your food in a container, away from your tent.

Don't count on stopping a bear with a handgun. In a well-known tale, a particularly large marauding bear terrified natives until they got the local priest to bless and sprinkle holy water over their bullets, finally downing the monster with a lucky shot to the eye. When they skinned him they counted 32 bullet holes in the hide from the bear's adventures over the years.

Bear Country - with berries on shore and salmon in the streams, many rivers and streams in western Alaska are prime territory for brown bears.

The cry of a loon is a particularly haunting sound. Young loons are sometimes carried on their parent's backs while swimming.

These aren't your regular trash cans. At many places in bear country, trash cans are of heavy steel, and bolted to the ground. If you hear a loud banging it's probably just a frustrated bear.

"September 14, 1997: I stayed at a big new lodge high on the hills above Talkeetna, and took mule ride tonight with a friend. Our "mule skinner" was a rough-hewn fellow, and as we meandered through the hills behind the lodge, he spoke of his years of experience hunting and trapping in the bush. He promised a Denali view we wouldn't forget, and he was right.

But for the dimmest color in the aspens, the low country was dark when we came to the view point. The sun was way off to the west, and its low slanting light putting all the valleys and low places in shadow. But we could make out Ruth and Tokositna Glaciers, Avalanche Spire, Windy Corner and Karsten's Ridge, all those places that had brought so much difficulty and heartbreak to climbers.

Beyond, and high above, a long snow-capped ridge, touched pink at the top with the sun's rays, rising to a marked high peak at its north end, was Denali, looking like the top of the continent that it was. We dismounted, set up a tripod to catch the moment, and then it was time to go, for the night was coming swiftly.

But on the way down, the mountain was always there, pink, in the fading light, above the trees. And I was reminded of the journals of the early travelers to Tibet and Nepal. Of how wherever they were, Everest was always there, seeming to loom over them."

"September 15, 1997: Up at first light, to climb just a half mile, to a high clearing. The sun had yet to crest Curry Ridge behind me, but like the night before, shone full and pink on the long snow covered ridge that was Denali, and only a long winding mist cloud showed where the Chulitna River threaded through the forest below the lodge.

"In the early afternoon, took kayaking excursion to Byers Lake. I've been around the water for decades, but in larger, powered craft. This business of sliding along, effortlessly, barely disturbing the water was an unexpected treat. There were just three of us, the lake glassy still, and now and again the haunting cry of the loon and the trumpeter swan. The magic of the afternoon was tangible; we spoke little, prefering to glide along the shore, on water as transparent as air. Near the lake's outlet, a school of sockeye salmon rippled the water, their bodies brillant red against the mottled browns and greens of the bottom. And there were Denali and her sisters, rising from the forest of yellow alder and dark larch and spruce, to reflect across the stillness.

"Lingered after dinner, with friends, the big fire to our backs and the last pink light on The High One out the tall windows to the west. We stayed until late, but when it was time to go, we went out to the wide deck for one last time, and there they were—splayed across the sky above the Alaska Range—the northern lights: pale greens and yellows, a boldly moving and changing pattern.

"There are some things you can only remember—pictures can't truly show, words can't fully describe, and this was one."

Caribou, like moose, are large members of the deer family. Both males and females have antlers. Caribou are much more likely to be found in groups than the more solitary moose.

North of Talkeetna, the railway follows the Susitna River to Gold Creek, then cuts north, through Chulitna Pass, along Summit Lake, and comes in to parallel the George Parks Highway again near **mile 280.** Look for the 918' Hurricane Gulch Bridge, at **mile 284.**

Low and treeless **Broad Pass** at **mile 304** was the major north and south route through these mountains long before roads or trains. Look for little cabins along the lake—they're shelters for stranded travelers and pilots.

The **Continental Divide** crosses Broad Pass somewhere in the Summit Lake area, near **mile 312**. This is a significant geographic locale—streams a hundred yards south drain eventually into Cook Inlet, near Anchorage, 140 miles south. But just a hundred yards north the streams drain into the Nenana River, that empties into the Tanana, which, many miles later, flows into the mighty Yukon, to flow to the Bering Sea, 800 miles away.

By the time you hit the Nenana River at around **mile 328**, there's enough slope to get the water moving pretty fast.

Denali National Park

The park was orginally established in 1917 as Mt. McKinley National Park, a wildlife preserve that didn't include the mountain for which it is named. Finally in 1980, the protected area was tripled in size, to include the entire mountain massif along with caribou herd winter range and calving grounds, and renamed Denali National Park and Preserve.

Travelers expecting the wide range of visitor services available in many "Lower 48" national parks might be disappointed here. For the park's true grandeur lies in its being, as much as is possible with the limited visitor access, an intact subarctic ecosystem. For many, Denali Park is experienced in a bus with a naturalist/driver. For others, a visit might include camping at Wonder Lake, with backpacking through the wilderness.

Beavers cut and dragged these logs to create a pond—a short walk across the river from the several lodges at the entrance to Denali National Park.

"...**Important Bear Notice** —now before we get out of the bus and walk around, listen up for some bear etiquette. If we should happen to encounter a bear in our little walk, the first thing you do is circle up and surround the bus driver."

—Heard on a Denali Park tour bus

"**In the bus, Denali National Park, Sept 17, 1997**: We didn't have to wait very long to see wildlife; just five minutes after entering the park, we stopped to watch two very big, brown, and somewhat dishelveled-looking moose wandering through the low bushes perhaps 25 yards from the bus. Big is the operative word here. Everyone is concerned about bears, but I wouldn't want to meet a moose face-to-face on a narrow trail either.

A little later our sharp-eyed driver pulled over again and directed our attention to a place on the hillside where something brown could be seen moving. This was nature in the raw—you needed binoculars to see it, but a big 'griz' was chowing down on what looked like a side of Dall sheep.

The next stop was a ranger's log cabin, and a presentation of winter life in the park, when rangers depend on dog teams for travel. (Motorized travel is restricted in much of the park during the winter.)

The bus continued, skirting the south side of Primrose Ridge, and a wide valley drained by the Savage River.

Here was no Yosemite Half Dome, Old Faithful, or yawning chasm of the Cororado River. But rather a stark, Arctic, almost otherworldly landscape, in which we humans felt

Crossing the Nenana River during a northbound trip on the Alaska Railroad, Sept 17, 1997

very much like only visitors.

Our turnaround was an overlook with a view across to the already wintry looking Alaska range. There was coffee and home made banana cake from the back of the bus. On the ride back, our driver spoke of his past, growing up in rural Oregon, and his Alaska dream—of coming North to share, in some way, his strong naturalist interests and abilities. His commitment to this land and to the Park's values were very evident; one felt fortunate to have him as guide."

The Seventy-Mile Kid: When the park was created in 1917, it was entirely fitting that Harry Karstens, known as the 'Seventy-Mile Kid,' was the first superintendant. Barely 19 when he came north with the Klondike Gold Rush, he got his nickname after he and a buddy pulled a dogsled themselves on a 40-day trip back into the Seventy-Mile River country of the upper Yukon. A few years later he got the 900-mile dog sled mail run contract from Gakona on the Copper River to Fort Gibbons on the Yukon, through the unmapped Alaska interior. His bitterly cold trips along this route became an Alaska legend.

"**Denali National Park, Sept. 17, 1997**, evening: the Nenana rushes by in the canyon below; across it the aspens are all bright orange, and the upper slopes dusted with snow. I feel the shadow of those who struggled in the high country beyond the ridge. Belmont Browne and his group—five months of hard traveling, only to be turned back just a few hundred yards from the top. Art Davidson and his

friends—caught in a 130 mph blow, in winter, out in the open, at 18,000 feet, chipping out a cave in the ice and managing to survive. And the many who didn't make it, swallowed up by the sea of crevasses, or simply disappeared. One feels humbled."

"**Waiting for the Alaska Railroad, Sept 17, 1997:** Our breath is white before us, whipped away quickly by the wind. We stand wrapped in coats, the last leaves, orange and yellow whirling around us. Fall is but a few short weeks in the Alaska Range; the heavy snows are waiting. Then the long mournful horn echoes from the hills across the river and the Northbound pulls into the station. Glad to get in, out of the cold, get a hot "Mt. McKinley" coffee and Yukon Jack liqueur—and just sit, watching the landscape flow past.

"The silty Nenana boils and rushes through the canyon below us. I imagine the little mining camps back in the draws, the men working all winter, to dig out the frozen earth, and pile it to wait for the spring thaw, when they can process the ore in the sluice boxes. The weather warms and the water begins to flow down through the riffles in the sluices, lifting away the dirt, until only the gold remains. Finally the gold is in the pokes (small canvas bags) and the men pack to go to town, drag the boats down to the shore, and slide into the current, to let the bucking Nenana take them to Tanana, or Fairbanks, with money to spend, maybe even a trip "outside" before winter."

Several families of reindeer herders from Lapland in northern Finland were brought to Alaska in the 1930s to establish herds of these caribou-like creatures.

Keep an eye peeled for river rafters in the Nenana River Canyon near here. Also moose are sometimes seen on the hillsides. The shallow winding sloughs of the lower Nenana were very difficult for early travelers.

UW Nowell 112

Somewhere on the lower Yukon the Saidie *transfers a load of freight to the Kobuk River-bound* John Reilly, *Sept 29, 1903.*

"Our train squeaks and squeals around the sharp bends above the river; if these bends were any sharper these long cars couldn't make it. Seven winding miles, and then the mountains flatten, become foothills, and the low taiga forest surrounds us."

The big weird thing near mile 362, as the train emerges from the Nenana River canyon is the Usibelli coal tipple. Inside is the equipment for filling the coal cars that run north to Fairbanks, or all the way south to Seward to be loaded aboard ships for the Orient.

The country changes substantially here as the trees seem to swallow us up until it seems we're traveling in a leafy canyon. This is all the northern tiaga—a taste of the vast, low, mixed black spruce and birch forests that cover much of the Yukon basin that drains interior Alaska. Plants and trees don't get very big here; the growing season is short and the ground has great frozen areas (permafrost) just below the surface.

Look for the Early Warning Missile Site, at **Clear, mile 392**. This one and two others, are all that remain of the DEW line—the array of radar sites, built during the Cold War across all of northern Alaska and Canada. Before sophisticated satellites, their job was to watch for Russian missiles coming in over the North Pole at North America.

The country is so flat here that the Nenana, barely thirty yards wide in places in the gorge, and rushing

along faster than a man can run, breaks into many branches like Seventeenmile and Lost Slough, and almost seems to just disappear into the flats before finally rejoining to enter the Tanana River at Nenana. Early travelers on rafts often had to pole tediously through miles of shallows here.

Winter was hard—sometimes the rivers froze quickly, trapping steamers far from any towns, forcing passengers to make their way overland, like this group, on the upper Yukon, in 1912.

The River Country

Look for the big black and white wooden tripod (about 30' high), between the tracks and the river at Nenana, **mile 411**. Each winter this tower is dragged out onto the frozen river for the Nenana Ice Classic, a uniquely Alaskan lottery. What folks are betting on is "Ice Out," the moment in spring when the frozen river breaks up.

It's entirely fitting that this be celebrated, for the rivers are the lifeblood for most of the towns in the immense drainage of the Yukon River.

Where there are no highways, the arrival of the first freight barge in the spring is always an exciting community event. This freight (usually in 40' containers or vans) usually begins its water journey from Seattle, stacked five and six high on a huge 400' oceangoing

Steam boats came in all sizes—this is the Steam ferry Keewalik Flyer, *near Candle, on the Yukon, 1903.*

barge, towed by a 5,000 horsepower tug. Somewhere near the mouth of the Yukon River, perhaps at St. Michaels, the containers would be hoisted onto a smaller barge, to be pushed upstream. Sometimes, for freight bound for communities on the smaller rivers, the container would be transferred a third time, onto a yet smaller barge, pushed by an even smaller tug.

Navigation is still tough—the river channels sometimes shift every few weeks; there are few buoys or navigational aids. Captains use hand drawn charts passed along from other captains and pilots. Sometimes the only way through is launching a skiff to sound out a particularly tricky channel before you entered it. Even then, groundings are routine.

The river as highway. Despite what you may hear, not everyone who lives out in the bush has a floatplane in their backyard. But the majority of villages and settlements in the vast country between the Alaska Range and the Bering Sea and Arctic Ocean lie along one of the many rivers with native and Russian names like Kitchatna, Tonzona, Kantishna, Hoholitna, and Chilikadrotna, Ugashik, Nushagak, and Kinak. When the ice is out, watercraft ranging from big tugs and barges to outboard jet boats move people and supplies around. When the ice is in, it is usually hard and smooth enough for vehicles.

It was during those in-between months, the short spring and falls, that travel was difficult:

"My brother had a hunting lodge, way up the Noatak, with a native partner. One fall, I went up to help them, that first year when they were putting it up. 'Course there's no roads anywhere up there...all the stuff came in by barge to the village and then we had to lug it all up the river in the big Lund outboards, loaded right to the gills with sheetrock, 2x6s, etc. It's almost forty miles up the river from the village to where the lodge is, and we reallyhad to get the main lodge framed up and closed in that fall—we put in a barrel stove [wood stove made from a 55-gallon drum, fairly common in rural Alaska,] and kept working right through October. But then when we headed out to go

home, the damn river was half froze up—maybe a hundred yards of ice, then fifty yards of water, then more ice! I thought we were screwed—that we'd have to leave the skiffs on the bank for the winter, and hike the 40 miles back along the shore.

The advent of small float planes made transportation in the bush a lot easier.

"But my brother's partner, a native, he cruised back and forth when we got to the first of the ice, checking it out, then called over to us, 'If this works, follow me...' I didn't have the faintest idea what he was going to try, but he swung around, got up to full throttle and headed right for the ice. Then, just as he hit, he killed the engine, and pulled it up and that aluminum skiff slid right up on top of that ice and skidded almost all the way across to the next open water! So we swung around, got a good run at it, and up we went too...

"That first time we were a little hesitant, but then after a few more tries we got the hang of it, and we could slide maybe 50 yards if we could get a good run at it...and a lot of them frozen places were 50 yards or less, so we'd just slide all the way across and into the water on the other side and just keep on going.

"What a kick—we got back to the village without having to push those boats over the ice hardly at all. But you could tell—another two or three days and we'd have been totally screwed."

— A friend

Many early area residents were involved in small gold mining operations such as this one with a rocker box located near a stream.

Suddenly, around mile 466, Civilization appears—houses, streets, and people mowing lawns. After what seems like the endless tiaga forest stretching unbroken to the horizon, coming upon civilization so suddenly is almost a shock. First is College, and the University of Alaska at **mile 467**, and then a few miles later, Fairbanks.

Fairbanks

The Wandering Trader—In the summer of 1901, E.T. Barnette was headed for the upper Tanana with a load of trading goods. Shallow water forced him to unload his goods right in front of what is now the Fairbanks Visitor's Bureau log cabin. He started to build an even shallower-draft vessel to keep going up the river, but when gold was discovered nearby, Barnette decided to build his trading post right where he was and Fairbanks was born.

Take the time to read the bronze plaques beneath the Pioneer's Memorial in downtown Fairbanks. It's a moving tribute to the courage and perseverence of the early settlers.

Fairbanks today has a more stable economy, with a large military contingent from nearby Fort Wainwright and Eielson Air Force Base. For much of the century, however, it went through the many boom and busts that characterize so much of Alaskan economy.

"Thirty below zero this morning. Frost has crept through the walls and caused the bedclothes to stick to the wall on that side and it is mortal agony to crawl out of the warm nest in the center of the bed when daddy called."

— Margaret Murie, *Two in The Far North*

Winter in Fairbanks lasts from October to April, and before the modern conveniences like plumbing, electricity and oil heat, these months were an unrelenting challenge for residents, especially for women, perhaps raising families with their men away. Margaret Murie, who came to Fairbanks in 1911 when she was nine, grew up with a keen memory of the routines and community activities that made life manageable for the women of Fairbanks:

"A regular routine, a definite project for each day, a regular program with other people – all that helps. It is all

part of the bulwark the women built, consciously or unconsciously, against the isolation, the wilderness, the cold, the difficulties of housekeeping..."
— Margaret Murie, *Two in The Far North*

The river was the highway, and the nearest town was ten days away by river boat. Between freeze-up in the fall and ice out in the spring, there was only the weekly horse-drawn mail sleigh that traveled a difficult trail through the mountains and over the frozen rivers to Valdez.

Ice out was a big event—notices were posted around town to keep residents informed: "Ice moved at Fort Gibbon this morning at 8 a.m.," for the first steamer of the season meant fresh vegetables, followed shortly therafter by the "slaughter-house boat" with its pens of cows, sheep, pigs, geese, and chickens, brought up from Seattle.

In a town of log homes that heated with wood, fire was always a worry. A big steam pump at the Northern Commercial Company power plant was always ready to pump river water from under the river ice to fight fires. On at least one occasion, when the wood-fired boilers couldn't keep up with the demands of a big fire, the cry went out to "Bring the bacon"—case after case of oily bacon was brought from the warehouse, thrown into the boilers, the steam pressure rose, the water flowed once more, and the fire was contained.

Today Fairbanks is the most northerly city in North America. There are many of the conveniences found elsewhere, but the long winters are still bitter, bitter cold, with all their unique problems like having your car go humpity bump in the mornings because of the frozen flat place in the tires from sitting on the street all night long.

As it was for many communities, it was gold that brought settlers here. There is an excellent excursion available here that includes a riverboat tour, a visit to the Alaska Pipeline and a visit to a gold mine, with gold panning available to visitors.

The Oil Rush

New Alaska Pioneer, 1974. The tens of thousands of people that came to Alaska during the Oil Rush years transformed the state in many ways.

Native land claims had to be resolved before the pipeline received all the necessary permits.

Every Thursday in Seattle in the winter of 1974-5, there was a curious sight at the Alaska Ferry Terminal at Pier 48. (Before it moved to Bellingham in 1985, the Alaska ferry left each week from downtown Seattle.) Dozens of old beat-up cars pulling trailers, or pick-up trucks with campers on the back, full of whole families and their possessions were lined up, waiting to get on the Alaska-bound ferry. One wondered how many had those $1,200-a-week jobs already lined up, or where those who didn't might end up.

It was no less than another Gold Rush, though with substantially less hardship and a lot more winners.

For Alaska and its citizens, the Oil Rush brought a sea change. The state's budget rose to unprecedented levels, affording programs found in few other states. But to many Alaskans it brought too many people, and too many new rules on what a person could or could not do on public land.

Before the Oil Rush, Federal land managers would sometimes turn a blind eye on squatters or trespassers, as long as they kept a low profile. But the state's new prominence brought many people north that found land or rents too expensive, and naturally wanted simply to set up camp on a piece of that vast land. What had worked for a few didn't for many, and agencies had to crack down.

The Trans Alaska Oil Pipeline

Pipeline visitor's area near Fairbanks. The odd structures at the top of the supports are part of a heat transfer system to keep the posts from melting the permafrost and sinking. Note also that the pipeline can move sideways on a track between the posts as it expands and contracts.

The good news for Alaska was the huge oil strike at Prudhoe Bay in 1968. The not-so-good part was that getting it out required building a 800-mile pipeline to the ice-free port of Valdez on Prince William Sound. The route had to cross two major mountain ranges, 350 rivers and streams, operate in bitter winter weather, and withstand possible earthquakes.

As well as an engineering challenge, it was a political challenge; taking almost five years for environmental and Native land claim issues to be resolved. In the interval the price boomed as well - from the first estimate of $900 millon dollars, to the final tab that would reach almost 8 billion before the first barrel of oil flowed in June, 1977.

The Oil Boom and the revenues it brought transformed the state in many ways, from social (see page to left) to economic. Governor Jay Hammond demonstrated exceptional foresight by

creating the Alaska Permanent Fund with excess oil revenues, whose investment income was to be distributed among all Alaskans via an annual dividend check.

A so-called pig, which can be used to seperate different kinds of oil passing through the pipeline as well as keeping the inside of the pipe clean.

Today Prudhoe Bay production is in decline, and despite very high oil prices, Alaska's incomefrom oil royalties has dropped substantially. There is, however, a very large resource of North Slope natural gas, and plans are in the works to construct another pipeline that could bring yet another boom to the state.

Riverboat Discovery III Scrapbook

The *Discovery III* is a diesel-powered stern-wheeler, similar to the steam-powered craft that were the lifeblood of the river country of interior Alaska for almost a hundred years. The vessel is operated by the Binkley family, the third generation of this family to be involved in Alaska paddle-wheelers.

Clockwise from upper left: We stop at an Athabascan native village for craft and culture presentations. Note very large cabbages in garden. A floating fishwheel on the Tanana River. Behind is a smoker and a traditional cache, for storing food out of the reach of predators. Three-time Iditarod dogsled race winner Susan Bucher shows new puppies at her riverside homestead. An Athabascan native discusses her culture.

Tundra stream and ponds. Much of the north is covered by this kind of terrain. Wide areas are sometimes covered with tussocks, little round elevated bits of soil and vegetation, which are particularly difficult to travel over, summer or winter.

The Far North

North of Fairbanks, the roads, for the most part, disappear: first they become gravel, then dirt tracks, then they simply stop. The taiga and tundra that covers the vast Yukon basin rises into the Brooks Range, falls away again to become the lonely north slope. Beyond is the austere Arctic—active for a few brillant months in summer with spectacular whales and bird life.

But frozen, seemingly abandoned in winter, the Arctic Coast stretches seamlessly from the shore to the very pole itself.

Olaus and Margaret Murie—Olaus Murie came to Alaska in 1921 as field biologist for the U.S. Fish & Wildlife Service. Over the next several decades he and his wife Margaret traveled through much of the far North, banding birds, exploring animal habitat, making records and writing journals that were to become classics of Alaska literature. Making friends like Supreme Court Justice and Mrs. William Douglas and bringing them to Alaska, Murie eventually became head of The Wilderness Society. The Muries and others were instrumental in creating much of the vast parkland, monuments, and refuges that today ensure the integrity of Alaska's ecosystems. Margaret Murie's book, *Two in The Far North,* published by Alaska Northwest Books, selections of which follow, gives a wonderful account of their travels together.

On the Trail— The Muries' many dogsled trips give a real flavor of those winter days when dogs and sleds were the only way to get around The North:

"It was...dark when we labored up the last steep pitch to the mail cabin. Twenty four miles from Alatna, dogs pulling and puffing, we pushing and puffing; and when we were within a few yards of the cabin, my legs seemed to go out from under me and I crawled the rest of the way and through the square door hole and collapsed on a straw-strewn bunk. Olaus, who is never 'all gone,' put up the dogs, brought in our beds and grub and started a fire."

Dangers – dog sled travelers were pretty much on their own, dependent on their skill and knowledge in a harsh environment. They also depended on the skills of their dogs. A well-trained dog team would keep its driver away from some of the unique hazards of the trail, like overflows. These were created when river ice reached the river bed causing what water was still liquid to come to the surface of the ice.

Many of Olaus Murie's early trips throughout Alaska were to determine the range and habits of the caribou.

Brenda Carney

"...the overflow is more deadly because it is accompanied by cold weather, and only those who have experienced it can appreciate the horror of a plunge into ice water in forty-below weather. This is another reason for the waterproof match safes and the candle stubs or can of Sterno which Olaus and other mushers carry in the big front pockets of their parkas."

On Northern Rivers – on a goose banding trip to the Old Crow River, the motor of their boat broke, and Margaret watched, day after day, from the confines of a 4'x4' mosquito net with their six-month-old son, as Olaus and Jesse, his native assistant, pulled and poled their boat upstream:

"By leaning forward and putting my eyes close to the netting I could catch glimpses of the outside world. It remained unvaried for five weeks: Jesse's booted legs, the tip of the red painted bow, a green blur of grass and willows on the shore, maybe a bit of sky. Sometimes I caught a view of Olaus, trudging along on shore, the line over his shoulder. He was 'pulling her by the whiskers,' as the trappers say. Jess, experienced with the pike pole, leaned his weight on every stroke, in a steady rhythm all day long."

The Mosquitoes of the Old Crow country were legendary. Mealtimes were a particular challenge:

"Some days we merely went ashore with the tin grub box and ate a bowl of stewed fruit or tomatoes with pilot biscuits or cold sourdough pancakes, and a bit of cheese. Bowl in hand, you loosened the string of the head net, poked the spoonful of food into your mouth and quickly let the net down again. It was the same with all the bites."

UW Nowell W5

Inupiat
Glimpses of an Eskimo Past

UW Thwaites 0134-493

Scattered along the northern and western coasts are the Eskimo communities. Traditionally dependent on seals, whales, and caribou, this was a culture in which winter was another word for hunger. Today's Eskimos are more apt to live in prefab houses delivered by the annual barge, and depend on seasonal construction or oil related work.

UW 17963

UW 17962

UWUW 17964

Clockwise from upper left: A umiak or traditional native craft made with sealskins stretched over a driftwood frame. In these boats Eskimos sometimes traveled long distances along the northern Alaska coast. Ivory carver and wife, in tent at Nome, circa 1910. Many Eskimos from King Island would travel to Nome each summer to carve and sell ivory to visitors. The long white object is a walrus tusk decorated as a cribbage board. Shopping, Eskimo style, circa 1910. This group is aboard one of the several trading schooners that traveled northern waters each year to trade food stuffs, rifles, etc. for ivory and furs. Eskimo group with fish drying on racks, near Cape Prince of Wales, circa 1915. A shaman in a mask and carved hands tries to exorcise evil spirits from a sick child. Shamans were unable to cure the diseases such as smallpox brought by the white explorers and lost much face in their villages.

Acknowledgments

I am indebted to a number of unusually talented people, without whom this book would have been far less than what it is.

In particular to my designer, Martha Brouwer, of Waterfront Press, for her skill and grace in taking a sheaf of text, maps and drawings and fashioning them page by page into art.

To artists John Horton, Rie Muñoz, Marvin Oliver, and Nancy Stonington for their very special talents and for allowing me to use examples of their fine work.

To my old pen pals, John and Peggy Hanson, for their ideas, and valuable suggestions.

To John J. O'Ryan, for allowing me to quote freely from his unusual book, *The Maggie Murphy*.

To Glenn Hartmann, for his excellent editing and valuable ideas.

To John Pappenheimer, of Waterfront Press, for his continual support, excitement, and direction.

To my family, for encouraging me through a long project.

To many friends and shipmates, in all manner of craft, in many a breezy cove and strait, for sharing so many stories of the coast.

And finally to old Mickey Hansen, passed away but not forgotten, for his kindness in taking a greenhorn kid under his wing aboard the old *Sydney,* in 1965, showing him the way of a ship and the true magic of The North.

Bibliography

Allen, Arthur, *A Whaler & Trader in the Arctic*. Anchorage: Alaska Northwest Books,1978.

Anderson, Barry, *Lifeline to the Yukon*. Seattle: Superior Publishing, 1983.

Armstrong, Robert H. *A Guide to the Birds of Alaska,* Seattle: Alaska Northwest Books, 1991.

Blanchet, M. Wylie. *The Curve of Time*, N. Vancouver: Whitecap Books Ltd., 1990.

Bohn, Dave. *Glacier Bay: The Land and the Silence*. New York: Ballantine Books, 1967.

Bolotin, Norm. *Klondike Lost*. Anchorage: Alaska Northwest Publishing, 1980.

Caldwell, Francis, *Land of the Ocean Mists*, Seattle: Alaska Northwest Books, 1986.

Canadian Hydrographic Service: *British Columbia Pilot, Vol I & II* . Ottowa, 1965

Craven, Margaret. *I Heard the Owl Call My Name*. New York: Doubleday,1972

Eppenbach, Sarah. *Alaska's Southeast*. Seattle: Pacific Search Press, 1990.

Farwell, Captain R.F. *Captain Farwell's Hansen Handbook*. Seattle: L&H Printing, 1951.

Gibbs, Jim. *Disaster Log of Ships*. Seattle: Superior Publishing, 1971.

Goetzmann, William & Sloan, Kay, *Looking Far North, The Harriman Expedition to Alaska*, 1899, Princeton: Princeton Univ. Press, 1982.

Graham, Donald. *Lights of the Inside Passage*. Madeira Park, British Columbia: Harbour Publishing, 1986.

Hill, Beth. *Upcoast Summers*. Ganges, British Columbia: Horsdal & Schubart, 1985.

Hoyt, Erich. *Orca: the Whale Named Killer*. Buffalo: Firefly Press, 1990.

Huntington, Sydney, *Shadows on the Koyukuk*, Seattle: Alaska Northwesst Books, 1993.

Iglauer, Edith. *Fishing With John*. New York: Farrar, Straus & Giroux, 1988.

Jackson, W.H. *Handloggers*. Anchorage: Alaska Northwest Publishing, 1974.

Jacobsen, Johan Adrian. *Alaskan Voyage 1881-1883*. Chicago: University of Chicago Press, 1977.

Janson, Lone, *The Copper Spike*, Anchorage: Alaska Northwest Books, 1973.

Jonaitis, Aldona, editor. *Chiefly Feasts*. Seattle: University of Washington Press, 1991.

Jonaitis, Aldona. *From the Land of the Totem Poles*. Seattle: University of Washington Press, 1988.

Kent, Rockwell, *Wilderness*, New Haven: Leete's Island Books, 1975.

Larssen, A.K., and Sig Jaeger. *The ABC's of Fo'c's'le Living*. Seattle: Madrona Publishers, 1976.

MacDonald, George, *Chiefs of the Land and Sky*, Vancouver: UBC Press, 1993.

Macfie, Matthew. *Vancouver Island and British Columbia*. London: 1865.

Mckeown, Martha. *The Trail Led North: Mont Hawthorne's Story*. Portland, Oregon: Binfords & Mort, 1960.

Moore, Terris, *Mt. McKinley, The Pioneer Climbs,* Seattle: The Mountaineers, 1981.

Muir, John. *Travels in Alaska.* Boston: Houghton, Mifflin Co., 1915.

Murie, Margaret, *Two in the Far North,* Portland: Alaska Northwest Books, 1975.

Murie, Olaus, *Journeys to the Far North,* Palo Alto: The Wilderness Society, 1973.

Newell, Gordon and Joe Williamson. *Pacific Tugboats.* Seattle: Superior Publishing, 1957.

Nicholson, George. *Vancouver Island's West Coast.* Victoria, British Columbia: Moriss Printing, 1965.

Ritter, Harry. *Alaska's History.* Portland: Alaska Northwest Books, 1993.

Rushton, Gerald. *Echoes of the Whistle.* Vancouver: Douglas & McIntyre, 1980.

Ryan, John J. *The Maggie Murphy.* New York: W.W. Norton & Co., 1951.

Sherwonit, Bill, *To The Top of Denali,* Seattle: Alaska Northwest Books, 1997.

U. S. Dept. of Commerce. *United States Coastal Pilot, Vol 8 & 9.* Washington, D.C. 1969.

Upton, Joe, *Alaska Blues.* Anchorage: Alaska Northwest Publishing, 1977.

Upton, Joe, *The Coastal Companion,* Bainbridge Island, WA: Coastal Publishing, 1995

Upton, Joe, *Journeys Through the Inside Passage.* Portland: Alaska Northwest Books, 1992.

Vancouver, George. *A Voyage of Discovery to the North Pacific Ocean and Round the World,* London, 1798.

Walbran, Captain John T. *British Columbia Coast Names.* Ottowa: Government Printing Bureau, 1909.

White, Howard, editor. *Raincoast Chronicles: Forgotten Villages of the B.C. Coast.* Madeira Park: Harbour Publishing, 1987.

Index

Alaska place names

Joe and Matthew Upton,
Katmai, Alaska, 1997

Traveling northwest waters as a commercial fisherman since 1965 in small craft and large, Joe Upton gained intimate knowledge of the coast from Puget Sound almost to the Arctic Circle.

In the 1970s Upton lived and fished out of a tiny island community in the roadless wilderness of Southeast Alaska. His first book, *Alaska Blues*, based on those years, was hailed as "One of those books you want to proclaim a classic" by the *Seattle Post Intelligencer*.

In 1995, Upton established Coastal Publishing to produce illustrated maps and guidebooks for Alaska cruise travelers.

Upton lives with his wife, Mary Lou and two children, on an island in Puget Sound, and spends much of his summers traveling and fishing along the northwest coast.